C O U N T R Y
Pubs & Inns of
YORKSHIRE

By Barbara Vesey

Regional Hidden Places

Cornwall
Devon
Dorset, Hants & Isle of Wight
East Anglia
Gloucs, Wiltshire & Somerset
Heart of England
Hereford, Worcs & Shropshire
Lake District & Cumbria
Lancashire & Cheshire
Northumberland & Durham
Peak District
Sussex
Yorkshire

National Hidden Places

England
Ireland
Scotland
Wales

Hidden Inns

East Anglia
Heart of England
North of England
South
South East
West Country
Yorkshire

Country Pubs & Inns

Cornwall
Devon
Sussex
Yorkshire
Wales

Country Living Rural Guides

East Anglia
Heart of England
Ireland
North East of England
North West of England
Scotland
South
South East
Wales
West Country

Published by: Travel Publishing Ltd, 7a Apollo House, Calleva Park, Aldermaston, Berkshire RG7 8TN

ISBN 1·904·43449·5

© Travel Publishing Ltd

Published 2006

Printing by: Scotprint, Haddington

Maps by: © Maps in Minutes ™ (2006)
© Crown Copyright, Ordnance Survey 2006

Editor: Barbara Vesey

Cover Design: Lines and Words, Aldermaston, Berkshire

Cover Photograph: The Street Head Inn, Newbiggin in Bishopdale, Wensleydale, North Yorkshire

Text Photographs: © www.britainonview.com

Foreword

The *Country Pubs & Inns of Yorkshire* is one of a series of guides which will eventually cover the whole of the UK. This guide provides details of pubs and inns (including hotels which welcome non-residents) situated in the countryside of Yorkshire. "Countryside" is officially defined by *The Office of National Statistics* as "settlements of less than 10,000 inhabitants".

There are of course many selectively-based pub guides covering the UK but each title in the Country Pubs & Inns series will provide the reader with the *most comprehensive* choice of pubs and inns in the countryside through handy-sized, county-based guides. The guide enables the reader to choose the pub or inn to visit based on his/her own criteria such as location, real ales served, food, entertainment etc.

This easy-to-use guide is divided into 13 sections which allows the reader to select the area of Yorkshire being visited. Each chapter begins with a map containing the numbered location of the pub or inn and a brief illustrated summary of the places of interest in the area. By using the number the reader can then find more information on their choice of pub or inn.

We do hope that you will enjoy visiting the pubs and inns contained in this guide. We are always interested in what our readers think of the pubs and inns covered (or not covered) in our guides so please do not hesitate to write to us using the reader reaction forms provided to the rear of the guide. Equally, you may contact us via our email address at info@travelpublishing.co.uk. This is a vital way of ensuring that we continue to provide a comprehensive list of pubs and inns to our readers.

Finally, if you are seeking visitor information on Yorkshire or any other part of the British Isles we would like to refer you to the full list of Travel Publishing guides to be found at the rear of the book. You may also find more information about any of our titles on our website at www.travelpublishing.co.uk

Travel Publishing

How to use the guide

The *Country Pubs & Inns of Yorkshire* provides details of pubs and inns (including hotels which welcome non-residents) situated in the countryside of Yorkshire. "Countryside" is defined by *The Office of National Statistics* as "settlements of less than 10,000 inhabitants" so much of North and East Yorkshire but a smaller part of West and South Yorkshire fulfills this definition!

This guide has been specifically designed as an easy-to-use guide so there is no need for complicated instructions. However the reader may find the following guidelines helpful in identifying the name, address, telephone number and facilities of the pub or inn.

Finding Pubs or Inns in a Selected Location

The guide is divided into 13 chapters (or sections) each covering a specific geographical area of Yorkshire. Identify the area and page number you require from the map and table of contents on the following pages and turn to the relevant chosen page.

At the beginning of each chapter there is a detailed map of the area selected. The villages and towns denoted by **red** circles are places of interest on which information is provided in the introduction to the chapter should you wish to explore the area further. The numbered boxes in *green* represent each pub or inn in the area selected. For more information on the pub or inn simply locate the same number within the chapter (to the left of the pub/inn name) to find the name, address, telephone number and facilities of the pub or inn.

Finding a Specific Pub or Inn

If you know the name of the pub or inn and its location then simply go to the relevant chapter where the names of the pubs are listed in alphabetical order.

Pub and Inn Information

All pubs or inns in the guide give details of the name, address, telephone number and whether they offer real ales, food, accommodation and no smoking areas.

The advertising panels found in each chapter provide more comprehensive information on the pub or inn such as contact details, location, interior and exterior facilities, real ales, opening times, food, entertainment, disabled access, credit cards and places of interest.

Location Map

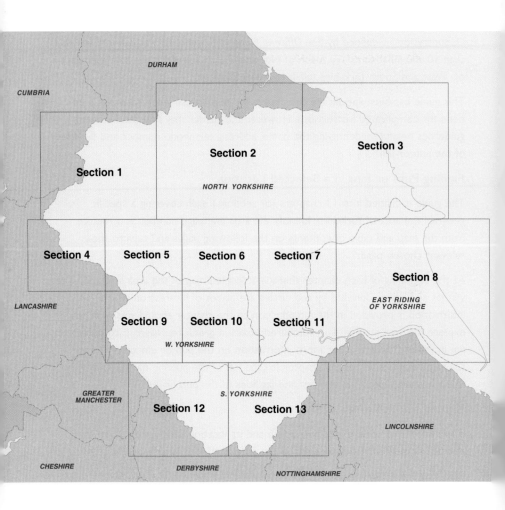

Contents

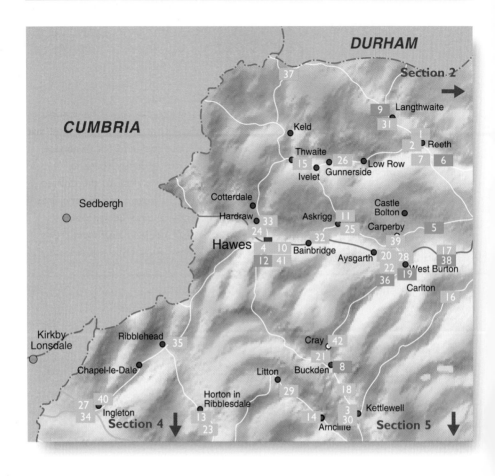

CUMBRIA

DURHAM

Section 2

Langthwaite 9

Keld
31

2 ▶ Reeth

Thwaite
15 26 ● Low Row 7 6
Ivelet Gunnerside

Cotterdale
Sedbergh
Hardraw 33 Askrigg 11 Castle Bolton ●
24 25 Carperby 5
32 39
Hawes 4 10 Bainbridge 20 28 17
12 41 Aysgarth 22 19 West Burton 38
36 Carlton 16

Kirkby Lonsdale Ribblehead 35 Cray 42
21
Chapel-le-Dale Litton Buckden 8
18
Horton in Ribblesdale 29 Kettlewell
27 40 13 3
34 Ingleton 14 30 Kettlewell
Section 4 23 Arncliffe Section 5

11	Pub or Inn Reference Number - Detailed Information
12	Pub or Inn Reference Number - Summary Entry
●■	Place of interest mentioned in the chapter introduction

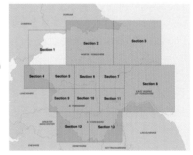

SECTION I

Arncliffe

Situated in Littondale, the village name dates back to Saxon times when the valley was referred to as Amerdale. This is a quiet, tranquil dale and life has remained the same here for many years in this small village.

Askrigg

Askrigg is bountifully supplied with footpaths radiating out to other villages, river crossings and farmsteads. One of the most scenic takes little more than an hour and takes in two impressive waterfalls, Whitfield Gill Force and Mill Gill Force. The route is waymarked from Mill Lane alongside the church.

Aysgarth

The village is famous for the spectacular **Aysgarth Falls** where the River Ure thunders through a rocky gorge and drops some 200 feet over three huge slabs of limestone which divide this wonderful natural feature into the Upper, Middle and Lower Falls.

Bainbridge

Back in the Middle Ages this area of Upper Wensleydale was a hunting forest, known as the Forest and Manor of Bainbridge and the village itself was established around the 12th century as a home for the foresters. Just to the east of Bainbridge is **Brough Hill** (private) where the Romans built a succession of forts known collectively as *Virosidum*. First excavated in the late 1920s, they now appear as overgrown grassy hummocks. Much easier to see is the Roman road that strikes southwestwards from Bainbridge, part of the trans-Pennine route to Lancaster. It passes close to the isolated lake of **Semer Water**, one of Yorkshire's only two natural lakes. Semer Water stretches half a mile in length and teems with wild fowl.

Buckden

Marking the beginning of Wharfedale proper, Buckden is the first full-sized village

Aysgarth Falls

of the dale and proudly boasts that it is also home to Wharfedale's first shop. The village is an excellent starting point for those wanting to climb Buckden Pike (2,302 feet), which lies to the east. The route to the summit takes in not only superb views but also several waterfalls.

Castle Bolton

Bolton Castle has dominated mid-Wensleydale for more than six centuries and is one of the major tourist attractions of the area. Vivid tableaux help bring history to life – the castle chaplain, the miller at work, the blacksmith at his forge – and there are regular living history events during the summer. If you climb to the battlements you will be rewarded with some breathtaking views along the dale.

Chapel-le-Dale

Whernside, to the north of the village, is the highest of the **Three Peaks**, at 2,418 feet, and also the least popular of the mountains – consequently there are few paths to the summit. Just below the top are a number of tarns.

Cotterdale

The small valley of Cotter Beck lies below the vast bulk of Great Shunner Fell which separates the head of Wensleydale from Swaledale. **Cotter Force**, although smaller than Hardraw, is extremely attractive though often neglected in favour of its more famous neighbour.

Gunnerside

The most impressive building in this charming Dales village in the heart of Swaledale is its **Methodist Chapel**, a classically elegant building, wonderfully light and airy.

At **The Old Working Smithy & Museum**, nothing has been bought in – all the artefacts on show are from the smithy itself; indeed many of them were actually made here. The smithy was established in 1795 and over the years little has been thrown away. Cartwheels, cobblers' tools, horseshoes, fireside implements and a miner's 'tub' (railway wagon) from a lead mine are just some of the vintage articles on show, and this is still a working smithy.

Hardraw

Located in a natural amphitheatre of limestone crags, **Hardraw Force** is the highest unbroken waterfall in England above ground, a breathtaking cascade 98 feet high.

Hawes

At 850 feet above sea level, Hawes is the highest market town in Yorkshire. Housed in the former railway station, the **Dales Countryside Museum** tells the story of how man's activities have helped to shape the Dales' landscape. Wensleydale's most famous product (after its sheep), is its soft, mild cheese, and at the **Wensleydale Cheese Experience** not only can you sample this delicacy but also learn about its history through a series of interesting displays.

Horton in Ribblesdale

This village is the ideal place from which to explore the limestone landscapes and green hills of Upper Ribblesdale. To the east lies **Pen-y-ghent** (2,273 feet high), one of the famous **Three Peaks**. The whole of this area has been designated as being of Special

Scientific Interest. This is an ancient landscape, well worth the efforts to preserve its ash woodlands, primitive earthworks, and rare birdlife such as peregrine falcon, ring ouzel, curlew and golden plover. There are also a great many caves in the area, which add to the sense of romance and adventure one feels in this place.

Ingleborough

Ingleton

Mentioned in the *Domesday Book* – the name means 'beacon town' – Ingleton is certainly one of the most visited villages in the Dales. From as long ago as the late 1700s, Ingleton has been famous for the numerous caves and other splendid scenery that lie within a short distance. The river, which is formed here by the meeting of the Rivers Twiss and Doe, is famous for its salmon leaps. **Ingleton Waterfalls** have been delighting visitors since 1885. Along the four miles of scenic walks, the stretch of waterfalls includes those with such interesting names as Pecca Twin Falls, Holly Bush Spout, Thornton Force, and Baxengill Gorge. Many thousands of years old, **White Scar Caves** were only discovered in 1923 by an adventurous student named Christopher Long. Finally, there is **Ingleborough** which, at 2,375 feet is the middle summit of the **Three Peaks**.

Ivelet

Just a few hundreds yard off the B6270, the 14th-century **Packhorse bridge** at Ivelet is regarded as one of the finest in Yorkshire. It's a very picturesque spot and you can also join a delightful riverside walk here.

Keld

Wain Wath Force, with rugged Cotterby Scar providing a fine backdrop, can be found alongside the Birkdale road. Catrake Force, with its stepped formation, can be reached from the cottages on the left at the bottom of the street in the village. For less adventurous pedestrians Kisdon Force, the most impressive waterfall in Swaledale, can be reached by a gentle stroll of less than a mile from the village along a well-trodden path. For really serious walkers, Keld is the most important crossroads in northern England. Here the south-to-north Pennine Way and the east-to-west Coast-to-Coast long-distance walks intersect.

Kettlewell

Surrounded by the beautiful countryside of Upper Wharfedale, Kettlewell is a popular centre for tourists and walkers. At the meeting-point of several old packhorse routes, which now serve as footpaths and bridleways, the village was a busy market centre and, at one time, the home of 13 public houses. Today, Kettlewell is a conservation area, a charming place of chiefly 17th- and 18th-century houses and cottages.

Langthwaite

Langthwaite, the main village of Arkengarthdale, will seem familiar to many who have never been here before as its bridge features in the title sequence of the popular television series *All Creatures Great and Small.*

Litton

This pretty village lends it name to the dale, **Littondale**, which is actually the valley of the River Skirfare. Once part of a Norman hunting forest, the dale was originally called Amerdale (meaning 'deep fork') and this ancient name is preserved in Amerdale Dub, where the River Skirfare joins the River Wharfe near Kilnsey.

Low Row

Located on the edge of this village, **Hazel Brow Organic Farm & Visitor Centre** is set in glorious Swaledale scenery. The 200-acre traditional family-run farm offers the opportunity to bottle-feed lambs, ride ponies or help to feed the calves, sheep and pigs.

Reeth

Considered the capital of Upper Swaledale, this small town is poised at the junction of the River Swale and its main tributary, Arkle Beck. The **Swaledale Folk Museum**, housed in what was once the old Methodist Sunday School, is the home for exhibits of local farming methods, crafts, and mining skills, as well as displays on local pastimes, the impact of Wesleyan Methodism, and the exodus of the population to the industrial areas of the south Pennines and America when the lead mines closed. This little town is also noted for its variety of craft shops. Running northwestwards from Reeth, Arkengarthdale is a small and remote valley, mostly treeless moorland.

Ribblehead

Lying close to the source of the River Ribble is the impressive structure, the **Ribblehead Viaduct**, which was built to carry the Settle-Carlisle Railway. Opened in 1876, after taking five years to construct, its 24 arches span the dark moorland and it is overlooked by Whernside. The **Ribblehead Station & Visitor Centre**, housed in former station buildings, presents an interpretive display showing the history of the line with special emphasis on the Ribblehead locality.

Thwaite

Surrounded by dramatic countryside which includes Kisdon Hill, Great Shunnor, High Seat, and Lovely Seat, this is a tiny village of ancient origins. To the southwest of the village lies **Buttertubs Pass**, one of the highest and most forbidding mountain passes in the country. From the south, as you crest the summit you will be rewarded with a stupendous view of Swaledale stretching for miles.

West Burton

One of the most picturesque villages in

Ribblehead Viaduct

Wensleydale, West Burton developed around its large central green where a busy weekly market used to take place. A distinctive feature of the green is its market 'cross'- actually a modestly sized pyramid erected here in 1820. Just to the east of the village a path leads across a small packhorse bridge to **Mill Force**, perhaps the most photogenic of the Wensleydale waterfalls.

5 The Bolton Arms

Hargill Lane, Redmire, North Yorkshire DL8 4EA
☎ 01969 624336 ⊕ www.bolton-arms.com

Real Ales, Bar Food, Restaurant Menu, Accommodation, No Smoking Area, Disabled Facilities

- ☛ 4½ miles west of Leyburn off the A684
- ☕ John Smiths, Black Sheet, guest ale
- ∥ 12-2 & 7-9
- ⊢ 5 en suite rooms
- ♫ Quiz night Thursdays
- ⚓ Car park, disabled access, patio, function room
- ⚡ All the major cards
- ⊘ No smoking in restaurant
- ⏱ Mon 7 p.m.-close; Tue-Fri 12-2.30 & 7 to close; weekends 12-close
- 🏛 Redmire Falls, Leyburn, Carlton-in-Coverdale, West Witton, Castle Bolton, West Burton

The pretty and tranquil hamlet of Redmire, surrounded by hundreds of acres of open

countryside, is home to The Bolton Arms, an impressive and welcoming stonebuilt inn dating back to 1790. Owned and personally run by John and Pam Berry, a charming couple whose hospitality is second to none, the inn is open Mondays from 7 p.m., every session Tuesday to Friday and all day at weekends and Bank Holidays.

This pristine inn offers three real ales – John Smiths, Black Sheep and a guest ale – and quality home-cooked food. Pam is a superb

cook, creating a range of dishes – her specialities include home-made steak and kidney pie, curries, chilli and lasagne – with something for everyone on the menu and specials board, all freshly prepared using the best ingredients, locally sourced wherever possible. Food is served in the lounge area and also in the elegant restaurant, which perfectly complements the quality of the food.

This fine inn also boasts five charming and supremely comfortable en suite guest bedrooms, tastefully furnished and decorated to a high standard of quality, three are housed in the former stable block which has been lovingly converted to offer first-class accommodation which is available all year round. The region is rich in wonders both scenic and urban, with stunning countryside, thunderous waterfalls, beautiful Dales vistas and centres at Leyburn, Hawes and Richmond.

1 Arkleside Hotel

Reeth, Richmond, North Yorkshire DL11 6SG
Tel: 01748 884200

Bar Food, Restaurant Menu, Accommodation,
No Smoking Area

2 The Black Bull Hotel

Reeth, Richmond, North Yorkshire DL11 6SZ
Tel: 01748 884213

Real Ales, Bar Food, Restaurant Menu,
Accommodation, No Smoking Area

3 Blue Bell Hotel

Middle Lane, Kettlewell, Skipton,
North Yorkshire BD23 5QX
Tel: 01756 760230

Real Ales, Bar Food, Restaurant Menu,
Accommodation, No Smoking Area

4 Board Hotel

Market Place, Hawes, North Yorkshire DL8 3RD
Tel: 01969 667223

Real Ales, Bar Food, Restaurant Menu,
Accommodation, No Smoking Area, Disabled Facilities

5 The Bolton Arms

Redmire, Leyburn, North Yorkshire DL8 4EA
Tel: 01969 624336

Real Ales, Bar Food, Restaurant Menu,
Accommodation, No Smoking Area, Disabled Facilities

See panel opposite

6 The Bridge Inn

Grinton, Richmond, North Yorkshire DL11 6HH
Tel: 01748 884224

Real Ales, Bar Food, Restaurant Menu,
Accommodation, No Smoking Area, Disabled Facilities

See panel below

6 The Bridge Inn

Grinton, Richmond, North Yorkshire DL11 6HH
☎ 01748 884224

⊕ www.bridgeinngrinton.co.uk

Real Ales, Bar Food, Restaurant Menu, Accommodation, No Smoking Area, Disabled Facilities

- On the B6270 1 mile south of Reeth
- Cumberland Ale, Cock-a-Hoop, Guest Ales
- 12-9.00
- 5 en suite rooms
- Regular quiz nights and live music
- Car park, outside eating/drinking, rod hire
- All major cards
- 12-12
- Richmond, Leyburn, Yorkshire Dales National Park, Swaledale

Situated on the banks of the beautiful River Swale in the heart of the Yorkshire Dales National Park, The Bridge Inn has a well-deserved reputation for excellent food and award winning ales. Licensee Andrew Atkin, together with his brother and resident chef, John Scott, provide fresh trout listed on the extensive menu. Just a small sample of the traditional and innovative dishes would include local roast pheasant with bacon-braised barley, casserole of venison with wild mushrooms and Grinton lamb and barley casserole. These can be accompanied by a choice of fine wines, ales, lagers, spirits and soft drinks. There are five en suite bedrooms all with TV and tea/coffee making facilities. You will be sure of a warm welcome at this 13th century coaching inn with its open fires and beautiful restaurant.

9 The Charles Bathurst Inn

Arkengarthdale, Richmond,
North Yorkshire DL11 6EN

☎ 01748 884567 ⊕ www.cbinn.co.uk

Real Ales, Bar Food, Restaurant Menu, Accommodation, No Smoking Area, Disabled Facilities

☛ A1 to A6108 from Scotch Corner to Richmond, B6270 to Reeth, right at Buck Hotel for Langthwaite (3 miles) past the church 150 yards

🍺 Black Sheep, John Smiths, Theakstons

🍴 12-2 & 6.30-9

🛏 18 en suite rooms

♫ Quiz night last Friday of the month, quoits, darts, pool table

⚓ Parking, disabled access, patio area, children's play area, terrace room for small parties and conferences

🛵 Not AMEX or Diner's

🏵 4 Diamonds ETC plus Silver Award for Dining, 4 Diamonds AA, 2006 Pub of the Year *Good Pub Guide*

🚫 All bedrooms and most dining areas no smoking

🕐 11-11

🏛 Hazel Brow Farm, Low Row, Richmond, Leyburn, Bowes Museum, Barnard Castle, Catterick, Pennine Way and Coast-to-Coast walks

The Charles Bathurst Inn is steeped in local history, dating back to the 1700s and located in the beautiful and remote Arkengarthdale. Tastefully refurbished using local wood and stone, and reopened in 1996, the interior boasts many original features including the open fires giving a welcoming atmosphere. Charles Bathurst was a land and mine owner and the son of Oliver Cromwell's physician, and the inn began life as his home. There are several cask-conditioned ales supplied by the Theakstons brewery, together with a good compliment of beers, wines, spirits and soft drinks. Bar meals at this superior inn include baguettes filled with bacon and cheddar, beef and Stilton and mushroom, tomato and mozzarella, and hearty fresh soups

such as leek and potato. Meals are served at lunch and dinner every day, and the impressive menu features tempting dishes such as shank of local lamb with lentils du pay and juniper jus, Aberdeen Angus sirloin steak, fillets of sea bass and guinea fowl. The starters and puddings – for example avocado and crab in a filo basket with lime mayonnaise, and lemon and almond macaroon served with crème fraiche and honey – are equally mouth-watering. All dishes are freshly prepared using local produce, cooked on the premises and expertly presented. The menu is written up daily on a large and handsome mirror hanging at the end of the bar, and changes

with the availability of fresh local ingredients. The accommodation at the inn continues the theme of excellence. Each of the 18 en suite guest bedrooms is individually designed and furnished with taste and style, ensuring guests' every comfort. The inn is a perfect base for exploring the many sights, attractions and outdoor pursuits in the area.

7 Buck Hotel

Reeth, Richmond, North Yorkshire DL11 6SW
Tel: 01748 884210

Real Ales, Bar Food, Restaurant Menu,
Accommodation, No Smoking Area, Disabled Facilities

8 The Buck Inn

Upper Wharfedale, Buckden, Skipton,
North Yorkshire BD23 5JA
Tel: 01756 760228

Real Ales, Bar Food, Restaurant Menu,
Accommodation, No Smoking Area, Disabled Facilities

See panel below

9 The Charles Bathurst Inn

Langthwaite, Arkengarthdale, Richmond,
North Yorkshire DL11 6EN
Tel: 01748 884567

Real Ales, Bar Food, Restaurant Menu,
Accommodation, No Smoking Area, Disabled Facilities

See panel opposite

10 Cocketts Hotel

Market Place, Hawes, North Yorkshire DL8 3RD
Tel: 01969 667312

Real Ales, Bar Food, Restaurant Menu,
Accommodation, No Smoking Area, Disabled Facilities

11 The Crown Inn

Main Street, Askrigg, Leyburn,
North Yorkshire DL8 3HQ
Tel: 01969 650298

Real Ales, Bar Food, Restaurant Menu,
No Smoking Area, Disabled Facilities

12 The Crown Hotel

Market Place, Hawes, North Yorkshire DL8 3RD
Tel: 01969 667212

Real Ales, Bar Food, Restaurant Menu,
Accommodation, No Smoking Area, Disabled Facilities

See panel on page 12

8 The Buck Inn

Buckden, Skipton, North Yorkshire BD23 5JA
☎ 01756 760228 🌐 www.thebuckinn.com

Real Ales, Bar Food, Restaurant Menu, Accommodation, No Smoking Area, Disabled Facilities

- ☛ On the B6160 9 miles northwest of Grassington
- 🍺 Black Sheep, Timothy Taylor Landlord, Theakstons, guest ale from local brewery
- 🍴 Breakfast, lunch (12.30-2.30) & dinner (6-9)
- 🛏 13 en suite rooms
- ⛱ Car park, patio garden
- 💳 All major cards
- 🏆 AA Rosette Award for Culinary Excellence
- 🚭 No smoking in restaurant
- 🕐 8.30-11
- 🏛 Grassington, Hawes, Leyburn, Skipton, Harrogate

The impressive Buck Inn is an internationally renowned traditional Georgian coaching inn boasting every modern comfort. Located in a tranquil village at the foot of Buckden Pike, it is a wonderful place to relax and unwind. Each of the guest bedrooms is individually designed and furnished to meet the inn's classic style and flair for matching comfort with luxury. Some have four-poster beds; all offer a haven of peace and comfort and magnificent views across the surrounding countryside. Breakfast features home-baked breads, cakes, biscuits and preserves; packed lunches are available on request. The lunchtime and evening menus at the award-winning Courtyard change weekly to take advantage of the freshest ingredients in season.

12 The Crown Hotel

Market Place, Hawes, North Yorkshire DL8 3RD
☎ 01969 667212

Real Ales, Bar Food, Restaurant Menu, Accommodation, No Smoking Area, Disabled Facilities

- 15½ miles west of Leyburn on the A684
- Theakstons, Old Peculiar, John Smiths Cask, guest ales
- 12-2.30 & 6.30-9
- 4 guest bedrooms
- Tues night quiz; ongoing theme nights
- Car park, disabled access, beer garden, small function room and outdoor catering
- All major cards
- No smoking in restaurant
- 5-12
- Dales Countryside Museum, Wensleydale Creamery, Hardraw Force, Aysgarth Falls

Occupying a central position on the Market Place in the ever-popular village of Hawes, The Crown Hotel is the perfect place to stop for an excellent drink or meal, and to use as a base while exploring the region. Dating back to 1776, this venerable former coaching inn is a handsome and elegant

brickbuilt establishment boasting many original features that add to its cosiness and comfort: big open fire, traditional décor and relaxed, friendly ambience. Real ales together with a range of lagers, cider, stout, wines, spirits and soft drinks ensure something to quench your thirst, while the extensive menus and daily specials offer a huge choice of hearty Yorkshire fare, all home-cooked and using the freshest local ingredients. A small sample from the menu includes turkey and leek pie, shoulder of lamb, hot or cold roast beef sandwiches and much more. The sweets, too, are well worth leaving room for, with tempting delights such as sticky toffee pudding and treacle tart on the menu.

There's a small function room and outside catering is welcome. Outside there's a large beer garden for fine days. Owners Jim and Judith Paredes, ably assisted by Jim's mum, Wendy, offer all their guests first-class service and hospitality. The inn also offers four excellent guest bedrooms, including a spacious family room, for anyone touring the Dales and the many historic and natural beauties – the Dales Countryside Museum, Braithwaite Hall (Coverham), Aysgarth Falls and Hardraw Force to name just four – of the area as well as Hawes itself and the other attractive towns and villages of the region, which include Leyburn, Castle Bolton, Constable Burton and Bainbridge.

13 Crown Inn

Horton-in-Ribblesdale, Settle,
North Yorkshire BD24 0HF
Tel: 01729 860209

Real Ales, Bar Food, Restaurant Menu,
Accommodation

14 The Falcon Inn

Arncliffe, Skipton, North Yorkshire BD23 5QE
Tel: 01756 770205

Real Ales, Bar Food, Restaurant Menu,
Accommodation, No Smoking Area, Disabled Facilities

15 Farmers Arms

Muker, Richmond, North Yorkshire DL11 6QG
Tel: 01748 886297

Real Ales, Bar Food, Restaurant Menu,
Accommodation, No Smoking Area, Disabled Facilities

16 Foresters Arms

Carlton, Leyburn, North Yorkshire DL8 4BB
Tel: 01969 640272

Real Ales, Bar Food, Restaurant Menu,
No Smoking Area, Disabled Facilities

17 The Fox & Hounds Inn

Main Street, West Witton, Leyburn,
North Yorkshire DL8 4LP
Tel: 01969 623650

Real Ales, Bar Food, Restaurant Menu, No Smoking
Area, Disabled Facilities

18 The Fox & Hounds Residential Inn

PO Box 17, Starbotton, Skipton,
North Yorkshire BD23 5WU
Tel: 01756 760269

Real Ales, Bar Food, Restaurant Menu,
Accommodation, No Smoking Area

19 The Fox & Hounds Inn

West Burton, Leyburn, North Yorkshire DL8 4JY
Tel: 01969 663111

Real Ales, Bar Food, Restaurant Menu,
Accommodation, No Smoking Area, Disabled Facilities

See panel on page 14

20 George & Dragon Inn

Aysgarth, Leyburn, North Yorkshire DL8 3AD
Tel: 01969 663358

Real Ales, Bar Food, Restaurant Menu,
Accommodation, No Smoking Area, Disabled Facilities

21 George Inn

Hubberholme, Skipton, North Yorkshire BD23 5JE
Tel: 01756 760223

Real Ales, Bar Food, Accommodation,
No Smoking Area

22 George Inn

PO Box 29, Thoralby, Leyburn,
North Yorkshire DL8 3YU
Tel: 01969 663256

Real Ales, Bar Food, Restaurant Menu,
Accommodation

23 Golden Lion Hotel

Horton-in-Ribblesdale, Settle,
North Yorkshire BD24 0HB
Tel: 01729 860206

Real Ales, Bar Food, Accommodation,
No Smoking Area

24 The Green Dragon

Hardrow, Hawes, North Yorkshire DL8 3LZ
Tel: 01969 667392

Real Ales, Bar Food, Accommodation,
No Smoking Area, Disabled Facilities

25 Kings Arms

Market Place, Askrigg, Leyburn,
North Yorkshire DL8 3HL
Tel: 01969 650817

Real Ales, Bar Food, No Smoking Area

26 Kings Head

Gunnerside, Richmond, North Yorkshire DL11 6LD
Tel: 01748 886261

Real Ales, Bar Food, Restaurant Menu,
No Smoking Area, Disabled Facilities

19 The Fox & Hounds Inn

West Burton, Leyburn, North Yorkshire DL8 4JY
☎ 01969 663111

Real Ales, Bar Food, Restaurant Menu, Accommodation, No Smoking Area, Disabled Facilities

☞ Off the B6160 7 miles west of Leyburn, 3
miles south of Aysgarth Falls (A684)

🍺 Black Sheet, Tetleys, John Smiths, Cooper
Dragon

🍴 12-2 & 6-8.30

🛏 6 en suite rooms

🎵 Quiz night Fridays

🅿 Car park, disabled access, patio area

💳 All the major cards

🏅 3 Diamonds ETC

🚫 No smoking in dining room

🕙 11-midnight (Sun and Bank Holidays to 11)

🏛 Mill Force, Leyburn, Aysgarth Falls, Bolton
Castle

In the centre of the unspoilt and picturesque
village of West Burton, The Fox & Hounds
Inn is a traditional Wensleydale pub with

immense charm. Andrew Landau and his
friendly, efficient staff provide a warm welcome
to all their guests at this stunning little pub,
where the low oak beams enhance the old-
world scene in the bar and dining room.

Traditional Yorkshire food is served here,
hearty, nourishing and delicious. All food is
prepared and cooked on the premises, and is
served in both the bar and dining room. The
extensive choice of daily specials are in
demand at lunchtime, and there's a light-bites
menu at lunchtime and a full menu in the
evening. Booking advised for evenings and
weekends. Hand-pulled ales include Cooper
Dragon, from Skipton, and are complemented
by a good range of bitters, lagers, cider, stout,
wines, spirits and soft drinks. Picnic tables at
the front of the pub overlook the lovely village
green.

Children are welcome, as are well-
behaved dogs. For visitors wishing to stay
in the area there are six comfortably
appointed and attractively decorated guest
bedrooms, with every facility guests could
expect. Two of the rooms are located on
the ground floor. Special one-night breaks
are offered. A tasty breakfast is included in
the tariff. The village of West Burton is one
of the prettiest in all of Wensleydale, lying
in a conservation area and best known for
its large and beautiful village green. The
village is also well placed for exploring the
many sights and attractions of the Dales.

27 Marton Arms Hotel
Thornton In Lonsdale, Ingleton, Carnforth,
Lancashire LA6 3PB
Tel: 01524 241281

Real Ales, Bar Food, Restaurant Menu,
Accommodation, No Smoking Area, Disabled Facilities

28 Palmer Flatt Hotel
Aysgarth, Leyburn, North Yorkshire DL8 3SR
Tel: 01969 663228

Real Ales, Bar Food, Restaurant Menu,
Accommodation, No Smoking Area

29 Queens Arms
Litton, Skipton, North Yorkshire BD23 5QJ
Tel: 01756 770208

Real Ales, Bar Food, Restaurant Menu,
No Smoking Area, Disabled Facilities

30 The Racehorses Hotel
Kettlewell, Skipton, North Yorkshire BD23 5QZ
Tel: 01756 760233

Real Ales, Bar Food, Restaurant Menu,
Accommodation, No Smoking Area, Disabled Facilities

31 Red Lion Inn
Langthwaite, Richmond, North Yorkshire DL11 6RE
Tel: 01748 884218

Real Ales, Bar Food, Restaurant Menu,
Accommodation, No Smoking Area, Disabled Facilities

32 Rose & Crown Hotel
Bainbridge, Leyburn, North Yorkshire DL8 3EE
Tel: 01969 650225

Real Ales, Bar Food, Restaurant Menu,
Accommodation, No Smoking Area, Disabled Facilities

33 Simonstone Hall
Simonstone, Hawes, North Yorkshire DL8 3LY
Tel: 01969 667255

Bar Food, Restaurant Menu, Accommodation,
Disabled Facilities

34 Springfield Country House Hotel
26 Main Street, Ingleton, Carnforth,
Lancashire LA6 3HJ
Tel: 01524 241280

Accommodation, No Smoking Area

35 Station Inn
Ribblehead, Ingleton, Carnforth,
Lancashire LA6 3AS
Tel: 01524 241274

Real Ales, Bar Food, Accommodation,
No Smoking Area, Disabled Facilities

36 **The Street Head Inn**
Newbiggin, Leyburn, North Yorkshire DL8 3TE
Tel: 01969 663282

Real Ales, Bar Food, Restaurant Menu,
Accommodation, No Smoking Area, Disabled Facilities

See panel on page 16

37 Tan Hill Inn
Richmond, North Yorkshire DL11 6ED
Tel: 01833 628246

Real Ales, Bar Food, Restaurant Menu,
Accommodation, No Smoking Area, Disabled Facilities

38 **The Wensleydale Heifer**
Main Street, West Witton, Leyburn,
North Yorkshire DL8 4LS
Tel: 01969 622322

Real Ales, Bar Food, Restaurant Menu,
Accommodation, No Smoking Area, Disabled Facilities

See panel on page 17

39 Wheatsheaf Hotel
Carperby, Leyburn, North Yorkshire DL8 4DF
Tel: 01969 663216

Real Ales, Bar Food, Restaurant Menu,
Accommodation, No Smoking Area, Disabled Facilities

36 The Street Head Inn

Newbiggin in Bishopdale, Wensleydale,
North Yorkshire DL8 3TE

☎ 01969 663282 ⊕ www.streetheadinn.co.uk

Real Ales, Bar Food, Restaurant Menu, Accommodation, No Smoking Area, Disabled Facilities

- 🚲 2 miles from West Burton on the B6160
- 🍺 Black Sheep, Theakstons, John Smiths
- 🍴 12-2 & 6-9
- 🛏 5 en suite rooms; old school bunkhouse (sleeps up to 20)
- 🅿 Car park, disabled access
- 💳 All major cards
- 🏆 4 Diamonds ETC
- 🕐 M-F 11.30-3 & 6-close; weekends all day
- 🏛 Richmond, Ripon, Castle Bolton, Barnard Castle, Jervaulx Abbey, Aysgarth Falls, Hardraw Falls and Kidson Force, Ingleton caves, Hawes, Reeth, Thirsk

Surrounded by beautiful scenery and some excellent walking country, The Street Head Inn is a convivial and welcoming place in the heart of Wensleydale. A genuine gem, this superb inn is situated in the unspoilt valley of

Bishopdale, some nine miles southwest of Leyburn on the B6160. There's great value food and drink here, with hearty and wholesome Yorkshire fare including fresh local beef and lamb and a wide choice of daily specials.

This early 18th-century coaching inn, built in 1730, is painted a brilliant white on the outside and has retained many original features, The warm and welcoming atmosphere at this spacious inn is enhanced by the beamed ceilings, beautiful antiques, open fires and

feature window created from the original coach entrance. Owners Nigel and Joanne Fawcett are very experienced in the trade, and bought these elegant premises in 2002. A farmer by occupation, Nigel's farm is within a short walk of the inn, and he has also run and owned different inns over the past 18 years in the nearby villages of Aysgarth, Reeth and Muker before arriving here.

Ably assisted by manager Joanne Harrington and head chef Trevor Bailey, the Fawcetts makes this a place that is convivial and welcoming, and have a wealth of local knowledge they are happy to share with guests. Cask ales are served in the cosy bar, together with a selection of lagers, cider, stout, wines, spirits and soft drinks.

There are five handsome and comfortable bedrooms, all with panoramic views over Bishopdale and each with a king-sized bed. Just a short walk from the inn, Nigel has converted the old school house into wonderful self-catering accommodation that sleeps up to 20 people, with one room sleeping eight and three rooms sleeping four. It is available all year round for individual, group or exclusive bookings, and has recently been refurbished to a high standard while retaining all of its original charm.

40 Wheatsheaf Inn & Hotel

22 High Street, Ingleton, Carnforth,
Lancashire LA6 3AD
Tel: 01524 241275

Real Ales, Bar Food, Restaurant Menu,
Accommodation, No Smoking Area

41 White Hart Inn

Main Street, Hawes, North Yorkshire DL8 3QL
Tel: 01969 667259

Real Ales, Bar Food, Restaurant Menu,
Accommodation, No Smoking Area

42 White Lion Inn

Buckden, Cray, Skipton, North Yorkshire BD23 5JB
Tel: 01756 760262

Real Ales, Bar Food, Restaurant Menu,
Accommodation, No Smoking Area

38 The Wensleydale Heifer

West Witton, North Yorkshire DL8 4LS
☎ 01969 622322
🌐 www.wensleydaleheifer.co.uk

Real Ales, Bar Food, Restaurant Menu, Accommodation, No Smoking Area, Disabled Facilities

- Off the A684 west of Leyburn
- John Smiths, Black Sheep, Theakstons
- 12-2.30, 6-7 (early bird) & 7-9.30
- 9 en suite rooms
- Car park, beer garden, function room
- All major cards
- No smoking in restaurant
- 11-close
- Leyburn, Hawes, Richmond, Northallerton, Ripon

The charming village of West Witton is home to The Wensleydale Heifer, a fine traditional inn dating back to 1643. From the outside it looks like a typical Yorkshire inn, but inside it has been fully refurbished to make the most of its original features while offering guests every modern comfort. The walls are painted in fresh pastel shades and the furniture is leather or wicker, while the state-of-the-art lighting add to the modern feel of the place. The accent is on the excellent food, with a distinguished menu of dishes such as Whitby cod, Aberdeen Angus rib steak, maple roast native lobster, slow-braised shoulder of West Burton lamb and their famous fish pie with a mature cheddar and nutmeg crust. The superb accommodation includes four-poster rooms and provides guests with every comfort.

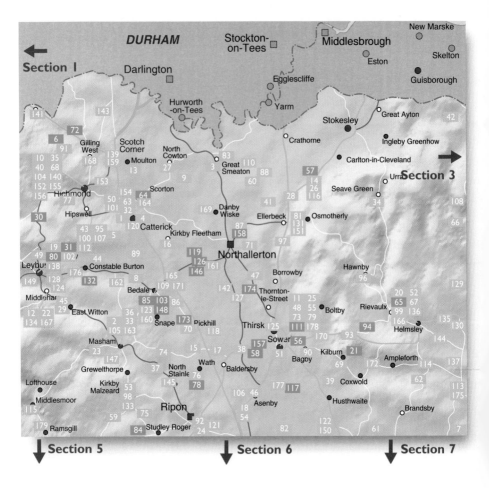

DURHAM

Section 1

Stockton-on-Tees

Middlesbrough

New Marske

Skelton

Eston

Darlington

Egglescliffe

Guisborough

Hurworth-on-Tees

Yarm

Great Ayton

141   143

72

6   91

Gilling West   Scotch Corner   North Cowton

10   35   139   168   159   Moulton
40   68   13
104 140
152 155   153
156   Richmond

50   63   64
101 32

Hipswell   1   4

43   95   120 Catterick
100 107   5

30

19   31   112

49   80   102
138

Leyburn   44   89

149 128   132   162   8

124   Bedale

Middleham   45   85   103   86

12   22   29   East Witton   36   123 148

134 167   2   33   160   Snape   173 Pickhill
105 163   70   118

Masham

23   147

Grewelthorpe   37   North Stainle   Wath

Lofthouse   Kirkby Malzeard   53

Middlesmoor   98   133

115   59   75

179 Ramsgill   84   Studley Roger

Section 5   Section 6   Section 7

Great Smeaton   110
88   57

60   14   26   116

41   28

Scorton   154   164

Danby Wiske

169   Ellerbeck   81   131
Kirkby Fleetham   158   151
16   87   97

119   71
126   161   Northallerton
146

47   Borrowby

165   109 171   142   174 Thornton-le-Street
127

11   25
48   55   Boltby
73   79

Thirsk   125   111 178

157   Sowerby   56   170   93
58   51   90
38   Bagby   Kilburn   21
69   172

145   Baldersby   39   Coxwold
78

106   46   177 117
18   Asenby   Husthwaite
54

92   121   122
24   82   150   61

Crathorne   Ingleby Greenhow

Carlton-in-Cleveland   Stokesley

Urra   Section 3
34

Seave Green   108

Osmotherly   66

Hawnby
96   129

20   52
65   67
Rievaulx   99   136
166   135
94   Helmsley   130   144

Ampleforth   114   137

62   113
Brandsby   175
7

Legend

11 Pub or Inn Reference Number - Detailed Information

12 Pub or Inn Reference Number - Summary Entry

● ■ Place of interest mentioned in the chapter introduction

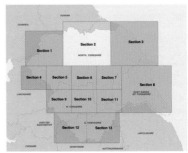

SECTION 2

Ampleforth

Set on the southern slopes of the Hambleton Hills, Ampleforth is perhaps best known for its Roman Catholic public school, Ampleforth College, established by the Benedictine community that came here in 1809, fleeing from persecution in post-revolutionary France. The monks built an austere-looking Abbey in the Romanesque style among whose treasures are an altar stone rescued from Byland Abbey and finely crafted woodwork by the 'Mouseman of Kilburn', Robert Thompson.

Bedale

This pleasant little market town with its many fine Georgian buildings and old coaching inns developed around the point where the Saxon track from Ripon joined the route from Northallerton to Wensleydale. The market cross still stands at the top of Emgate, a narrow street leading from the river to the marketplace. The curving main street leads to the beautiful parish **Church of St Gregory** at the northern end. Across the road from the church is **Bedale Hall**, a Palladian-style mansion with a superb ballroom.

Boltby

Boltby is an engaging village tucked away at the foot of the Hambleton Hills, close to where the oddly-named Gurt of Beck tumbles down the hillside and, depending on how much rain has fallen on the moors, passes either under or over a little humpback bridge.

Carlton in Cleveland

A pleasing little village just inside the National Park, Carlton has a haunted Manor House and a church which was destroyed by fire in 1874 just weeks after its rector had spent years restoring it with his own hands.

Catterick Village

Catterick Village's connections with Nelson are not immediately obvious but it was Alexander Scott, vicar of Catterick in 1816, who was at Nelson's side when he died at Trafalgar. Also, the Admiral's sister-in-law, Lady Tyrconnel, lived at nearby **Kiplin Hall**, a beautiful Jacobean country home famed for its wonderful interior plasterwork and medieval fishponds.

Constable Burton

Surrounded by walled and wooded parkland **Constable Burton Hall** is famous for its gardens (open March to October) and in particular its spacious, romantic terraces. The house itself is not open to the public but its stately Georgian architecture provides a magnificent backdrop to the fine gardens, noble trees and colourful borders.

Coxwold

Coxwold enjoys a particularly lovely setting in the narrow valley that runs between the Hambleton and Howardian Hills. At the western end of the village stands the 500-year-old **Shandy Hall**, home of Laurence Sterne, vicar of Coxwold in the 1760s. Just to the south of Coxwold is **Newburgh Priory,** founded in 1145 as an Augustinian monastery and now a mostly Georgian country house with fine interiors and a beautiful water garden. From Coxwold, follow the minor road northeastwards towards Ampleforth. After about two miles, you will see the lovely, cream-coloured ruins of **Byland Abbey** (English Heritage).

Danby Wiske

This pleasant little village takes its name from the Danby family, once great landowners with huge properties across North Yorkshire, and the little River Wiske. It has a moated former rectory and a village green overlooked by a traditional hostelry.

East Witton

An attractive village set beside the confluence of the rivers Cover and Ure, just to the west of the village is **Jervaulx Abbey**, one of the great Cistercian sister houses to Fountains Abbey. Despite its ruination, Jervaulx is among the most evocative of Yorkshire's many fine abbeys. The grounds have been transformed into beautiful gardens with the crumbling walls providing interesting backdrops for the sculptured trees and colourful plants and shrubs.

Grewelthorpe

North of the village are the beautiful **Hackfall Woods** through which the River Ure flows. During the 19th century the Victorians developed the woodland, creating waterfalls and transforming the 18th-century follies that had been built here into splendid vantage points. Following a period of neglect which began with the sale of the woodland in the 1930s, the Hackfall Woods are now in the care of the Woodland Trust and the area is being gradually restored to its 19th-century condition.

Guisborough

The stark ruins of **Gisborough Priory** (English Heritage) stand on an elevated site overlooked by the Cleveland Hills. Founded by a great landowner in the region, Robert de Brus II, in 1119 the monastery became one of the most powerful in Yorkshire. It was extended in 1200 but almost a century later the whole complex was destroyed by fire. Rebuilding took several generations and was not completed until the late 1300s. Of the priory itself, the great arch of the east end is the most striking survival, an outstanding example of Gothic architecture. The priory grounds are a popular venue for picnics.

Helmsley

One of North Yorkshire's most popular and attractive towns, Helmsley lies on the banks of the River Rye on the edge of the North York Moors National Park. The spacious cobbled market square has an astonishingly ornate Gothic memorial designed by Sir Giles Gilbert Scott and looking like a smaller version of his famous memorial to Sir Walter Scott in Edinburgh. The Earls of Feversham lived at **Duncombe Park** whose extensive grounds sweep up to within a few yards of the Market Place, a beautifully restored house with 35 acres of lovely gardens and a further 400 acres of superbly landscaped grounds. With Helmsley Castle as its backdrop, **Helmsley Walled Garden** offers five acres of lovely

Rievaulx Abbey

gardens containing many unusual varieties of flowers, vegetables and herbs. Just to the west of Helmsley rise the indescribably beautiful remains of **Rievaulx Abbey** (English Heritage), standing among wooded hills beside the River Rye – 'the most beautiful monastic site in Europe.' Looking down on the extensive remains of the Abbey is **Rievaulx Terrace** (National Trust), a breathtaking example of landscape gardening completed in 1758.

Husthwaite

Old stone houses mingle with mellow Victorian and Edwardian brick and overlooking the village green, where three lanes meet, the Church of St Nicholas still retains its original Norman doorway. Just outside the village, on the road to Coxwold, there's a stunning view across to the Hambleton Hills and the White Horse of Kilburn.

Ingleby Greenhow

Located on the very edge of the National Park, Ingleby Greenhow enjoys a favoured position, protected from east winds by the great mass of Ingleby Moor. The beckside church looks small and unimposing from the outside, but inside there is a wealth of rugged Norman arches and pillars, the stonework carved with fanciful figures of grotesque men and animals.

Kilburn

Kilburn was the home of one of the most famous of modern Yorkshire craftsmen, Robert Thompson – the **'Mouseman of Kilburn'**. Robert's father was a carpenter but he apprenticed his son to an engineer. At the age of 20 however, inspired by seeing the medieval wood carvings in Ripon Cathedral, His work can be seen in more than 700 churches, including Westminster Abbey and York Minster. Each piece bears his 'signature' – a tiny carved mouse placed in some inconspicuous corner of the work. You can see several of the Mouseman's creations in Kilburn village church – there's one perched on the traceried pulpit, another clinging to a desk in the sanctuary, and a third sitting cheekily on the lectern.

Leyburn

The main market town and trading centre of mid-Wensleydale, Leyburn is an attractive town with a broad marketplace lined by handsome late-Georgian and Victorian stone buildings.

On the eastern edge of the town is Leyburn Station. The **Wensleydale Railway** offers regular services to Bedale and Leeming Bar, a 12-mile route through pretty countryside.

The Shawl, to the west of the town, is a mile-long limestone scarp along which runs a footpath offering lovely panoramic views of the dale.

Lofthouse

This small Dales' village lies in the upper valley of the River Nidd and, unlike neighbouring Wharfedale, the stone walls and rocky outcrops are of millstone grit though the valley bottom consists of limestone. Nearby **How Stean Gorge** is often called Yorkshire's Little Switzerland, and for good reason. This spectacular limestone gorge, which is up to 80 feet deep in places, through which the Stean Beck flows is a popular tourist attraction. A narrow path with footbridges guide the visitor along the gorge where the waters rush over the large boulders below. However, there are also many sheltered areas of calm water where fish hide under the rocks. As well as taking a stroll up this fascinating path, visitors can also step inside Tom Taylor's Cave and, along the walk, marvel at the wide variety of plant life that grows in this steep ravine.

Masham

Set beside the River Ure, Masham (pronounced *Massam*) is a very picturesque place with a huge marketplace at its heart. The ancient Church of St Mary stands in one corner, a school founded in 1760 in another, while at the centre is the market cross surrounded by trees and flowers. The size of the marketplace reflects Masham's historical importance as a market town and its position, between the sheep-covered hills and the corn growing lowlands, certainly helped to support its flourishing trade. The town is famed for its beer, boasting two celebrated breweries – Theakston's and Black Sheep.

Middlesmoor

This tucked-away village of stonebuilt cottages and houses lies at the head of Upper Nidderdale and is reached by a single, winding road. The existence of ancient settlers can be seen in the present 19th-century Church of St Chad where an early 10th- or 11th-century preaching cross, bearing the inscription *Cross of St Ceadda* can be seen.

Moulton

This small village is home to two fine 17th-century manor houses that were built by members of the Smithson family. The Manor House, in the village centre, was originally built in the late-16th century and was improved greatly in the mid-17th century. Just to the south lies **Moulton Hall**, built by George Smithson following his marriage to Eleanor Fairfax in 1654. Similar in size to the original Smithson family home and somewhat resembling it, Moulton Hall is now in the hands of the National Trust.

Northallerton

The county town of North Yorkshire, Northallerton was an important stop on the route from Newcastle to London and several old coaching inns still stand along the High Street. Northallerton has many old buildings of interest, including an ancient Grammar School whose history goes back to at least 1322. The town also boasts a grand medieval church, a 15th-century almshouse and, of more recent provenance, a majestic County Hall

Richmond Castle

built in 1906 and designed by the famous Yorkshire architect Walter Brierley. The oldest private house in Northallerton is Porch House, which bears a carved inscription with the date 1584. According to tradition, Charles I came here as a guest in 1640 and returned seven years later as a prisoner.

Osmotherley

Long-distance walkers will be familiar with this attractive moorland village since it is the western starting point for the Lyke Wake Walk, which winds for more than 40 miles over the moors to Ravenscar on the coast. At the centre of the village is a heavily carved cross and, next to it, a low stone table which was probably once a market stall and also served John Wesley as a pulpit. About a mile northeast of the village, **Mount Grace Priory** (English Heritage & National Trust) is a 14th-century building set in tranquil surroundings.

Ramsgill

This pleasant village, clustered around its well-kept green, is situated at the head of **Gouthwaite Reservoir**, a popular and important site for wildfowl.

Richmond

The former county of Richmondshire (which still survives as a parliamentary constituency) once occupied a third of the North Riding of Yorkshire. Alan Rufus, the 1st Earl of Richmond, built the original **Richmond Castle** in 1071 and the site, 100 feet up on a rocky promontory with the River Swale passing below, is imposing and well chosen. The keep rises to 109 feet with walls 11 feet thick, while the other side is afforded an impregnable defence by means of the cliff and the river. Richmond Castle was the first Norman castle in the country to be built, right from the foundations, in stone. Additions were made over subsequent years but it reached its final form in the 14th century.

Ripon

This attractive cathedral city, on the banks of the Rivers Ure, Skell, and Laver, dates from the 7th century. A striking survival of the Saxon cathedral is the 1,300-year-old Crypt. At its northeast corner is a narrow passage known as The Needle. The Crypt is all that remains of St Wilfrid's church but the magnificent **Cathedral of St Peter and St Wilfrid**, which now stands on the site, is certainly well worth visiting. Situated at the edge of the Market Square are the picturesque, half-timbered 14th-century **Wakeman's House** and the attractive Georgian **Town Hall**. To the southeast of the city is one of the area's finest stately homes, **Newby Hall**, built in the 18th century and designed by Robert Adam. The award-winning **Newby Hall Gardens** are extensive and well designed.

Snape

This quiet and unspoilt village, where the original timber-framed cottages stand side by side with their more modern neighbours, is still dominated by **Snape Castle**. Set in over 1,000 acres of parkland, **Thorp Perrow Arboretum** is unique to Britain, if not Europe, in that it was the creation of one man, Col. Sir Leonard Ropner (1895-1977). Sir Leonard travelled all over the world collecting rare and unusual species for Thorp Perrow and today the hundreds of trees he enthusiastically collected are in their prime.

Sowerby

In Sowerby, Georgian houses stand beneath a majestic avenue of lime trees, an old packhorse bridge crosses Cod Beck, footpaths lead across fields and alongside the quiet stream, and Millgate Gardens provide a peaceful refuge.

Stokesley

This lovely market town lies beneath the northern edge of the moors, its peace only troubled on market day which has taken place here every Friday since its charter was granted in 1223. Nikolaus Pevsner called Stokesley 'one of the most attractive small towns in the county'. There are rows of elegant Georgian and Regency houses reached by little bridges over the River Leven which flows through the town, and an old water wheel which marks the entrance to the town.

Studley Roger

The magnificent **Studley Royal Gardens** were created in the early 18th century before they were merged with nearby Fountains Abbey in 1768. With a network of paths and the River Skell flowing through the grounds, it is well worth exploring these superb gardens. A National Trust property, like the adjoining gardens, **Fountains Abbey** is the pride of all the ecclesiastical ruins in Yorkshire and the only World Heritage Site in Yorkshire. **Fountains Hall** is a magnificent Elizabethan mansion which still stands in the Abbey's grounds and part of which is open to the public.

Sutton-under-Whitestonecliff

Boasting the longest place-name in England, Sutton is more famous for the precipitous cliff that towers above it, **Sutton Bank**.

For one of the grandest landscape views in England, go to the top of Sutton Bank and look across the vast expanse of the Vale of York to the Pennine hills far away to the west. There's a National Park Information Centre at the summit of Sutton Bank and a well-marked Nature Trail leads steeply down to, and around, **Lake Gormire**, an Ice Age lake trapped here by a landslip. Gormire is one of Yorkshire's only two natural lakes, the other being Semer Water in Wensleydale. Gormire is set in a large basin with no river running from it: any overflow disappears down a 'swallow hole' and emerges beneath White Mare Cliffs.

Fountains Abbey, Studley Roger

Thirsk

Thirsk has become famous as the home of veterinary surgeon Alf Wight, better known as James Herriot, author of *All Creatures Great and Small*, who died in 1995. **The World of James Herriot** is housed in the original surgery in Kirkgate and offers visitors a trip back in time to the 1940s, exploring the life and times of the world's most famous country vet. This pleasant small town of mellow brick houses has a sprawling Market Place and the magnificent 15th-century **St Mary's Church** which is generally regarded as the finest parish church in North Yorkshire.

Sion Hill Hall, about four miles northwest of Thirsk, is celebrated as the 'last of the great country houses'. Its light, airy and well-proportioned rooms, all facing south, are typical of the work of the celebrated Yorkshire architect, Walter Brierley. In the Hall's Victorian Walled Garden is another major visitor attraction – **Falconry UK's Bird of Prey and Conservation Centre**.

Wath

The stately home of **Norton Conyers** boasts fine paintings, furniture and costumes, and there's a lovely 18th-century walled garden within the grounds.

6 | Bay Horse Inn

Ravensworth, Richmond,
North Yorkshire DL11 7ET
☎ 01325 718328

Real Ales, Bar Food, Restaurant Menu, No Smoking Area, Disabled Facilities

- ☛ Off the A66 close to Scotch Corner
- 🍺 Bombardier, Theakstons Best
- 🍴 Mon & Weds-Sun 12-1.30 & 6-9.30
- 🍴 Car park, beer garden, disabled access
- 💳 All major cards
- 🕐 Tues 6-11; Mon & Weds-Sat 12-2 & 6-11 (Sun and Bank Holidays to 10.30)
- 🏛 Barnard Castle, Easby Abbey, Richmond, the River Swale

The Bay Horse Inn makes a very pretty picture overlooking the village green, with its mellow stone walls, cobbled front patio, colourful hanging baskets and tubs of flowers, all against a backdrop of mature trees. The

interior is just as inviting. A stone door case, dating from the 1600s or possibly even earlier, was almost certainly salvaged from Ravensworth Castle; the rest of the building dates back to 1743. The bar is traditional without sacrificing any comforts, decorated with an eclectic mix of mementos that add to the homeliness and welcoming ambience of the place.

The dining room/restaurant is ornamented with a collection of 'horsey' memorabilia, including that associated with the great horse and Grand National near-winner 'Crisp', whom owner Sue used to look after. Your hosts Sue and Charlie bought the inn nine years ago when it had fallen on hard times. They have transformed the Bay Horse into a justly popular hostelry with an enviable reputation for good ale and excellent food. Charlie's very extensive menu caters for all palates, including those of vegetarians and children. Cheese soufflé, Thai fishcakes and Yorkshire puddings are among the starters; home-made beef crumble, duck breast in orange sauce and lamb hot pot are just three of the many main courses, together with delicious fresh fish dishes including salmon and dill lasagne and stuffed trout, curries, salads, sandwiches and hearty favourites such as liver, bacon and onion casserole and shepherd's pie. The irresistible choice of desserts includes gold-rush pie, baked Alaska, pecan toffee sponge and a range of ice-creams. The restaurant seats 50; booking is advised for Saturday evening and Sunday lunchtime. Children welcome.

1 Angel Hotel

High Street, Catterick, Richmond,
North Yorkshire DL10 7LL
Tel: 01748 818490

Real Ales, Bar Food, Restaurant Menu,
Accommodation, No Smoking Area

2 The Bay Horse Inn

Silver Street, Masham, Ripon,
North Yorkshire HG4 4DX
Tel: 01765 689236

Real Ales, Bar Food, Accommodation,
No Smoking Area, Disabled Facilities

3 Bay Horse Inn

Great Smeaton, Northallerton,
North Yorkshire DL6 2EQ
Tel: 01609 881466

Real Ales, Bar Food, Restaurant Menu,
No Smoking Area

4 The Bay Horse Inn

38 Low Green, Catterick, Richmond,
North Yorkshire DL10 7LP
Tel: 01748 811383

Real Ales, Bar Food, Restaurant Menu,
No Smoking Area, Disabled Facilities

5 Bay Horse Inn

Tunstall, Richmond, North Yorkshire DL10 7QS
Tel: 01748 818564

Real Ales, Bar Food, Restaurant Menu,
No Smoking Area, Disabled Facilities

6 Bay Horse Inn

Ravensworth, Richmond,
North Yorkshire DL11 7ET
Tel: 01325 718328

Real Ales, Bar Food, Restaurant Menu,
No Smoking Area, Disabled Facilities

See panel opposite

7 Bay Horse Inn

Terrington, York, Yorkshire YO60 6PP
Tel: 01653 648416

Real Ales, Bar Food, Restaurant Menu,
No Smoking Area, Disabled Facilities

8 Bay Horse Inn

The Green, Crakehall, Bedale,
North Yorkshire DL8 1HP
Tel: 01677 422548

Real Ales, Bar Food, Restaurant Menu,
No Smoking Area, Disabled Facilities

9 The Beeswing Inn

East Cowton, Northallerton,
North Yorkshire DL7 0BD
Tel: 01325 378349

Real Ales, Bar Food, Restaurant Menu,
No Smoking Area, Disabled Facilities

10 Bishop Blaize Hotel

Market Place, Richmond,
North Yorkshire DL10 4QG
Tel: 01748 823065

Real Ales, Bar Food, Restaurant Menu,
Accommodation, No Smoking Area, Disabled Facilities

11 Black Bull

75 Market Place, Thirsk, North Yorkshire YO7 1EY
Tel: 01845 525310

Real Ales, Bar Food, Restaurant Menu,
No Smoking Area, Disabled Facilities

12 Black Bull Inn

East Witton Road, Middleham, Leyburn,
North Yorkshire DL8 4NX
Tel: 01969 623669

Real Ales, Bar Food, Accommodation

13 Black Bull Inn

Moulton, Richmond, North Yorkshire DL10 6QJ
Tel: 01325 377289

Real Ales, Bar Food, Restaurant Menu,
No Smoking Area, Disabled Facilities

14 The Black Horse

23 High Street, Swainby, Northallerton,
North Yorkshire DL6 3ED
Tel: 01642 700436

Bar Food, No Smoking Area

21 The Black Swan Country Inn

Oldstead, Coxwold, North Yorkshire YO61 4BL
☎ 01347 868387
🌐 www.theblackswaninn.com

Real Ales, Bar Food, Restaurant Menu, Accommodation, No Smoking Area, Disabled Facilities

- 👉 6 miles east of Thirsk off the A170
- 🍺 John Smiths and guest ale
- 🍴 12-2 & 6-9
- 🛏 6 en suite rooms
- 🅿 Car park, disabled access, function room
- 💳 All the major cards
- 🚫 No smoking in restaurant
- 🕐 12-11 (Sundays to 10.30)
- 🏛 Shandy Hall, Newburgh Priory, Byland Abbey (Coxwold), The White Horse (Kilburn)

The lovely village of Oldstead is home to The Black Swan Country Inn, a traditional country pub set in the rolling countryside on the southern edge of the North Yorkshire National Park, making an ideal base for touring by car, cycle or via the numerous footpaths on foot. This charming place has great character,

and the hospitality offered is second to none. Overlooking rolling meadows and woodland, the inn was built in the 1700s to serve cattle-drovers on their way from the North Yorkshire moors to the Vale of York. Nestled in a valley sheltered by the prominent White Horse escarpment, it is a haven of peace and quiet yet is within easy reach of many of Yorkshire' best-loved sightseeing locations and attractions. Just a short walk from historic Byland Abbey,

this relaxed and welcoming inn offers real ales together with a full complement of lagers, cider, stout, wines, spirits and soft drinks. The Drovers Bar has open fires, stone-flagged floor and beamed ceiling, and is a cosy setting for enjoying traditional hand-pulled ales are served from the Robert 'Mousey' Thompson built wooden bar, which features the famous Thomson mouse. The food is simply delicious, guests choosing from a range of menus (including an outstanding vegetarian one) from a range of freshly prepared main courses. The upstairs dining room features a wooden floor with part wood surround and a beamed ceiling. There is a comfortable seating area where diners may sit and relax either before or after their meal. The dining room is a no smoking. The comprehensive menu comprises of a blend of traditional homemade Yorkshire fare together with more international dishes.

This superb inn also boasts six handsome en suite guest bedrooms. Here in Herriot Country, the sights and attractions are many and anyone staying at this fine inn will have a wealth of daytrips to enjoy taking in such historic and beautiful venues as Sion Hill Hall, Sutton Park, Monk Park Farm Visitor Centre and the World of James Herriot .

15 The Black Horse

The Green, Kirklington, Bedale,
North Yorkshire DL8 2ND
Tel: 01845 567122

Real Ales, Bar Food, Restaurant Menu,
No Smoking Area, Disabled Facilities

16 The Black Horse Inn

7 Lumley Lane, Kirkby Fleetham, Northallerton,
North Yorkshire DL7 0SH
Tel: 01609 748008

Real Ales, Bar Food, Restaurant Menu,
Accommodation, No Smoking Area, Disabled Facilities

17 Black Horse Inn

Aínderby Quernhow, Thirsk,
North Yorkshire YO7 4HX
Tel: 01845 567796

Real Ales, Bar Food, Restaurant Menu,
No Smoking Area, Disabled Facilities

18 Black Swan

Dishforth, Thirsk, North Yorkshire YO7 3JU
Tel: 01845 577627

Real Ales, Bar Food, No Smoking Area,
Disabled Facilities

19 The Black Swan

Market Place, Leyburn, North Yorkshire DL8 5AS
Tel: 01969 623131

Real Ales, Bar Food, Restaurant Menu,
Accommodation, No Smoking Area, Disabled Facilities

20 Black Swan

Market Place, Helmsley, York, Yorkshire YO62 5BJ
Tel: 01439 770466

Real Ales, Bar Food, Restaurant Menu,
Accommodation, No Smoking Area, Disabled Facilities

21 The Black Swan Country Inn

Main Street, Oldstead, York, Yorkshire YO61 4BL
Tel: 01347 868387

Real Ales, Bar Food, Restaurant Menu,
Accommodation, No Smoking Area, Disabled Facilities

See panel opposite

22 Black Swan Hotel

Market Place, Middleham, Leyburn,
North Yorkshire DL8 4NP
Tel: 01969 622221

Real Ales, Bar Food, Restaurant Menu,
Accommodation, No Smoking Area, Disabled Facilities

23 Black Swan Hotel

Fearby, Ripon, North Yorkshire HG4 4NF
Tel: 01765 689477

Real Ales, Bar Food, Restaurant Menu,
No Smoking Area, Disabled Facilities

24 Black-A-Moor Inn

Boroughbridge Road, Bridge Hewick, Ripon,
North Yorkshire HG4 5AA
Tel: 01765 603511

Real Ales, Restaurant Menu, Accommodation,
No Smoking Area, Disabled Facilities

25 Blacksmiths Arms

83 Market Place, Thirsk, North Yorkshire YO7 1ET
Tel: 01845 522173

Real Ales, Bar Food, Accommodation,
Disabled Facilities

26 The Blacksmiths Arms

2 Black Horse Lane, Swainby, Northallerton,
North Yorkshire DL6 3EW
Tel: 01642 700303

Real Ales, Bar Food, Restaurant Menu,
No Smoking Area, Disabled Facilities

27 The Blacksmiths Arms

Myton Terrace, North Cowton, Northallerton,
North Yorkshire DL7 0EU
Tel: 01325 378310

Real Ales, Bar Food, Restaurant Menu,
No Smoking Area, Disabled Facilities

28 Blue Bell Inn

Ingleby Cross, Northallerton,
North Yorkshire DL6 3NF
Tel: 01609 882272

Real Ales, Bar Food, Accommodation,
No Smoking Area

30 **The Bolton Arms**

Downholme Village, Richmond,
North Yorkshire DL11 6AE
☎ 01748 823716

Real Ales, Bar Food, Restaurant Menu, Accommodation, No Smoking Area, Disabled Facilities

- ☛ On the A6108 a few miles southwest of Richmond
- 🍺 Black Sheep and guest ales
- 🍴 Weds-Mon 12-2 & 6.30-9 (No food on Tuesdays)
- 🛏 2 guest bedrooms
- ⛽ Car park, beer garden, function room
- 💳 All major cards
- 🕐 Mon, Wed, Thur, Fri & Sat 11-3 & 6-close, Tues 6.30-Close, Sun 12-3 & 6-Close
- 🏛 Richmond, Catterick, Leyburn

The Bolton Arms is a handsome and impressive stonebuilt inn dating back to the 18th century. The inn commands excellent views over Swaledale, and makes a perfect base for exploring the region – there are two attractive and comfortable guest bedrooms, tastefully decorated and furnished. One room boasts a four-poster bed. The interior of this inn is warm and welcoming, and the well-stocked bar has a range of real ales, lagers, spirits, good wines and soft drinks. To eat there's an excellent menu of home-cooked dishes at lunch and evening. Daily specials include kleftico – a traditional Cypriot lamb dish – prime fillet of beef, duck breast and venison casserole.

31 **The Bolton Arms**

Market Place, Leyburn, North Yorkshire DL8 5BW
☎ 01969 623327

Real Ales, Bar Food, Restaurant Menu, No Smoking Area, Disabled Facilities

- ☛ On the A684
- 🍺 John Smiths, Black Sheep and Guest Beer
- 🍴 12-2.30 & 6-8.30
- 🎵 Jazz night Tuesday; occasional live music
- ⛽ Car park, patio garden, disabled access, quoits pitch
- 💳 All major cards
- 🚫 No smoking in restaurant
- 🕐 Mon-Thurs 11-11; Fri & Sat 10-12.30; Sun 12-close
- 🏛 Leyburn, Castle Bolton, Aysgarth, Hawes

Built in 1783, The Bolton Arms is an elevated stonebuilt inn overlooking Leyburn's busy market square. This convivial and welcoming place is owned and run by Rachel Lambie, who together with her friendly, attentive staff offer all guests a warm welcome. The inn boasts a proud history of providing excellent food and drink to regular customers and visitors, meals are served every lunchtime and most evenings, with an impressive menu of hearty favourites and daily specials, available to eat in the bar or beautiful non-smoking bistro. The popular, traditional carvery , served Sunday lunchtime, offers a trio of roast meat and wide selection of trimmings using only local produce.

29 Blue Lion Inn
East Witton, Leyburn, North Yorkshire DL8 4SN
Tel: 01969 624273
Real Ales, Bar Food, Restaurant Menu,
Accommodation, No Smoking Area

30 The Bolton Arms
Downholme, Richmond, North Yorkshire DL11 6AE
Tel: 01748 823716
Real Ales, Bar Food, Restaurant Menu,
Accommodation, No Smoking Area, Disabled Facilities
See panel opposite

31 The Bolton Arms
Market Place, Leyburn, North Yorkshire DL8 5BW
Tel: 01969 623327
Real Ales, Bar Food, Restaurant Menu,
No Smoking Area, Disabled Facilities
See panel opposite

32 Bridge House Hotel
Catterick Bridge, Richmond,
North Yorkshire DL10 7PE
Tel: 01748 818331
Real Ales, Bar Food, Restaurant Menu,
Accommodation, No Smoking Area

33 Bruce Arms Public House
3 Little Market Place, Masham, Ripon,
North Yorkshire HG4 4DY
Tel: 01765 689372
Real Ales, Restaurant Menu, Accommodation,
No Smoking Area, Disabled Facilities

34 Buck Inn
Chop Gate, Middlesbrough, Cleveland TS9 7JL
Tel: 01642 778334
Bar Food, Restaurant Menu, Accommodation,
No Smoking Area

35 Buck Inn
27 Newbiggin, Richmond,
North Yorkshire DL10 4DX
Tel: 01748 822259
Real Ales, Bar Food, Restaurant Menu

36 The Buck Inn
Thornton Watlass, Ripon,
North Yorkshire HG1 1AH
Tel: 01677 422461
Real Ales, Bar Food, Restaurant Menu,
Accommodation, No Smoking Area, Disabled Facilities

37 Bull Inn
Church Street, West Tanfield, Ripon,
North Yorkshire HG4 5JQ
Tel: 01677 470678
Real Ales, Bar Food, Restaurant Menu,
Accommodation, No Smoking Area, Disabled Facilities

38 Busby Stoop Inn
Busby Stoop Road, Thirsk,
North Yorkshire YO7 4EQ
Tel: 01845 587235
Real Ales, Bar Food, Restaurant Menu,
Accommodation, No Smoking Area, Disabled Facilities

39 Carlton Inn
Main Street, Carlton Husthwaite, Thirsk,
North Yorkshire YO7 2BW
Tel: 01845 501265
Real Ales, Bar Food, Restaurant Menu,
No Smoking Area, Disabled Facilities

40 The Castle Tavern
Market Place, Richmond,
North Yorkshire DL10 4HU
Tel: 01748 823187
Real Ales, Bar Food, Accommodation,
No Smoking Area

41 Cat & Bagpipes Inn
East Harlsey, Northallerton,
North Yorkshire DL6 2DW
Tel: 01609 882301
Real Ales

42 Cleveland Inn
Commondale, Whitby, North Yorkshire YO21 2HG
Tel: 01287 660214
Real Ales

56 Divan Hotel Thirsk

Sutton Road, Thirsk, North Yorkshire YO7 2ER
☎ 01845 522293

Real Ales, Bar Food, Restaurant Menu, Accommodation, No Smoking Area, Disabled Facilities

- ☛ On the A170 about 1½ miles east of Thirsk
- 🍺 John Smiths
- ᛁ 12-2 & 6-10 (to 9 p.m. Sundays)
- 🛏 12 en suite rooms
- ⚒ Car park, disabled access, garden, function room
- 💳 All major cards
- 🚫 No smoking in bedrooms; no-smoking areas throughout
- 🏛 Thirsk, Sutton Bank, Sion Hill, Ripon, Northallerton, Rievaulx Abbey

All-day light bites (salads, sandwiches, baked potatoes and more) are complemented by complete menus at lunch and dinner where the accent is on the freshest ingredients used to create tempting dishes including steaks, a selection of chicken, fish, seafood and pasta dishes and a choice of Mediterranean specialities such as deep-fried filo pastry rolls stuffed with feta and parsley or roasted mixed Mediterranean vegetables served with garlic yogurt. The function room accommodates small weddings and other celebrations, while the accommodation comprises 12 attractive and very comfortable en suite guest bedrooms. Ideally placed for touring the Dales, this charming hotel is owned and run by Helen Green, a young and enthusiastic host who takes great pride in offering all her guests a warm welcome and genuine hospitality.

58 Dog & Gun

Carlton Miniott, Thirsk, North Yorkshire YO7 4NJ
☎ 01845 522150

Real Ales, Bar Food, Restaurant Menu, No Smoking
Area, Disabled Facilities

- ☛ Carlton Miniott is on the A61 two miles southwest of Thirsk
- 🍺 John Smiths, Theakstons, Deuchers and rotating guest ales
- ᛁ 12-2 & 6-9
- 🎵 Sunday quiz night, occasional live music
- ⚒ Car park, beer garden
- 💳 All major cards
- 🕐 12-3 & 5.30-11; Sat 12-11; Sun and Bank Holidays 12-10.30
- 🏛 Thirsk, Sion Hill, Sutton Bank, Ripon, Northallerton, Rievaulx Abbey

Oak beams, open fires and traditional comforts aplenty can be found at the Dog & Gun, where you can enjoy a warm welcome and friendly atmosphere together with excellent real ales and great food. Homemade dishes feature on the menu, with steak and Guinness pie just one of the hearty favourites at this fine pub, together with an excellent baby lamb and many other choices of daily specials. Guests can enjoy their meal in the huge conservatory-style restaurant. The real stars here are the staff – friendly, helpful, offering a high standard of service and hospitality. There are smoking and no-smoking areas, a lovely beer garden and ample parking. Families are more than welcome – there's a separate children's menu available.

43 Colburn Lodge

Catterick Road, Catterick Garrison,
North Yorkshire DL9 4QX
Tel: 01748 832349

Bar Food, Restaurant Menu, No Smoking Area,
Disabled Facilities

44 Countrymans Inn

Hunton, Bedale, North Yorkshire DL8 1PY
Tel: 01677 450554

Real Ales, Bar Food, Restaurant Menu,
Accommodation, No Smoking Area, Disabled Facilities

45 The Coverbridge Inn

East Witton, Leyburn, North Yorkshire DL8 4SQ
Tel: 01969 623250

Real Ales, Bar Food, Accommodation,
No Smoking Area, Disabled Facilities

46 Crab & Lobster

Dishforth Road, Asenby, Thirsk,
North Yorkshire YO7 3QL
Tel: 01845 577286

Real Ales, Bar Food, Restaurant Menu,
Accommodation, No Smoking Area, Disabled Facilities

47 The Crosby

Thornton Le Beans, Northallerton,
North Yorkshire DL6 3SP
Tel: 01609 772776

Real Ales, Bar Food, Restaurant Menu,
No Smoking Area, Disabled Facilities

48 Cross Keys Inn

Kirkgate, Thirsk, North Yorkshire YO7 1PL
Tel: 01845 522550

Real Ales

49 Cross Keys Inn

Bellerby, Leyburn, North Yorkshire DL8 5QS
Tel: 01969 622256

Real Ales, Bar Food, Restaurant Menu,
No Smoking Area, Disabled Facilities

50 The Crown

Richmond Road, Brompton On Swale, Richmond,
North Yorkshire DL10 7HE
Tel: 01748 811666

Real Ales, Bar Food, Restaurant Menu,
No Smoking Area, Disabled Facilities

51 Crown & Anchor

138 Front Street, Sowerby, Thirsk,
North Yorkshire YO7 1JN
Tel: 01845 522448

Real Ales, Restaurant Menu, No Smoking Area

52 The Crown Hotel

Market Place, Helmsley, York, Yorkshire YO62 5BJ
Tel: 01439 770297

Real Ales, Bar Food, Restaurant Menu,
Accommodation, No Smoking Area

53 Crown Inn

Grewelthorpe, Ripon, North Yorkshire HG4 3BS
Tel: 01765 658210

Real Ales, Bar Food, Restaurant Menu,
No Smoking Area, Disabled Facilities

54 Crown Inn

Dishforth, Thirsk, North Yorkshire YO7 3JU
Tel: 01845 577398

Real Ales, Bar Food, Restaurant Menu,
No Smoking Area, Disabled Facilities

55 The Darrowby Inn

47 Market Place, Thirsk, North Yorkshire YO7 1HA
Tel: 01845 523222

Real Ales, Bar Food, Accommodation,
No Smoking Area

56 Divan Hotel Thirsk

Sutton Road, Thirsk, North Yorkshire YO7 2ER
Tel: 01845 522293

Real Ales, Bar Food, Restaurant Menu,
Accommodation, No Smoking Area, Disabled Facilities

See panel opposite

57 The Dog & Gun Country Inn

Cooper Lane, Potto, North Yorkshire DL6 3HQ
☎ 01642 700232
🌐 www.dogandguncountryinn.co.uk

Real Ales, Bar Food, Restaurant Menu, Accommodation, No Smoking Area, Disabled Facilities

- Off the A19 southbound towards Northallerton
- Black Sheep, guest ale
- Tues-Sat 12-3 & 6-9; Sunday Carvery 12-4
- 5 en suite rooms
- Quiz night Sundays, regular live music
- Car park, disabled access, beer garden, function suite
- All major cards
- AA 3 Diamonds
- No smoking areas
- Tues-Sat 12-3 & 6-11 (Sun and Bank Holidays to 10.30)
- Northallerton, Darlington, Stokesley, North Yorks Moors National Park

character of a traditional inn. The interior features oak-beamed ceilings while there's also a four-level restaurant, separate traditional carvery and new conservatory. The Watsons take justified pride in the variety and freshness of the food and drink on offer, which includes a tempting Sunday carvery and menus at lunch and dinner Tuesday to Saturday. Booking is advised, particularly for Friday and Saturday evenings and Sunday lunch.

Located in the pretty North Yorkshire hamlet of Potto six miles from the centre of Middlesbrough, The Dog & Gun Country Inn is a charming family inn owned and run by Esmond and Jeanne Watson and their daughters. They and the rest of their staff welcome all their guests warmly and offer the highest standard of quality and service.

The inn retains its original charm and elegance while also boasting modern comforts. Parts of the building date back to the early 1700s, and the décor throughout retains the

There are two real ales on tap (including one changing guest ale) together with a good selection of lagers, stout, cider, wines, spirits and soft drinks. And whether you're after a light lunch or a fine dinner with all the trimmings, this fine inn is well worth seeking out. Awarded 3 Diamonds by the AA, this superb inn five gracious, elegant and supremely comfortable guest bedrooms, recently refurbished to the highest standards and in keeping with the rest of the inn. Scenic countryside surrounds the inn, which makes a perfect base for exploring the many natural beauties and man-made attractions of the region.

57 The Dog & Gun Country Inn

Cooper Lane, Potto, Northallerton,
North Yorkshire DL6 3HQ
Tel: 01642 700232

Real Ales, Bar Food, Restaurant Menu,
Accommodation, No Smoking Area, Disabled Facilities

See panel opposite

58 Dog & Gun

Carlton Miniott, Thirsk, North Yorkshire YO7 4NJ
Tel: 01845 522150

Real Ales, Bar Food, Restaurant Menu,
No Smoking Area, Disabled Facilities

See panel on page 32

59 The Drovers Inn

Dallowgill, Kirkby Malzeard, Ripon,
North Yorkshire HG4 3RH
Tel: 01765 658510

Real Ales, Bar Food, Restaurant Menu,
No Smoking Area, Disabled Facilities

60 Duke Of Wellington Inn

Welbury, Northallerton, North Yorkshire DL6 2SG
Tel: 01609 882464

Real Ales, Restaurant Menu, No Smoking Area

61 Durham Ox

West Way, Crayke, York, Yorkshire YO61 4TE
Tel: 01347 821506

Real Ales, Bar Food, Restaurant Menu,
Accommodation, No Smoking Area, Disabled Facilities

62 Fairfax Arms

Main Street, Gilling East, York, Yorkshire YO62 4JH
Tel: 01439 788212

Real Ales, Bar Food, Restaurant Menu,
No Smoking Area, Disabled Facilities

63 Farmers Arms

Gatherley Road, Brompton On Swale, Richmond,
North Yorkshire DL10 7HZ
Tel: 01748 818062

Real Ales, Bar Food, Restaurant Menu,
No Smoking Area, Disabled Facilities

64 The Farmers Arms Inn

Northside, Scorton, Richmond,
North Yorkshire DL10 6DW
Tel: 01748 812533

Real Ales, Bar Food, Restaurant Menu,
No Smoking Area, Disabled Facilities

See panel on page 37

65 The Feathers Hotel

Market Place, Helmsley, York, Yorkshire YO62 5BH
Tel: 01439 770275

Real Ales, Bar Food, Restaurant Menu,
Accommodation, No Smoking Area, Disabled Facilities

See panel on page 36

66 Feversham Arms

Church Houses, Farndale, Kirkbymoorside,
York YO62 7LF
Tel: 01751 433206

Real Ales, Bar Food, Restaurant Menu,
Accommodation, No Smoking Area

67 Feversham Arms Hotel

1 High Street, Helmsley, York, Yorkshire YO62 5AE
Tel: 01439 770766

Real Ales, Bar Food, Restaurant Menu,
Accommodation, No Smoking Area

68 Fleece Hotel

5 Victoria Road, Richmond,
North Yorkshire DL10 4DW
Tel: 01748 825733

Real Ales, Bar Food, Restaurant Menu,
No Smoking Area, Disabled Facilities

69 Foresters Arms

Kilburn, York, Yorkshire YO61 4AH
Tel: 01347 868386

Real Ales, Bar Food, Restaurant Menu,
Accommodation, No Smoking Area, Disabled Facilities

70 Fox & Hounds

Carthorpe, Bedale, North Yorkshire DL8 2LG
Tel: 01845 567433

Real Ales, Bar Food, Restaurant Menu,
No Smoking Area, Disabled Facilities

65 The Feathers Hotel

Market Place, Helmsley, York,
North Yorkshire YO62 5BH
☎ 01439 770275

🌐 www.feathershotelhelmsley.co.uk

Real Ales, Bar Food, Restaurant Menu, Accommodation, No Smoking Area, Disabled Facilities

- ☛ On the A170 between Thirsk and Pickering
- 🍺 Tetleys, Black Sheep, guest ales
- 🍴 12-2.30 & 5.30-8.30
- 🛏 16 en suite rooms
- 🎵 Occasional live bands
- 🅿️ Car park, disabled access, function suite
- 💳 All major cards (except Amex)
- 🚫 No smoking in restaurant
- 🕐 Mon-Sat 11-11, Sun 12-11
- 🏛 Helmsley Castle, Duncombe Park, Ryedale, Rievaulx Abbey, North Yorks Moors Railway, Whitby, Scarborough

Taste and elegance are the bywords at The Feathers Hotel in Helmsley, a gracious and

impressive place offering the best in food, drink and accommodation. Dating back to the 15th century, it began life as two distinct buildings that were later joined into one.

Set in the heart of the picturesque market town of Helmsley, where it overlooks the market square, the hotel retains much of its original character and charm while offering the most up-to-date comforts to all its guests. The ambience is always warm, friendly and relaxed.

The décor is just one of many draws here, as the hotel houses one of the finest collections of Mouseman furniture in the nation, including the bar top in the famous Pickwick Bar – the largest single piece of oak that the Mouseman ever worked upon. Mouseman was the sobriquet of Robert Thompson, the famous craftsman who would add the distinctive 'signature' of a crouching mouse to all his work.

There's something to quench every thirst in the bar, from real ales and a very good wine list to lagers, spirits, cider, stout and soft drinks. And to eat? The Feathers enjoys an enviable reputation for serving up hearty portions of fresh, quality local produce, expertly prepared and presented. Meals are served in the (no-smoking) Feversham Lounge, a spacious, tasteful and attractive room where you can dine in comfort. The accommodation at this fine hotel is simply superb, with 16 en suite guest bedrooms furnished with understated elegance. Some rooms feature four-poster beds.

64 The Farmers Arms

Scorton, Richmond, North Yorkshire DL10 6DW
☎ 01748 812533

Real Ales, Bar Food, Restaurant Menu, No Smoking Area, Disabled Facilities

☞ On the Northallerton Road exiting Brompton-on-Swale

🍺 John Smiths Cask, Black Sheep, guest ale

🍴 Mon 6.30-9; Tues-Sun 12-2.30 & 6.30-9; all-day snacks

🛏 3 en suite rooms

🎵 Thurs night quiz (fortnightly)

⛳ Car park, disabled access, beer garden, function room

💳 All major cards

🚫 No smoking in restaurant

🕐 Mon 6-close; Tues-Fri 12-3 & 6-11; Sat 12-11; Sun 12-10.30

🏛 Richmond, Scotch Corner, Northallerton

The Farmers Arms enjoys a well-earned reputation for great food. The menus and daily specials offer a huge choice of excellent dishes. A small sample of the meals served here includes salmon fillet with asparagus, pheasant breast, pork medallions, steaks, duck breast, grilled swordfish and lamb Henri. Dating back to the 1700s, this handsome village inn is comfortable and cosy, and well worth seeking out while exploring the region.

Real ales are served alongside lagers, wines, spirits, cider, stout and soft drinks, and your drink or meal can be enjoyed in the lovely beer garden on fine days. This superior inn also has three brand new guest bedrooms, which are comfortable and provide guests with every facility and amenity they could expect.

71 Fox & Hounds Inn

Bullamoor, Northallerton,
North Yorkshire DL6 3QP
Tel: 01609 772257

Real Ales, Bar Food, Restaurant Menu,
Accommodation, No Smoking Area, Disabled Facilities

72 The Fox Hall Inn

East Layton, Richmond,
North Yorkshire DL11 7PW
Tel: 01325 718262

Real Ales, Bar Food, Restaurant Menu,
Accommodation, No Smoking Area, Disabled Facilities

See panel on page 39

73 Frankland Arms

Ingramgate, Thirsk, North Yorkshire YO7 1DF
Tel: 01845 522027

Real Ales

74 Freemasons Arms

Nosterfield, Bedale, North Yorkshire DL8 2QP
Tel: 01677 470548

Real Ales, Bar Food, Restaurant Menu,
Accommodation, No Smoking Area, Disabled Facilities

75 Galphay Inn

Galphay, Ripon, North Yorkshire HG4 3NJ
Tel: 01765 650133

Real Ales, Bar Food, Restaurant Menu,
No Smoking Area, Disabled Facilities

76 George & Dragon Inn

Melmerby, Ripon, North Yorkshire HG4 5HA
Tel: 01765 640970

Real Ales, Bar Food, Restaurant Menu,
No Smoking Area

78 The George Country Inn

Main Street, Wath, Ripon,
North Yorkshire HG4 5EN
☎ 01765 640202

Real Ales, Bar Food, Restaurant Menu, Accommodation, No Smoking Area, Disabled Facilities

☛ Off the A61 3 miles north of Ripon, after about 1 mile turn left onto the minor road signposted Wath or turn left 1 mile further along and reach Wath via Melmerby; can also be reached east off the A6108, turning at West Tanfield

🍺 Tetleys, Black Sheep, guest ale

🍴 Winter: Mon & Weds-Thurs 6-9, Fri-Sat 6-10, Sun 12-3; Summer: Weds-Sat 12-3 & 6-9; Sun 12-3

🛏 4 en suite rooms

♫ Weds night quiz

🚗 Parking, disabled access, beer garden

💳 All major cards

🚫 No smoking in restaurant

🕐 Winter: Mon & Weds-Thurs 5-11, Fri-Sun 12-3 & 5-11; Summer: 12-close 7 days a week

🏛 Norton Conyers, Ripon, North Stainley, Lightwater Theme Park

The eye-catching exterior of The George Country Inn in the heart of the village of Wath is a welcoming sight. A hub of village life, this attractive inn – which dates back to the 1700s – has picnic tables and tubs of flowers outside, while inside all is warm, cosy and comfortable. Combining the best of ancient and modern, The George is a marvellous traditional inn with an Eastern flavour: hearty English favourites vie with superb Thai food on the menu here. The décor is the best of Yorkshire, with comfortable seating, an understated elegance and always a friendly and welcoming ambience.

Owners Roger and Vanna offer all their guests a warm welcome and their very best in food, drink and accommodation. At Thai at the George, a superb restaurant and takeaway, the Thai chef creates an impressive range of expertly prepared dishes such as curries, stir fries, noodles and rice dishes, vegetarian options and more. English meals are also available. For Sunday lunch there's a choice between an 'all you can eat' Thai buffet or a traditional English roast with all the trimmings. Thursdays are steak night. The cuisine here has earned high praise from local and national food critics.

The restaurant doubles as a function room and seats 80 guests. Booking required at weekends. To drink, there are several real ales together with a good selection of wines, spirits, lagers, cider, stout and soft drinks. This fine inn also boasts four excellent guest bedrooms – two doubles, one single and a family room – all spacious and comfortable. The tariff includes a hearty breakfast.

72 The Fox Hall Inn

East Layton, Richmond, North Yorkshire DL11 7PW
☎ 01325 718262

Real Ales, Bar Food, Restaurant Menu, Accommodation, No Smoking Area, Disabled Facilities

- ☞ On the A66 close to Scotch Corner
- 🍺 Black Sheep, Theakstons, guest ale
- 🍴 12-9
- 🛏 10 guest bedrooms (8 en suite)
- ♫ Regular theme nights; clay pigeon shooting; pool, darts
- ⛴ Car park, disabled access, beer garden, patio
- 💳 All major cards
- 🚫 No smoking in restaurants
- 🕐 11-11
- 🏛 River Swale, Easby Abbey, Richmond, Reeth, Leyburn

A handsome coaching inn dating back to the 1500s, The Fox Hall Inn is a spacious and welcoming place with all-day food, drink and accommodation.

The accent is on excellent food here, with a menu and specials board of tasty and hearty favourites served in one of two restaurant areas. The bar is cosy and comfortable, and serves up a selection of real ales, lagers, wines, spirits and soft drinks. The beer garden is the perfect place to enjoy a relaxing drink or meal on fine days, and the inn also offers 10 guest bedrooms for anyone wanting a handy base from which to explore the many beautiful sights and attractions of the region.

77 George & Dragon Inn

Hudswell, Richmond, North Yorkshire DL11 6BL
Tel: 01748 823082

Real Ales, Bar Food, Restaurant Menu, No Smoking Area, Disabled Facilities

78 The George Country Inn

Main Street, Wath, Ripon,
North Yorkshire HG4 5EN
Tel: 01765 640202

Real Ales, Bar Food, Restaurant Menu, Accommodation, No Smoking Area, Disabled Facilities

See panel opposite

79 Golden Fleece

42 Market Place, Thirsk, North Yorkshire YO7 1LL
Tel: 07623 523108

Real Ales, Restaurant Menu, Accommodation, Disabled Facilities

80 The Golden Lion Hotel

Market Place, Leyburn, North Yorkshire DL8 5AS
Tel: 01969 622161

Real Ales, Bar Food, Restaurant Menu, Accommodation, No Smoking Area, Disabled Facilities

See panel on page 40

81 Golden Lion

6 West End, Osmotherley, Northallerton,
North Yorkshire DL6 3AA
Tel: 01609 883526

Real Ales, Bar Food, Restaurant Menu, No Smoking Area, Disabled Facilities

82 Golden Lion Inn

Main Street, Helperby, York, Yorkshire YO61 2NT
Tel: 01423 360870

Real Ales, Bar Food, Restaurant Menu, No Smoking Area, Disabled Facilities

80 The Golden Lion Hotel

Market Place, Leyburn, North Yorkshire DL8 5AS

☎ 01969 622161 ⊚ www.thegoldenlion.co.uk

Real Ales, Bar Food, Restaurant Menu, Accommodation, No Smoking Area, Disabled Facilities

☛ At the junction of the A684 (Northallerton-Hawes) and the A6108 (Ripon-Richmond)

🍺 Theakstons, Black Sheep, guest ale

🍴 12-2 & 6-8.30

🛏 15 en suite rooms

♿ Disabled access, car park, function room, patio

💳 All the major cards

🏆 1 Star AA

🚭 No-smoking areas

🕐 11-12 (Sun and Bank Holidays to 11.30)

🏛 Aysgarth Falls, Middleham Castle, Jervaulx Abbey

Built in the mid-1700s, The Golden Lion Hotel is a classically typical Yorkshire roadhouse – spacious, handsome and very welcoming. The food and drink on hand are of excellent quality and are very good value. Everything on the menu is locally sourced and

home-made, and the real ales and other thirst-quenchers – lagers, cider, stout, wines, spirits, soft drinks – never fail to deliver. This traditional family hotel lies on the broad market place of Leyburn. Dating from 1765, the impressive exterior includes lovely green and gold ironwork and large bay windows. Anne Wood's superior hotel offers facilities usually associated with larger establishments. The 15 tasteful and comfortable en suite guest bedrooms (doubles, twins, family and single

rooms) have TV, telephone, radio and tea-making kit, and a lift to the upper floors enables access for guests with disabilities, for whose needs many of the rooms have been adapted. The tariff includes a delicious breakfast, and special breaks are available throughout the year. In the 70-cover restaurant, murals of Dales scenes by local artist Lynn Foster provide a pleasant backdrop to a wonderful dining experience: good, wholesome Yorkshire fare freshly prepared from local ingredients. Diners can choose between a la carte and fixed-price menus, or something lighter from the informal bar snack menu. Among the favourites are home-made beef and Guinness pie, braised lamb, and roast beef. There's also a tempting Sunday dinner menu, and children's meals. Booking is required for Friday and Saturday evening and for Sunday lunch.

Guests can enjoy a quiet drink in one of the oak-panelled bars, in the restaurant or, on fine days, outside on the patio. Anne and her dedicated team provide excellent service and hospitality to all their guests. Leyburn is a perfect base for exploring the Dales.

85 The Green Dragon

Market Place, Bedale, North Yorkshire DL8 1EQ
☎ 01677 425246

Real Ales, Accommodation, Disabled Facilities

☞ On the High Street in Bedale, 7½ miles southwest of Northallerton on the A684

🍺 Guest ales

🛏 7 en suite bedrooms

⚒ Beer garden

💳 All major cards

🕐 Mon-Thurs 4-close; Fri-Sun 12-close

🏛 Bedale Beck, Bedale Hall, Northallerton, Catterick

A handsome town centre inn in the heart of Bedale, The Green Dragon is elegant and charming inside and out. Real ales are served alongside a good range of wines, spirits, lagers, cider, stout and soft drinks. This superior inn also boasts seven pristine guest bedrooms, decorated and furnished to a high standard of comfort and quality – a happy marriage of traditional features and modern amenities. And of course Bedale makes an excellent base from which to explore the many delights of the region, from Bedale itself to the River Swale and Swaledale, Northallerton, Thirsk and Ripon. Gateway to the Dales and 5 minutes from the A1.

83 The Grange Arms

Hornby, Northallerton, North Yorkshire DL6 2JQ
Tel: 01609 881249

Real Ales, Bar Food, Restaurant Menu,
No Smoking Area

84 The Grantley Arms

Grantley, Ripon, North Yorkshire HG4 3PJ
Tel: 01765 620227

Real Ales, Bar Food, Restaurant Menu,
No Smoking Area, Disabled Facilities

See panel on page 42

85 The Green Dragon

Market Place, Bedale, North Yorkshire DL8 1EQ
Tel: 01677 425246

Real Ales, Accommodation, Disabled Facilities

See panel above

86 Green Dragon Inn

High Row, Exelby, Bedale,
North Yorkshire DL8 2HA
Tel: 01677 422233

Real Ales, Bar Food, Restaurant Menu,
Accommodation, No Smoking Area, Disabled Facilities

87 Green Tree Inn

Stokesley Road, Brompton, Northallerton,
North Yorkshire DL6 2UA
Tel: 01609 780251

Real Ales, Bar Food, No Smoking Area,
Disabled Facilities

88 Grey Horse Inn

West Rounton, Northallerton,
North Yorkshire DL6 2LW
Tel: 01609 882750

Real Ales, Bar Food, Restaurant Menu,
No Smoking Area, Disabled Facilities

84 The Grantley Arms

High Grantley, Ripon, North Yorkshire HG4 3PJ

☎ 01765 620227 ⊕ www.grantleyarms.com

Real Ales, Bar Food, Restaurant Menu, No Smoking Area, Disabled Facilities

- ☞ Off the B6265 below Ripon
- 🍺 Black Sheep, guest ales
- 🍴 12-2 & 5.30-9
- 🅿 Car park, disabled access, patio, function room
- 💳 All the major cards
- 🚫 No smoking in restaurants or at Sunday Lunch; no pets
- 🕐 Tues-Sat 12-2.30 & 5.30-close; Sunday 12-10.30
- 🏛 Ripon, North Stainley, Fountains Abbey, Boroughbridge, Hackfall Woods

The Grantley Arms is a fine traditional inn boasting excellent food. Dating back to

the mid-1600s, the inn is set in the picturesque village of High Grantley and enjoys a well-earned reputation for the quality of its food, drink and hospitality. Popular with locals and visitors alike, the pub's handsome décor, comfort and spotlessness are just three of its many attractions, and all add to its warm and welcoming ambience.

The bar areas are spacious, while the attractive and elegant restaurant is air-

conditioned and seats 30. The food comes highly recommended with an excellent range of dishes such as lamb noisettes, pheasant, steaks and halibut steak. Guests select from the à la carte menu or specials board. Special two- or three-course lunches are available, and there's an evening 'early bird' menu between 5.30 and 7 Tuesday to Friday. Booking is advised. To complement your meal there's a good range of draught ales and an excellent selection of wines.

Anyone exploring the many sights and attractions of the region – Fountains Abbey, the Devil's Arrows, Lightwater Valley, Marmion Tower, the River Ure, Nidderdale and much more – would be well advised to stop here for a quiet drink or memorable meal in supremely tasteful and convivial surroundings.

89 Greyhound Country Inn
Hackforth, Bedale, North Yorkshire DL8 1PB
Tel: 01748 811415

Real Ales, Bar Food, Restaurant Menu,
Accommodation, No Smoking Area, Disabled Facilities

90 The Greyhound Inn
Bagby, Thirsk, North Yorkshire YO7 2PF
Tel: 01845 597315

Restaurant Menu, No Smoking Area

91 Hack & Spade
Whashton, Richmond, North Yorkshire DL11 7JL
Tel: 01748 823721

Restaurant Menu, No Smoking Area

92 Half Moon Inn
Sharow, Ripon, North Yorkshire HG4 5BP
Tel: 01765 600291

Real Ales, Bar Food, Restaurant Menu,
Accommodation, No Smoking Area

93 Hambleton Inn
Hambleton, Thirsk, North Yorkshire YO7 2HA
Tel: 01845 597202

Real Ales, Bar Food, Restaurant Menu,
No Smoking Area

94 The Hare Inn
Scawton, Thirsk, North Yorkshire YO7 2HG
Tel: 01845 597524

Real Ales, Bar Food, Restaurant Menu,
No Smoking Area, Disabled Facilities

See panel on page 44

95 Harry's
Shute Road, Catterick Garrison,
North Yorkshire DL9 4AE
Tel: 01748 836232

Real Ales, Bar Food, No Smoking Area,
Disabled Facilities

96 Hawnby Hotel
Hill Top, Hawnby, York, Yorkshire YO62 5QS
Tel: 01439 798202

Bar Food, Restaurant Menu, Accommodation,
No Smoking Area, Disabled Facilities

97 The Haynes Arms
Kirby Sigston, Northallerton,
North Yorkshire DL6 3TD
Tel: 01609 883383

Real Ales, Bar Food, Restaurant Menu, No Smoking
Area

98 The Henry Jenkins Inn
Main Street, Kirkby Malzeard, Ripon,
North Yorkshire HG4 3RY
Tel: 01765 658557

Real Ales, Bar Food, Restaurant Menu,
No Smoking Area

99 J A & D L Rivis
10 Castlegate, Helmsley, York, Yorkshire YO62 5AB
Tel: 01439 770304

Bar Food

100 J.T'S Bar
21 Hildyard Row, Catterick Garrison,
North Yorkshire DL9 4DH
Tel: 01748 833899

Disabled Facilities

101 King William Iv
1 Station Road, Brompton on Swale, Richmond,
North Yorkshire DL10 7HN
Tel: 01748 811416

Real Ales, Bar Food, Restaurant Menu,
No Smoking Area

102 The Kings Head
3 Grove Square, Leyburn,
North Yorkshire DL8 5AE
Tel: 01969 622272

Real Ales, Bar Food, Restaurant Menu,
No Smoking Area

103 The King's Head
40 Market Place, Bedale, North Yorkshire DL8 1EQ
Tel: 01677 422763

Real Ales, Bar Food, Restaurant Menu,
Accommodation, No Smoking Area, Disabled Facilities

See panel on page 45

94 The Hare Inn

Scawton, Thirsk, North Yorkshire YO7 2HG
☎ 01845 597524

Real Ales, Bar Food, Restaurant Menu,
No Smoking Area, Disabled Facilities

- ☞ 1 mile off the A170 Thirsk-Helmsley Road close to Sutton Bank.
- ☕ Black Sheep, John Smiths Cask, guest ale
- 🍴 Weds-Sat 12-3 & 6.30-9; Sun 12-4
- 🅿 Parking, disabled access, front garden
- 💳 All major cards
- ♟ *Good Pub Guide 2005*
- 🚫 No smoking in restaurant
- ⏰ Winter: Weds-Sat 12-3 & 6.30 to close, Sun 12-4; Summer: all day 7 days a week
- 🏛 Rievaulx Abbey, Helmsley, Thirsk, Castle Howard, Malton, Pickering

It is said that stones left over from the construction of Rievaulx Abbey were used to

build The Hare Inn as far back as the 12th century. This distinguished inn is well worth seeking out for its excellent food, drink and hospitality.

The chef creates a range of marvellous dishes using the very freshest local ingredients, with delights such as rump of Yorkshire Dales lamb, organic salmon, thyme and root vegetable risotto and steak-and-kidney pudding all expertly prepared and presented. The starters and puddings are no less

impressive, and children's portions are available for most dishes.

Occupying a very scenic, secluded location, this spacious and welcoming inn is mentioned in the Domesday Book and has an understated elegance throughout. Its handsome interior is divided into several charming and cosy rooms with original features such as low beams and flagstone floors, which add to the welcoming ambience and traditional feel of the place.

Owner Ken Moore and his friendly, capable staff offer a good standard of service and quality to all their guests, and the inn is justly popular with locals and visitors alike. Handy for a drink or meal while exploring the many sights and attractions of the region – which include Scawton's own local and ancient church of St Mary and, of course, Rievaulx Abbey nearby – stopping at this fine inn will please even the most discerning diner.

103 The King's Head

40 Market Place, Bedale, North Yorkshire DL8 1EQ
☎ 01677 422763

Real Ales, Bar Food, Restaurant Menu, Accommodation, No Smoking Area, Disabled Facilities

☛ On the main street of Bedale, which is 7½ miles southwest of Northallerton on the A684

🍺 John Smiths, Black Sheep, guest ale

🛏 5 en suite rooms

🎵 Karaoke Thurs night; live DJ Fri & Sat; live music Sun

⚓ Car park, beer garden

🕐 Mon-Thurs 4-11; Fri-Sat 11a.m.-2 a.m.; Sun 12-12

🏛 Bedale, Crakehall, Northallerton

Located in the heart of Bedale, an excellent base from which to explore the Dales and beyond, The King's Head is a spacious and welcoming inn serving great real ales and offering very comfortable accommodation. Owned and run by Steve Reed, this fine inn at the gateway to the Dales specialises in golf packages and is a convivial place to enjoy a relaxing drink amid comfortable surroundings. Real ales include John Smiths and Black Sheep, together with a rotating guest ale, as well as a good range of lagers, cider, stout, wines, spirits and soft drinks. Other diversions at the inn include live televised sport and two full-sized snooker tables. The accommodation comprises five handsome and comfortable en suite guest bedrooms.

104 The Kings Head Hotel

10 Market Place, Richmond,
North Yorkshire DL10 4HS
Tel: 01748 850220

Real Ales, Bar Food, Restaurant Menu, Accommodation, No Smoking Area, Disabled Facilities

105 Kings Head Hotel

40 Market Place, Masham, Ripon,
North Yorkshire HG4 4EF
Tel: 01765 689295

Real Ales, Bar Food, Restaurant Menu, Accommodation, No Smoking Area, Disabled Facilities

106 The Lamb Inn

Rainton, Thirsk, North Yorkshire YO7 3PH
Tel: 01845 577284

Real Ales, Bar Food, Restaurant Menu, No Smoking Area, Disabled Facilities

107 Le Maginot

4-6 Byng Road, Catterick Garrison,
North Yorkshire DL9 4DJ
Tel: 01748 832404

108 Lion Inn

High Blakey, Kirkbymoorside, Blakey Ridge,
York YO62 7LQ
Tel: 01751 417320

Real Ales, Bar Food, Restaurant Menu, Accommodation, No Smoking Area

109 The Lodge

North Road, Hackforth, Bedale,
North Yorkshire DL8 1NP
Tel: 01677 422122

Real Ales, Bar Food, Restaurant Menu, Accommodation, No Smoking Area

117 The Moor & Pheasant

Dalton, Dalton Moor, North Yorkshire YO7 3JD
☎ 01845 577268

Real Ales, Bar Food, Restaurant Menu, Disabled Facilities

- Off the A168 via J49 of the A1/M1 4 miles south of Thirsk
- John Smiths Cask, Titanic guest ale
- Mon-Thurs 12-3 & 6-9; Fri 7 Sat 12-3 & 5.30-8.30; Sun 12-8; all-day light bites
- Small caravan site
- Saturday night quiz; Friday night bingo
- Car park, disabled access, beer garden, children's play area
- All major cards
- Mon-Thurs 11 a.m.-midnight; Fri & Sat 11 a.m. to 2 a.m.; Sun 10 a.m. to midnight
- Thirsk, Ripon, Northallerton, Rievaulx Abbey

Dating back to the 1780s, The Moor & Pheasant is a true hidden gem yet is just off the A1/M1 a few miles from Thirsk. It has changed over the years to stay up to date with offering guests every modern comfort. The food, drink and hospitality are first class, with owner Paul Murray and his friendly, conscientious staff offering a high standard of service.

There are always two real ales on tap, together with a good range of lagers, wines, spirits, soft drinks, cider and stout. Light bites are served throughout the day, and there's also a good menu and specials board with hearty favourites cooked to order. The children's menu ensures that young diners will find something to please their palates.

The interior is warm and cosy, with a large brickbuilt fire and other traditional features adding to the relaxed and welcoming ambience at this superior pub. For fine days there's a lovely beer garden complete with children's play area where guests can enjoy a very pleasant drink or meal.

To the rear of the pub there's a small caravan site for guests exploring the region – and of course there's much to explore here, with sights and attractions that include Thirsk, Sion Hill, Sutton Bank, Ripon, Northallerton and Rievaulx Abbey. Thirsk has become famous as the home of veterinary surgeon Alf Wight, author of *All Creatures Great and Small*, and is surrounded by some of the most beautiful countryside in England.

110 The Lord Nelson Inn

Front Street, Appleton Wiske, Northallerton,
North Yorkshire DL6 2AD
Tel: 01609 881351

Real Ales, Bar Food, No Smoking Area

111 The Lord Nelson

St James Green, Thirsk, North Yorkshire YO7 1AQ
Tel: 01845 522845

Real Ales, Restaurant Menu, Disabled Facilities

See panel adjacent

112 Louies Bar

Kitchener Road, Catterick Garrison,
North Yorkshire DL9 4HE
Tel: 01748 836611

Disabled Facilities

113 The Malt Shovel

Main Street, Hovingham, York, Yorkshire YO62 4LF
Tel: 01653 628264

Real Ales, Bar Food, Restaurant Menu,
No Smoking Area

114 The Malt Shovel Inn

Oswaldkirk, York, Yorkshire YO62 5XT
Tel: 01439 788461

Real Ales, Bar Food, No Smoking Area

115 Middlesmoor Crown

Middlesmoor, Harrogate, North Yorkshire HG3 5ST
Tel: 01423 755204

Real Ales, Bar Food, Restaurant Menu,
Accommodation, No Smoking Area, Disabled Facilities

116 Miners Arms

124 High Street, Swainby, Northallerton,
North Yorkshire DL6 3DG
Tel: 01642 700457

No Smoking Area

117 The Moor & Pheasant

Dalton Moor, Dalton, Thirsk,
North Yorkshire YO7 3JD
Tel: 01845 577268

Real Ales, Bar Food, Restaurant Menu

See panel opposite

111 The Lord Nelson

St James Green, Thirsk, North Yorkshire YO7 1AQ
☎ 01845 522845

Real Ales, Restaurant Menu, Disabled Facilities

☛ On the outskirts of the centre of Thirsk –
follow the signs for the A170

🍺 Black Sheep, Riggwelter and 1 rotating guest
ale

🛏 3 en suite rooms

🎵 Acoustic night Sunday; monthly comedy night;
occasional live music

♨ Car park; disabled access; games room;
function room

🕐 12-11 (Sun and Bank Holidays to 10.30)

🏛 Thirsk, Sion Hill, Sutton Bank, Ripon,
Northallerton, Rievaulx Abbey

The Lord Nelson is a well-looked-after and
charming inn that makes a perfect base for
exploring Thirsk and the surrounding region,
with three en suite rooms that are
comfortable and attractive. This inn also offers
great real ales and tasty all-day snacks. Next
door, owners Katy and Jamie Pearson display
the work of local artists for sale.

118 Nags Head

Pickhill, Thirsk, North Yorkshire YO7 4JG
Tel: 01845 567391

Real Ales, Bar Food, Restaurant Menu,
Accommodation, No Smoking Area, Disabled Facilities

119 The New Inn

Thrintoft, Northallerton,
North Yorkshire DL7 0PN
Tel: 01609 777060

Real Ales, Bar Food, Restaurant Menu,
No Smoking Area, Disabled Facilities

See panel on page 48

120 The Oak Tree

Low Green, Catterick, Richmond,
North Yorkshire DL10 7LU
Tel: 01748 818233

Real Ales, Bar Food, Restaurant Menu,
No Smoking Area, Disabled Facilities

119 The New Inn

Moor Lane, Thrintoft, Northallerton, North
Yorkshire DL7 0PN
☎ 01609 777060

Real Ales, Bar Food, Restaurant Menu, No Smoking Area, Disabled Facilities

☛ Off the main Bedale-Northallerton Road close to the A1

🍺 John Smiths, Black Sheep, Websters

🍴 12-2 & 6-9

⚒ Car park, disabled access, beer garden

💳 All major cards

🕐 Tues-Sun 11.30-3 & 6-11

🏛 Bedale, Northallerton, Moulton, Aldbrough

Truly excellent food is the hallmark at The New Inn, a divine village pub that looks picture-perfect from the outside and gets even better once you're inside. Dating back to 1776, it is pretty, pristine and spacious. The menu and specials board includes tempting dishes such as home-made steak and kidney pie, lamb shank, poached salmon, grills and delicious hot and cold salads. The vegetarian options include leek and mushroom crumble and brie and broccoli parcels. The Sunday roasts are worth making a special journey for.

The atmosphere at this inn is always convivial and welcoming, and owners Alan and Joy Woods are enthusiastic and friendly hosts who spare no effort in providing all their guests with first-class food, drink and hospitality.

126 The Old Royal George

Morton on Swale, Northallerton,
North Yorkshire DL7 9QS
☎ 01609 780254

Real Ales, Bar Food, Restaurant Menu, No Smoking Area

☛ On the A684 2 miles southwest of Northallerton

🍺 Marstons Pedigree

🍴 12-2 & 6-9

🎵 Quiz night Thursdays

⚒ Car park, beer garden

💳 All major cards

🚫 No smoking areas

🕐 12-2 & 6-close

🏛 Northallerton, Bedale, Crakehall, Sion Hill, Thirsk, Catterick

Dating back to the 1800s, The Old Royal George is a delightful inn, pristine and welcoming. Now in the capable hands of Mike Miles, who has many years' experience in the trade, this fine inn has been totally refurbished to maintain all its period charm while incorporating every modern comfort. With a range of lagers, real ale, wines, spirits and other drinks, the inn also boasts great food at lunch and dinner every day. The menu and specials board feature tempting bar meals and main courses including scampi with home-made chips and salad, Cumberland sausage with mash and red onion marmalade, lobster, king prawns, Mediterranean vegetables, swordfish, New Zealand green-lipped mussels, slow-roasted lamb, roast duck, steaks and much more.

121 Oak Tree Inn

Copt Hewick, Ripon, North Yorkshire HG4 5BY
Tel: 01765 603578

Real Ales, Bar Food, Restaurant Menu,
No Smoking Area, Disabled Facilities

122 Old Black Bull

North End, Raskelf, York, Yorkshire YO61 3LF
Tel: 01347 821431

Real Ales, Bar Food, Restaurant Menu,
Accommodation, No Smoking Area, Disabled Facilities

123 The Old Black Swan

Market Place, Bedale, North Yorkshire DL8 1ED
Tel: 01677 422973

Real Ales, Bar Food, No Smoking Area,
Disabled Facilities

124 Old Horn Inn

Spennithorne, Leyburn, North Yorkshire DL8 5PR
Tel: 01969 622370

Real Ales, Bar Food, Restaurant Menu,
Accommodation, No Smoking Area, Disabled Facilities

125 Old Oak Tree

South Kilvington, Thirsk, North Yorkshire YO7 2NL
Tel: 01845 523276

Real Ales, Bar Food, No Smoking Area,
Disabled Facilities

126 The Old Royal George

Morton On Swale, Northallerton,
North Yorkshire DL7 9QS
Tel: 01609 780254

Real Ales, Bar Food, Restaurant Menu,
No Smoking Area

See panel opposite

127 Otterington Shorthorn Inn

Otterington Shorthorn, South Otterington,
Northallerton, North Yorkshire DL7 9HP
Tel: 01609 773816

Real Ales, Bar Food, Restaurant Menu,
No Smoking Area, Disabled Facilities

128 Pheasant Inn

Harmby, Leyburn, North Yorkshire DL8 5PA
Tel: 01969 622223

Real Ales, Disabled Facilities

129 Plough Inn

Main Street, Fadmoor, York, Yorkshire YO62 7HY
Tel: 01751 431515

Real Ales, Bar Food, Restaurant Menu,
No Smoking Area, Disabled Facilities

130 The Plough Inn

Main Street, Wombleton, York,
Yorkshire YO62 7RW
Tel: 01751 431356

Real Ales, Bar Food, Restaurant Menu,
No Smoking Area, Disabled Facilities

131 Queen Catherine

West End, Osmotherley, Northallerton,
North Yorkshire DL6 3AG
Tel: 01609 883209

Real Ales, Bar Food, Restaurant Menu,
Accommodation, No Smoking Area, Disabled Facilities

132 Queens Head

West Moor Lane, Finghall, Leyburn,
North Yorkshire DL8 5ND
Tel: 01677 450259

Real Ales, Bar Food, Restaurant Menu,
Accommodation, No Smoking Area, Disabled Facilities

See panel on page 50

133 The Queens Head

Main Street, Kirkby Malzeard, Ripon,
 North Yorkshire HG4 3RS
Tel: 01765 658497

Real Ales, Bar Food, Restaurant Menu,
No Smoking Area

134 Richard III Hotel

Market Place, Middleham, Leyburn,
North Yorkshire DL8 4NP
Tel: 01969 623240

Real Ales, Bar Food, Restaurant Menu,
Accommodation, No Smoking Area, Disabled Facilities

132 Queens Head

West Moor Lane, Finghall,
North Yorkshire DL8 5ND
☎ 01677 450259

Real Ales, Bar Food, Restaurant Menu, Accommodation, No Smoking Area, Disabled Facilities

☛ Off the A684 east of Leyburn

🍺 John Smiths, Theakstons, Black Sheep, Daleside, guest ales

🍴 Breakfast, lunch (12-2.30) & dinner (6-9.30)

🛏 5 en suite rooms

♫ Quiz every other Friday evening from 9 p.m.

🅿 Car park, disabled access, function room, beer gardens, children's play area

💳 All major cards

🏆 *Good Pub Guide 2006*

🚫 No smoking in restaurant

🕐 8-close

🏛 Leyburn, Richmond, Hawes, Ripon, Northallerton, Pateley Bridge

A superb country inn dating back to the 15th century in the quiet village of Finghall, just off the A684 east of Leyburn, The Queens Head is owned and run by Sharon and Peter Farhall, who arrived in 2001 and who have nearly 30 years' experience in the trade. This cosy pub is comfortable and welcoming, and retains much of its historic charm and character. From the excellent gardens to the rear of the premises visitors can see Wyvill Hall – reputedly the inspiration for Toad Hall, home of Toad in Wind in the Willows. Open from 8 in the morning seven days a week, the inn serves breakfast as well as lunch and dinner, and stays open late. In addition to the real ales on tap at this Free House there is also a good range of lagers, cider, stout, wines, spirits and soft drinks.

Head chef Andrew Megson has built up a fine and deserved reputation for his menus, which offer a range of freshly prepared home-cooked dishes to suit all tastes and appetites. Favourites include hot chicken salad, pork fillets and pan-fried sea bass. The daily specials

complement the huge range of mouth-watering dishes served here. The dining room is stylish and handsome, and seats 55. Booking is essential at weekends, though food can also be enjoyed in the bar areas. Children are welcome in the restaurant until around 9 p.m. During the lifetime of this edition, chalet-style accommodation will be available with five purpose-built rooms offering every modern comfort and amenity. Please ring for details.

Finghall makes a good touring base, handy for the many sights and attractions of the region including Leyburn, Richmond and Wensleydale.

135 The Rose & Crown

Main Road, Nawton, York, Yorkshire YO62 7RD
Tel: 01439 771247

Real Ales, Bar Food, No Smoking Area

136 The Royal Oak

Market Place, Helmsley, York,
Yorkshire YO62 5BL
Tel: 01439 770450

Real Ales, Bar Food, Restaurant Menu,
Accommodation, No Smoking Area

137 Royal Oak Inn

Church Street, Nunnington, York,
Yorkshire YO62 5US
Tel: 01439 748271

Real Ales, Bar Food, Restaurant Menu,
No Smoking Area, Disabled Facilities

138 Sandpiper Inn

Railway Street, Leyburn, North Yorkshire DL8 5AT
Tel: 01969 622206

Real Ales, Bar Food, Restaurant Menu,
Accommodation, No Smoking Area, Disabled Facilities

139 Scotch Corner Hotel

Scotch Corner, Middleton Tyas, Richmond,
North Yorkshire DL10 6NR
Tel: 01748 850900

Real Ales, Bar Food, Restaurant Menu,
Accommodation, No Smoking Area, Disabled Facilities

140 Ship Inn

93 Frenchgate, Richmond, North Yorkshire DL10 7AE
Tel: 01748 823182

Real Ales

141 Smailways Country Inn

Smallways, Richmond, North Yorkshire DL11 7QW
Tel: 01833 627225

Real Ales, Bar Food, No Smoking Area,
Disabled Facilities

142 Solberge Hall Hotel

Newby Wiske, Northallerton,
North Yorkshire DL7 9ER
Tel: 01609 779191

Bar Food, Restaurant Menu, Accommodation,
No Smoking Area, Disabled Facilities

143 The Stanwick Arms

Aldbrough St John, Richmond,
North Yorkshire DL11 7SZ
Tel: 01325 374258

Real Ales, Bar Food, Restaurant Menu,
Accommodation, No Smoking Area

144 Star Inn & Cross House Lodge

High Street, Harome, York, Yorkshire YO62 5JE
Tel: 01439 770397

Real Ales, Bar Food, Restaurant Menu,
Accommodation, No Smoking Area, Disabled Facilities

145 Staveley Arms

North Stainley, Ripon, North Yorkshire HG4 3HT
Tel: 01765 635439

Real Ales, Bar Food, Restaurant Menu,
No Smoking Area, Disabled Facilities

146 The Swaledale Arms

Morton On Swale, Northallerton,
North Yorkshire DL7 9RJ
Tel: 01609 774108

Real Ales, Bar Food

See panel on page 52

147 Swinton Park

Swinton, Ripon, North Yorkshire HG4 4JH
Tel: 01765 680900

Real Ales, Bar Food, Restaurant Menu,
Accommodation, No Smoking Area, Disabled Facilities

148 The Three Coopers

2 Emgate, Bedale, North Yorkshire DL8 1AL
Tel: 01677 422153

Real Ales, Bar Food, Restaurant Menu,
No Smoking Area, Disabled Facilities

See panel on page 52

146 The Swaledale Arms

Morton on Swale, Northallerton,
North Yorkshire DL7 9RJ
☎ 01609 774108

Real Ales, Bar Food

- ☛ On the A684 2 miles southwest of Northallerton
- 🍺 Black Sheep, John Smiths
- 🍴 11.30-2 & 6.30-9 Mon-Thurs (to 9.30 Fr & Sat)
- 🅿 Car park, disabled access, function room
- 💳 All major cards
- 🕐 11.30-3 & 6.30-12
- 🏛 Northallerton, Bedale, Crakehall, Sion Hill, Thirsk, Catterick

The Swaledale Arms is a charming village pub with great food, drink and hospitality. With real ales on tap together with lagers, cider, stout, wines, spirits and soft drinks, there's something to quench every thirst, while the daily menus and specials board offer an outstanding selection of dishes using the freshest local ingredients. The spacious lounge has a roaring open fire and the ambience is always friendly and welcoming. Run by Laura and Mark, engaging and conscientious hosts, this inn makes a perfect place to stop for a relaxing drink or meal while exploring the Dales.

148 The Three Coopers

Emgate, Bedale, North Yorkshire DL8 1AL
☎ 01677 422153

Real Ales, Bar Food, Restaurant Menu, No Smoking Area, Disabled Facilities

- ☛ 7½ miles southwest of Northallerton on the A684
- 🍺 Cumberland, Lakeland, guest ales
- 🍴 12-7.30 in season; 12-2 off-season
- 🎵 Quiz fortnightly Sundays; live music monthly
- 🕐 Sun-Thurs 11 a.m.-midnight; Fri & Sat 11 a.m.- 1 a.m.
- 🏛 Bedale, Crakehall, Catterick, Northallerton

The Three Coopers is a lovely 17th-century village pub hidden just off Bedale's main street. Pristine and delightful inside and out, this convivial pub is always warm and welcoming. The décor is traditional, with several original features including the large open fire and wealth of warm woods throughout.

There are several real ales to choose from together with a good choice of lagers, cider, stout, wines, spirits and soft drinks. All the food is home-cooked, from the delicious soups to pies, fresh fish dishes, steaks and more. Wednesday is steak night, with a range of sirloin, fillet and rump steaks as well as 16-ounce T-bones.

149 Three Horse Shoes
Wensley, Leyburn, North Yorkshire DL8 4HJ
Tel: 01969 622327

Real Ales, Bar Food, Restaurant Menu,
No Smoking Area, Disabled Facilities

150 Three Tuns
North End, Raskelf, York, Yorkshire YO61 3LF
Tel: 01347 821335

Real Ales, Bar Food, Restaurant Menu,
No Smoking Area, Disabled Facilities

151 Three Tuns Restaurant
9 South End, Osmotherley, Northallerton,
North Yorkshire DL6 3BN
Tel: 01609 883301

Real Ales, Bar Food, Restaurant Menu,
Accommodation, No Smoking Area, Disabled Facilities

152 Town Hall Hotel
Market Place, Richmond,
North Yorkshire DL10 4QL
Tel: 01748 822068

Real Ales, Bar Food, Restaurant Menu,
No Smoking Area, Disabled Facilities

153 Travellers Rest
20 Richmond Road, Skeeby, Richmond,
North Yorkshire DL10 5DS
Tel: 01748 822030

Real Ales, Bar Food, Restaurant Menu,
Accommodation, No Smoking Area, Disabled Facilities

154 Tudor Hotel
Gatherley Road, Brompton On Swale, Richmond,
North Yorkshire DL10 7JF
Tel: 01748 818021

Real Ales, Bar Food, Restaurant Menu,
Accommodation, No Smoking Area, Disabled Facilities

155 Turf Hotel
Victoria Road, Richmond,
North Yorkshire DL10 4DW
Tel: 01748 829011

Bar Food, Accommodation

156 The Unicorn Inn
2 Newbiggin, Richmond,
North Yorkshire DL10 4DT
Tel: 01748 823719

Real Ales, Disabled Facilities

157 The Vale Of York
Carlton Miniott, Thirsk,
North Yorkshire YO7 4LX
Tel: 01845 523161

Real Ales, Bar Food, Restaurant Menu,
Accommodation, No Smoking Area, Disabled Facilities

See panel on page 55

158 The Village Inn
88 Water End, Brompton, Northallerton,
North Yorkshire DL6 2RL
Tel: 01609 771660

Real Ales, Bar Food, Restaurant Menu,
Accommodation, No Smoking Area, Disabled Facilities

See panel on page 54

159 Vintage Hotel
Scotch Corner, Middleton Tyas, Richmond,
North Yorkshire DL10 6NP
Tel: 01748 824424

Bar Food, Restaurant Menu, Accommodation,
No Smoking Area, Disabled Facilities

160 Waggon & Horses Inn
20 Market Place, Bedale, North Yorkshire DL8 1EQ
Tel: 01677 424333

Real Ales, Bar Food, Restaurant Menu,
Accommodation, No Smoking Area, Disabled Facilities

161 Wellington Heifer
Ainderby Steeple, Northallerton,
North Yorkshire DL7 9PU
Tel: 01609 775542

Real Ales, Bar Food, Restaurant Menu,
Accommodation, No Smoking Area, Disabled Facilities

162 The Wheatsheaf Hotel
Bedale Road, Newton Le Willows, Bedale,
North Yorkshire DL8 1SG
Tel: 01677 450211

Real Ales, Bar Food, Restaurant Menu,
No Smoking Area

158 The Village Inn

Water End, Brompton, Northallerton,
North Yorkshire DL6 2RL
☎ 01609 771660

Real Ales, Bar Food, Restaurant Menu, Accommodation, No Smoking Area, Disabled Facilities

☛ Off the A167 2 miles north of Northallerton

🍺 John Smiths Cask, Black Sheep

🍴 Mon-Sat 12-2 & 5-9.30; Sun 12-3 & 6-9.30

🛏 7 en suite chalets

♫ Theme nights, monthly quiz or music

⛴ Car park, disabled access, function suite

💳 All major cards

🚫 No smoking areas

🕐 11.30-12 (Sun and Bank Holidays to 12.00)

🏛 Northallerton, Catterick, Thirsk, North Yorks Moors National Park, Leyburn

A bit like the Tardis, The Village Inn looks deceptively small on the outside but extends well back inside. Overlooking the pretty village green, this inn boasts a welcoming and charming interior, and is

adorned with the largest selection of jugs in the north of England, with 648 jugs and counting. The restaurant and function room are located upstairs.

All-day snacks and light bites are complemented by several comprehensive menus and daily specials board crammed full of delicious dishes at lunch and dinner seven days a week. There's a huge choice of fresh food made with the finest local ingredients. Monday and Tuesday night are steak nights and the Sunday carvery is worth a special trip. The

atmosphere at this friendly inn is always relaxed, while owners Martin and Olwyn and their conscientious staff offer all their guests a warm welcome and genuine Yorkshire hospitality. Entertainment at this fine inn includes regular ongoing theme nights such as sixties nights, held monthly, and a regular quiz night.

The car park is large and spacious with room for coaches, and the function suite is perfect for family gatherings, celebrations and conferences. The inn is also unique in having its own dedicated taxi service, so guests can leave their car at home and enjoy themselves in the knowledge there'll be safe, efficient transport home. And for anyone wanting to prolong their stay in this beautiful part of the world, there are seven neat chalets set back from the main inn building, all en suite, offering comfortable and tasteful accommodation. Located just a couple of miles from Northallerton, the inn makes an excellent base from which to explore the Dales and the North Yorks Moors National Park as well as the centres at Thirsk and Catterick and the many picturesque villages and breathtaking scenery of the region.

157 The Vale of York

Carlton Road, Carlton Miniott, Thirsk,
North Yorkshire YO7 4LX
☎ 01845 523161

Real Ales, Bar Food, Restaurant Menu, Accommodation, No Smoking Area, Disabled Facilities

- ☛ A61 Ripon Road exiting at Thirsk
- 🍺 Timothy Taylor Landlord, Black Sheep, John Smiths Cask, Samuel Smiths Cask
- 🍴 Mon-Sat 12-2 & 5-9; Sun 12-3.30
- 🛏 12 en suite rooms
- ♿ Parking, disabled access
- 💳 All major cards
- 🚫 No smoking in restaurant
- 🕐 9 a.m.-2 a.m.
- 🏛 Thirsk Race Course & Rail Station, York, Dales

The Vale of York is a traditional pub with original features such as log-burning fire, cosy ambience and an attractive and comfortable décor. Situated next to the racecourse at Thirsk, the inn makes a perfect place to enjoy a relaxing drink or meal while enjoying the sights and attractions of the region. The fully-stocked bar features several real ales together with a good range of lagers, cider, stout, wines, spirits and soft drinks.

Bar snacks are complemented by a fine menu of home-cooked dishes served at lunch and evenings. A small sample from the menu includes traditional steak pie, fresh haddock, buffalo steaks, famous mixed grill and many more. This superb inn offers accommodation in 12 comfortable guest bedrooms, tastefully decorated and furnished.

163 The White Bear

Crosshills, Masham, Ripon,
North Yorkshire HG4 4EN
Tel: 01765 689319

Real Ales, Bar Food, Restaurant Menu,
No Smoking Area, Disabled Facilities

164 White Heifer

High Row, Scorton, Richmond,
North Yorkshire DL10 6DH
Tel: 01748 811357

Real Ales, Bar Food, Restaurant Menu,
Accommodation, No Smoking Area

165 The White Rose Hotel

12 Bedale Road, Leeming Bar, Northallerton,
North Yorkshire DL7 9AY
Tel: 01677 422707

Real Ales, Bar Food, Restaurant Menu,
Accommodation, No Smoking Area

166 White Swan

5-6 Market Place, Helmsley, York,
Yorkshire YO62 5BH
Tel: 01439 788239

Real Ales, Bar Food, Restaurant Menu,
No Smoking Area, Disabled Facilities

167 The White Swan Hotel

Market Place, Middleham, Leyburn,
North Yorkshire DL8 4PE
Tel: 01969 622093

Real Ales, Bar Food, Accommodation,
No Smoking Area, Disabled Facilities

168 White Swan Inn

51 High Street, Gilling West, Richmond,
North Yorkshire DL10 5JG
Tel: 01748 821123

Real Ales, Bar Food, Restaurant Menu,
No Smoking Area, Disabled Facilities

169 White Thorne

Wiske View, Danby Wiske, Northallerton,
North Yorkshire DL7 0NJ
Tel: 01609 770122

Real Ales, Bar Food, Restaurant Menu,
Accommodation, Disabled Facilities

170 Whitestonecliffe Inn

Whitestonecliffe, Sutton, Thirsk,
North Yorkshire YO7 2PR
Tel: 01845 597271

Real Ales, Bar Food, Restaurant Menu,
Accommodation, No Smoking Area, Disabled Facilities

171 The Willow Tree Inn

Roman Road, Leeming, Northallerton,
North Yorkshire DL7 9SN
Tel: 01677 423903

Real Ales, Bar Food, Restaurant Menu,
No Smoking Area, Disabled Facilities

172 Wombwell Arms

Wass, York, Yorkshire YO61 4BE
Tel: 01347 868280

Bar Food, Restaurant Menu, Accommodation,
No Smoking Area, Disabled Facilities

173 The Woodman Inn

Burneston, Bedale, North Yorkshire DL8 2HX
Tel: 01677 422066

Real Ales, Bar Food, Restaurant Menu,
Accommodation, No Smoking Area, Disabled Facilities

See panel below

174 Woody's At The Black Swan

Main Street, Thornton Le Moor, Northallerton,
North Yorkshire DL7 9DN
Tel: 01609 774117

Real Ales, Bar Food, Restaurant Menu,
No Smoking Area, Disabled Facilities

See panel opposite

---

173 The Woodman Inn

Burneston, Bedale, North Yorkshire DL8 2HX
☎ 01677 422066

Real Ales, Bar Food, Restaurant Menu, Accommodation, No Smoking Area, Disabled Facilities

- 🖝 Off the A1 northbound ½ mile from Bedale
- 🍺 Jennings, Cumberland and guest ale
- 🍴 12-2.30 & 6-9; Sun 12-4
- 🛏 4 luxury chalets
- 🎵 Quiz night Thursday, folk night Wednesday, Occasional – please ring for details, occasional live music
- ⚓ Car park, full disabled access, beer gardens
- 💳 All major cards
- 🚫 No smoking in restaurant
- 🕐 Summer: 12-12; winter: seasonal hours
- 🏛 Bedale, Crakehall, Northallerton, North Yorks Moors National Park

Dating back to the late 1600s, The Woodman Inn is everything you'd want in a traditional country inn – supremely comfortable, welcoming and friendly, with a great selection of drinks and food. This Jennings pub features three real ales and a good range of lagers, cider, stout, wines, spirits and soft drinks. Everything on the menu is home-cooked using all local produce, and the menu includes hearty favourites and creative specials. Tuesday is steak night. The accommodation comprises four chalets offering every luxury, and Burneston makes a very handy base for exploring the region. One of the chalets is suitable for guests with disabilities.

175 Worsley Arms

High Street, Hovingham, York, Yorkshire YO62 4LA
Tel: 01653 628234

Real Ales, Bar Food, Restaurant Menu,
Accommodation, No Smoking Area

176 Wyvill Arms

Constable Burton, Leyburn,
North Yorkshire DL8 5LH
Tel: 01677 450581

Real Ales, Bar Food, Restaurant Menu,
Accommodation, No Smoking Area, Disabled Facilities

177 Ye Jolly Farmers Inn

Dalton, Thirsk, North Yorkshire YO7 3HY
Tel: 01845 577359

Real Ales, Bar Food, Restaurant Menu,
Accommodation, No Smoking Area, Disabled Facilities

178 Ye Old Three Tuns Inn

Finkle Street, Thirsk, North Yorkshire YO7 1DA
Tel: 01845 523291

179 Yorke Arms Hotel

Ramsgill, Harrogate, North Yorkshire HG3 5RL
Tel: 01423 755243

Real Ales, Restaurant Menu, Accommodation,
No Smoking Area, Disabled Facilities

174 Woody's at The Black Swan

Main Street, Thornton le Moor, Northallerton,
North Yorkshire DL7 9DN
☎ 01609 774117

Real Ales, Bar Food, Restaurant Menu, No Smoking Area, Disabled Facilities

- On the A19 close to Northallerton
- John Smiths, 2 guest ales
- 12-2 & 6.30-9
- Quiz night third Weds of the month
- Car park, function room
- All major cards
- No smoking in restaurant
- 12-2 & 6.30-close
- Northallerton, Bedale, Crakehall, Catterick, North Yorks Moors National Park

Dating back to 1700 the excellent village inn The Black Swan is located on the edge of the tranquil little hamlet of Thornton le Moor. Quiet and removed from the hustle and bustle yet within easy reach of Northallerton and the many other sights and attractions of North Yorkshire, this inn boasts Woody's at the Black Swan, a simply superb restaurant with comprehensive menus at lunch and dinner seven days a week. Chef Peter uses the freshest local ingredients to create tempting light lunches and main courses that include mixed grills, seafood, pasta, vegetarian dishes and speciality entrees such as roast rump of lamb, beef stroganoff, pork and apple sausage, duck breast and much more. Well worth seeking out, this welcoming inn is a relaxing and welcoming place to enjoy an excellent drink or meal amid picturesque surroundings.

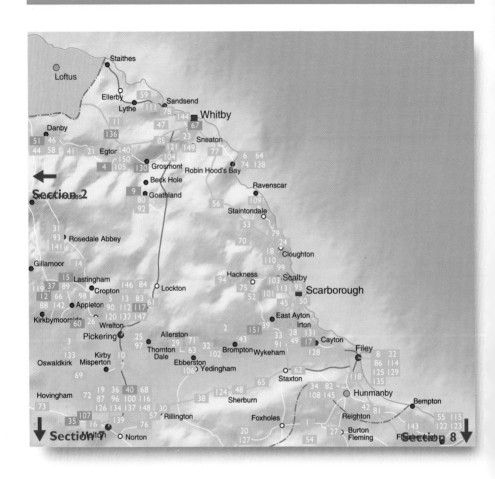

Loftus

Staithes

Ellerby
59
Lythe
11
Sandsend
78
144
67
Whitby

Danby
11
47
136
23
Sneaton
85
121 149
Egtor 140
77
6 64
150
104
74 138
4 105 130 Grosmont
Robin Hood's Bay
Beck Hole
Ravenscar
9
80 Goathland
109
92
56
Staintondale
53
31
79
93 Rosedale Abbey
70
24
141
18
110 Cloughton
Gillamoor 14
99
15 Lastingham
Hackness 103
Scalby
119 37 89 146 84
94
75
113 95
Scarborough
12 66 98 Cropton
5 13 83
52 101 45 50
88 142 Appleton 90 112 117 61
Kirkbymoorside 120 132 147
East Ayton
60 26 Wrelton
2
Irton
Pickering 25 Allerston
151 39
28 131
3 97
29 71
43
33 49 17 Cayton
133 Kirby 10 Thornton 63 32
91
128
Oswaldkirk Misperton 7 Dale
102 Brompton Wykeham
Filey 8 22
69 Ebberston
86 114
106 Yedingham
125 129
65
118 135
34 82
Hovingham 72 19 36 40 68
Staxton
108 145 Hunmanby
73 87 96 100 116
124 48
126 134 137 148 30
38 Sherburn
42 81
35 107 57 Rillington
Reighton
Bempton
16 139 76
20
55 115
Malton Norton
127
27 Burton
143 122 123
Foxholes
Fleming
54

Section 2 · Section 7 · Section 8

11 Pub or Inn Reference Number - Detailed Information

12 Pub or Inn Reference Number - Summary Entry

● ■ Place of interest mentioned in the chapter introduction

SECTION 3

Appleton-le-Moors

Located just inside the southern boundary of the Moors National Park, Appleton-le-Moors is noted for its fine church whose tower and spire provide a landmark for miles around. It was built in Victorian times to a design by J L Pearson, the architect of Truro Cathedral, and it reflects the same Gothic style as the Cornish cathedral.

Beck Hole

A mile or so up the dale from Goathland is the pretty little hamlet of Beck Hole. When the North Yorkshire Moors Railway was onstructed in the 1830s, at Beck Hole there was a 1-in-15 incline up to Goathland so the carriages had to be hauled by a complicated system of ropes and water-filled tanks. The precipitous incline caused many accidents so, in 1865, a 'Deviation Line' was blasted through solid rock. The original 1-in-15 incline is now a footpath.

Bempton

Bempton Cliffs, 400 feet high, mark the northernmost tip of the great belt of chalk that runs diagonally across England from the Isle of Wight to Flamborough Head. The sheer cliffs at Bempton provide an ideal nesting place for huge colonies of fulmars, guillemots, puffins and Britain's largest seabird, the gannet. Bempton Cliffs are now an RSPB bird sanctuary, a refuge during the April to August breeding season for more than 200,000 seabirds. The RSPB provides safe viewpoints allowing close-up watching and there's also a visitor centre, shop and refreshments.

Brompton-by-Sawdon

It was in the medieval church of this small village, on an autumn day in 1802, that William Wordsworth was married to Mary Hutchinson whose family lived at nearby Gallows Hill Farm. Mary's home, now the Wordsworth Gallery, plays host to an exhibition on the poets Wordsworth and Coleridge, while the medieval barn is now filled with designer gifts, ladies clothes and licensed tea rooms. The gallery is open Tuesday to Saturday all year round.

Castleton

Spread across the hillside above the River Esk, Castleton is a charming village which was once the largest settlement in Eskdale. The village's amber-coloured **Church of St Michael and St George** was built in memory of the men who fell during the First World War; inside there is some fine work by Robert Thompson, the famous 'Mouseman of Kilburn'. The benches, organ screen and panelling at each side of the altar all bear his distinctive 'signature' of a crouching mouse.

Cayton

Cayton is one of only 31 'Thankful Villages' in England, so-named after the First World War because all of their men came back safely from that horrific conflict. An unusual attraction here is the **Stained Glass**

Centre where stained glass and leaded lights are created for churches, hotels, restaurants, public houses and homes throughout the country. Visitors can watch the craftspeople at work, browse in the showroom and examine the exhibition of stained glass.

Church Houses

Set beside the River Dove is one of the Moors most famous beauty spots, **Farndale**. In spring, some six miles of the river banks are smothered in thousands of wild daffodils, a short-stemmed variety whose colours shade from a pale buttercup yellow to a rich orange-gold. The flowers, once mercilessly plundered by visitors, are now protected by law with 2,000 acres of Farndale designated as a local nature reserve.

Cropton

This tiny village, records hold, has been brewing ales from as far back as 1613 even though home-brewing was illegal in the 17th century. Despite a lapse in the intervening decades, brewing returned to the village when, in 1984, the cellars of the village pub were converted to accommodate Cropton Brewery, a micro-brewery with visitors' centre, guided tours and regional dishes.

Danby

A visit to **The Moors Centre** at Danby Lodge provides an excellent introduction to the North York Moors National Park. The Centre is housed in a former shooting lodge and set in 13 acres of riverside, meadow, woodland, formal gardens and picnic areas. Inside the Lodge, exhibits interpret the natural and local history of the moors. Open February-December. Downstream from The Moors Centre is a superb 14th-century packhorse bridge, one of three to be found in Eskdale.

East Ayton

Victorian visitors to Scarborough, occasionally tiring of its urban attractions, welcomed excursions to beauty spots such as the Forge Valley near East Ayton. Aeons ago, a sharp-edged glacier excavated the valley; then centuries of natural growth softened its hills, clothed them with over-arching trees and, quite by chance, created one of the loveliest woodland walks in England.

Ebberston

About a mile to the west of Ebberston, in 1718, Mr William Thompson, MP for Scarborough, built for himself what is possibly the smallest stately home in England, **Ebberston Hall**. From the front, the house appears to be just one storey high, with a pillared doorway approached by a grand flight of stone steps flanked by a moderately sized room on each side. Open to visitors only by appointment.

Egton Bridge

This little village tucked around a bend in the River Esk plays host each year to the famous **Gooseberry Show.** Established in 1800, the show is held on the first Tuesday in August. The village is dominated by the massive **Church of St Hedda** built in 1866. It has a dazzling roof painted blue with gold stars, and the altar incorporates some distinguished Belgian terracotta work.

Filey

With its six-mile crescent of safe, sandy beach, Filey was one of the first Yorkshire resorts to benefit from the early 19th-century craze for sea bathing. Filey's popularity continued throughout Victorian times but the little town always prided itself on being rather more select than its brasher neighbour just up the coast. Just to the north of town, **Filey Brigg** strikes out into the sea, the southern starting point for the **Cleveland Way**, which follows the coast as far north as Saltburn-by-the-Sea then turns south to Roseberry Topping and the Cleveland Hills, finally ending up at Helmsley.

Flamborough

At **Flamborough Head**, gigantic waves remorselessly wash away the shoreline. Paradoxically, the outcome of this elemental conflict is to produce one of the most picturesque locations on the Yorkshire coast, much visited and much photographed. Just to the north of Flamborough is **Danes Dyke**, a huge rampart four miles long designed to cut off the headland from hostile invaders. The Danes had nothing to do with it; the dyke was in place long before they arrived. Sometime during the Bronze or Stone Age, early Britons constructed this extraordinary defensive ditch. A mile and a quarter of its southern length is open to the public as a Nature Trail.

Gillamoor

This pleasant little village is well worth a

Flamborough Head

visit to see its very rare and very elegant four-faced sundial erected in 1800, and to enjoy the famous **Surprise View**. This is a ravishing panoramic vista of Farndale with the River Dove flowing through the valley far below and white dusty roads climbing the hillside to the heather-covered moors beyond.

Glaisdale

From Lealholm a country lane leads to Glaisdale, another picturesque village set at the foot of a narrow dale beside the River Esk, with Arncliffe Woods a short walk away. The ancient stone bridge here was built around 1620.

Goathland

Goathland attracts thousands of visitors each year, not least for **Goathland Station** on the North Yorkshire Moors Railway. This attractive village 500 feet up on the moors, where old stone houses are scattered randomly around spacious sheep-groomed greens, is also home to **Mallyan Spout**, a 70-foot high waterfall locked into a crescent of rocks and trees. In the award-winning **Goathland Exhibition Centre** you'll find a information about the many walks in the area.

Goldsborough

Just outside this small village are the remains of one of five signal stations built by the Romans in the 4th century when Saxon pirates were continually raiding the coastal towns. The stations were all built to a similar design with a timber or stone watchtower surrounded by a wide ditch.

Grosmont

Grosmont is the northern terminus of the **North Yorkshire Moors Railway**, the nation's most popular heritage railway, and houses the vintage steam locomotives that ply the 18-mile-long route. The station itself has been restored to the British Railways style of the 1960s and contains a tea room and a two shops with a wide variety of rail-related and other items on sale. In high season as many as eight trains a day in each direction are in service and there are many special events throughout the year.

Hutton-le-Hole

Long regarded as one of Yorkshire's prettiest villages, facing Hutton-le-Hole's green is the **Ryedale Folk Museum**, an imaginative celebration of 4,000 years of life in North Yorkshire. Among the 13 historic buildings is a complete Elizabethan Manor House, a medieval crofter's cottage with a thatched, hipped roof, peat fire and garth, and the old village shop and post office fitted out as it would have looked in 1953.

Kirby Misperton

The 375 acres of wooded parkland surrounding Kirby Misperton Hall provide the setting for **Flamingoland**, a zoo and fun park that is home to more than 1,000 birds, animals and

North Yorkshire Moors Railway

reptiles. With more than 100 different attractions, including a fun fair with some truly scary rides, an adventure playground and a real working farm, it's no surprise to learn that Flamingoland is the 4th most visited theme park in the country.

Kirkbymoorside

Set quietly off the main road, this agreeable market town of fine Georgian houses, narrow twisting lanes, family-owned shops and a cobbled marketplace, straggles up the hillside. After you pass the last house on the hill, you enter the great open spaces of the North Yorkshire Moors National Park, 553 square miles of outstanding natural beauty which, since they were accorded the status of a National Park in 1952, have been protected from insensitive encroachments.

Lealholm

From The Moors Centre at Danby a scenic minor road winds along the Esk Valley and brings you to the attractive village of Lealholm, its houses clustering around a 250-year-old bridge over the Esk. A short walk leads to some picturesque stepping stones across the river.

Levisham

Just to the west of the village, in the scenic valley of Newton Dale, lies Levisham Station, one of several that lie on the route of the North Yorkshire Moors Railway. This stop is the ideal location for walking with a wide variety of wildlife and flowers within a short distance of the station.

Lockton

About three miles north of Lockton, the **Hole of Horcum** is a huge natural amphitheatre which, so the story goes, was scooped out of Levisham Moor by the giant Wade. It is now a popular centre for hang gliders. Lockton village itself is set high above a deep ravine, boasts one of the few duck ponds to have survived in the National Park, and offers some fine walks.

Lythe

Perched on a hill top, Lythe is a small cluster of houses with a sturdy little church which is well worth a visit. Just south of the village is **Mulgrave Castle**, hereditary home of the Marquis of Normanby. The Castle grounds, which are open to the public, contain the ruins of Foss Castle built shortly after the Norman Conquest.

Malton

The River Derwent was vitally important to Malton. The river rises in the moors near Scarborough, then runs inland through the Vale of Pickering, bringing an essential element for what was once a major industry in Malton – brewing. In the 19th century there were nine breweries here; now only the Malton Brewery Company survives. Old Malton is located just to the north of the Roman Fort, an interesting and historic area on the edge of open countryside. Nearby villages such as Settrington and their secluded country lanes are home to many famous racehorse stables: if you are up and about early enough you will see the horses out on their daily exercises. A mile or so north of Old Malton is **Eden Camp**, a theme museum dedicated to re-creating the dramatic experiences of ordinary people living through the Second World War. Right next door is **Eden Farm Insight**, a working farm with a fascinating collection of old farm machinery and implements.

Nunnington

Nunnington Hall (National Trust) is a late 17th-century manor house in a beautiful setting beside the River Rye with a picturesque packhorse bridge within its grounds. Inside, there is a magnificent panelled hall, fine tapestries and china, and the famous Carlisle collection of miniature rooms exquisitely furnished in different period styles to one-eighth life size.

Pickering

Pickering is the largest of the four market towns in Ryedale and possibly the oldest, claiming to date from 270 BC.

The parish church of **St Peter and St Paul** is well worth visiting for its remarkable 15th-century murals. Also not to be missed in Pickering is the **Beck Isle Museum** housed in a gracious Regency mansion. Pickering is also the southern terminus of the **North York Moors Railway** and here you can board a steam-drawn train for an 18-mile journey along one of the oldest and most dramatically scenic railways in the country. Just up the road, at the **Pickering Trout Lake**, you can hire a rod and tackle and attempt to beat the record for the largest fish ever caught here – it currently stands at a mighty 25lb 4oz (11.45 kg).

Ravenscar

The coastline around Ravenscar is particularly dramatic and, fortunately, most of it is under the protection of the National Trust. There are some splendid cliff-top walks and outstanding views across

Robin Hood's Bay. Ravenscar is the eastern terminus of the 42-mile hike across the moors to Osmotherley known as the **Lyke Wake Walk**.

Robin Hood's Bay

Artists never tire of painting this 'Clovelly of the North', a picturesque huddle of red-roofed houses clinging to the steep face of the cliff. The most extraordinary building in Bay Town, as locals call the village, is undoubtedly **Fyling Hall Pigsty**. It was built in the 1880s in the classical style although the pillars supporting the portico are of wood rather than marble. Detailed information about the village and the Bay is on display at the **Old Coastguard Station** on The Dock. This National Trust property also houses the National Park Visitor and Education Centre. Also worth a visit are the **Robin Hood's Bay Museum**.

Rosedale Abbey

To the east of Farndale is another lovely dale, Rosedale, a nine-mile-long steep-sided valley through which runs the River Seven. The largest settlement in the dale is Rosedale Abbey which takes its name from the small nunnery founded here in 1158. High on these moors stands **Ralph Cross**, nine feet tall and erected in medieval times as a waymark for travellers. When the North York Moors National Park was established in 1952, the Park authorities adopted Ralph Cross as its emblem.

Runswick Bay

A little further down the coast, Runswick Bay is another picturesque fishing village with attractive cottages clinging to the steep sides of the cliff.

Sandsend

From Runswick Bay, the A174 drops down the notoriously steep Lythe Bank to Sandsend, a pretty village that grew up alongside the Mulgrave Beck as it runs into the sea at 'sands' end' – the northern tip of the long sandy beach that stretches some two and a half miles from here to Whitby. The Romans had a cement works nearby, later generations mined the surrounding hills for the elusive jet stone and for alum, and the Victorians built a scenic railway along the coast. Sections of the route now form part of the Sandsend Trail, a pleasant and leisurely two-and-a-half hour walk around the village.

Scarborough

With its two splendid bays and dramatic cliff-top castle, Scarborough was targeted by the early railway tycoons as the natural candidate for Yorkshire's first seaside resort. **Scarborough Castle** dates to the decade between 1158 and 1168 and was built on the site of a Roman fort and signal station. Its gaunt remains stand high on Castle Rock Headland, dominating the two sweeping bays. **Peasholm Park**, the **Rotunda Museum**, **Scarborough**

Art Gallery and **The Stephen Joseph Theatre in the Round** are just a few of the sights of this superb town.

Sinnington

At Sinnington the River Seven drops down from the moors and the valley of Rosedale into the more open country of the Vale of Pickering. The stream passes through this tiny village, running alongside a broad green in the centre of which stands a graceful old packhorse bridge. At one time this medieval bridge must have served a useful purpose but whatever old watercourse that once flowed beneath it has long since disappeared – thus the bridge is known as the 'dry' bridge.

Staithes

Visitors to this much-photographed fishing port leave their cars at the park in the modern village at the top of the cliff and then walk down the steep road to the old wharf. Staithes is still a working port with one of the few fleets in England still

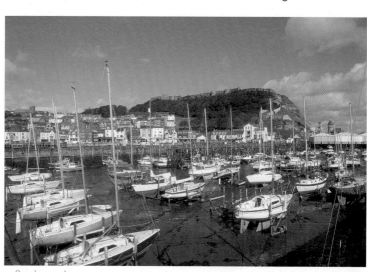

Scarborough

catching crabs and lobsters. Nearby is a small sandy beach, popular with families (and artists), and a rocky shoreline extending north and south pitted with thousands of rock pools hiding starfish and anemones. The rocks here are also rich in fossils. A little further up the coast rises Boulby Cliff, at 666 feet (202m) the highest point on the east coast of England.

Thornton-le-Dale

As long ago as 1907, a *Yorkshire Post* poll of its readers acclaimed Thornton-le-Dale as the most beautiful village in Yorkshire. Despite stiff competition for that title, most visitors still find themselves in agreement.

Just off the A170 near the parish church of All Saints you'll find one of the most photographed houses in Britain, a thatched cottage set beside a sparkling beck. On the nearby village green there's an ancient cross and a set of wooden stocks. About three miles north of Thornton-le-Dale, the Dalby Visitor Centre is the starting point for the

Dalby Forest Drive (toll payable), a nine-mile circuit through what was once the royal hunting Forest of Pickering.

Whitby

Whitby is one of North Yorkshire's most historic and attractive towns, famed as one of the earliest and most important centres of Christianity in England and as Captain James Cook's home port. High on the cliff that towers above the old town stand the imposing and romantic ruins of **Whitby Abbey** (English Heritage), while a short walk from the Abbey is **St Mary's Church**, a unique building 'not unlike a house outside and very much like a ship inside.' The **Whitby Archives Heritage Centre** holds an exhibition of local photographs, local history research facilities, a shop and heritage gallery. The **Museum of Victorian Whitby** has a re-creation of a 19th-century lane in the town complete with interiors and shop windows along with miniature rooms and settings.

1 Anvil Arms

Bridlington Road, Wold Newton, Driffield,
North Humberside YO25 3YL
Tel: 01262 470279

Real Ales, Bar Food, Restaurant Menu

2 Anvil Inn

Main Street, Sawdon, Scarborough,
North Yorkshire YO13 9DY
Tel: 01723 859896

Real Ales, Restaurant Menu, No Smoking Area

3 Appletree Inn & Restaurant

Marton, Sinnington, Pickering, York YO62 6RD
Tel: 01751 431457

Real Ales, Bar Food, Restaurant Menu,
No Smoking Area, Disabled Facilities

4 The Arncliffe Inn

Glaisdale, Whitby, North Yorkshire YO21 2QL
Tel: 01947 897555

Real Ales, Bar Food, Restaurant Menu,
Accommodation, Disabled Facilities

See panel on page 68

5 Bay Horse

8 Market Place, Pickering,
North Yorkshire YO18 7AA
Tel: 01751 472526

Real Ales, Bar Food, Restaurant Menu,
No Smoking Area

6 Bay Hotel

The Dock, Robin Hoods Bay, Whitby,
North Yorkshire YO22 4SJ
Tel: 01947 880278

Real Ales, Bar Food, Accommodation,
No Smoking Area

7 Bean Sheaf Hotel

Malton Road, Kirby Misperton, Malton,
North Yorkshire YO17 6UE
Tel: 01653 668614

Bar Food, Restaurant Menu, Accommodation,
No Smoking Area

8 Bellvue Bar

Belle Vue Street, Filey, North Yorkshire YO14 9HU
Tel: 01723 513721

Real Ales, Bar Food, No Smoking Area

9 The Birch Hall Inn

Goathland, Beckhole, Whitby,
North Yorkshire YO22 5LE
Tel: 01947 896245

Real Ales, Bar Food, Restaurant Menu

See panel below

10 Black Bull Inn

Malton Road, Pickering, North Yorkshire YO18 8EA
Tel: 01751 475258

Real Ales, Bar Food, Restaurant Menu,
Accommodation, No Smoking Area, Disabled Facilities

9 The Birch Hall Inn

Beck Hole, Goathland, Whitby,
North Yorkshire YO22 5LE
☎ 01947 896245

Real Ales, Bar Food, Restaurant Menu

☛ Off the A169 9 miles south of Whitby, 15 miles north of Pickering

🍺 Black Sheep, guest ales

🍴 All day snacks

🛏 Self-catering cottage (sleeps 4)

⛲ Garden

🕐 11-11 (summer); 11-3 & 7.30-11 (winter)

🏛 River Ellerbeck, Mallyan Spout, Wade's Way, North Yorkshire Moors Railway

Licensed since 1860, The Birch Hall Inn is an astonishing tiny village inn that draws customers from all over Yorkshire. Charming and welcoming. As well as ales and simple snacks, between the two bars owners Glenys and Neil Crampton have their own sweet shop with tempting confectionery to please every palate. Next door there's excellent self-catering accommodation.

4 The Arncliffe Inn

Arncliffe Terrace, Glaisdale, Whitby,
North Yorkshire YO21 2QL
☎ 01947 897555

**Real Ales, Bar Food, Restaurant Menu,
Accommodation, Disabled Facilities**

- Off the A171 10 miles southwest of Whitby
- Black Sheep, Theakstons, guest ale
- 12-2.30 & 6-8.45; bistro Tues-Sat 7-9
- 4 en suite rooms
- Sun night quiz
- Parking, disabled access, patio
- All major cards
- 12-3 & 6-11; Sat & Sun 12-11; closed Mon in winter
- Beggar's Bridge, Arncliffe Woods, Lealholm, Egton Bridge, Danby, Castleton

The Arncliffe Inn is a superb place with excellent food, drink and accommodation. The accent is firmly on great food here, with a menu and specials board of home-cooked dishes. In addition to the restaurant, where dishes such as home-made steak and mushroom pie, marinated chargrilled breast of chicken, steaks and salmon fillet tempt the palate, owners Graham and Marie Benn have also opened, new for 2005, a bistro on the premises called Café Glas and serving excellent dishes including the house speciality, San Franciscan fish stew – a melange of half-lobster, mussels, giant tiger prawns, squid, salmon, sole and clams in a marvellous tomato and chilli broth with potatoes, rice and olive oil bread.

To drink there are real ales together with a good complement of lagers, a fine wine list, cider, stout, spirits and soft drinks. The accommodation comprises four attractive and comfortable en suite guest bedrooms, and the inn makes an excellent touring base.

Glaisdale itself has many attractions, not least of which are the River Esk with its ancient stone Beggar's Bridge, dating back to 1620, and Arncliffe Woods. Nearby are the picturesque villages of Lealholm and Egton Bridge. Eskdale is the largest and one of the loveliest of the dales within the North York Moors National Park and is also unusual in that it runs west to east – the Esk being the only moorland river that does not find its way to the River Humber. Glaisdale branches off from Eskdale, and the Esk is famed for its salmon fishing (permit required). Walkers will appreciate the Esk Valley Walk, a group of ten linking walks that traverse the length of the valley.

11 Black Bull Inn

Ugthorpe, Whitby, North Yorkshire YO21 2BQ
Tel: 01947 840286

Real Ales, Bar Food, Restaurant Menu, No Smoking
Area

12 The Black Swan

11 Market Place, Kirkbymoorside,
Yorkshire YO62 6AA
Tel: 01751 431305

Bar Food, Restaurant Menu, Accommodation,
No Smoking Area, Disabled Facilities

See panel below

13 Black Swan

Birdgate, Pickering, North Yorkshire YO18 7AL
Tel: 01751 472286

Real Ales, Bar Food, Restaurant Menu,
Accommodation, No Smoking Area, Disabled Facilities

14 Blacksmith Country Inn

Hartoft, Pickering, North Yorkshire YO18 8EN
Tel: 01751 417331

Real Ales, Bar Food, Restaurant Menu,
Accommodation, No Smoking Area

15 The Blacksmiths Arms

Front Street, Lastingham, York, Yorkshire YO62 6TL
Tel: 01751 417247

Real Ales, Bar Food, Restaurant Menu,
Accommodation, No Smoking Area

See panel on page 70

16 Blacksmiths Arms

Malton Road, Swinton, Malton,
North Yorkshire YO17 6SQ
Tel: 01653 693629

Real Ales, Bar Food, Restaurant Menu,
No Smoking Area

---

12 The Black Swan

11 Market Place, Kirkby Moorside,
North Yorkshire YO62 6AA
☎ 01751 431305

**Bar Food, Restaurant Menu, Accommodation, No
Smoking Area, Disabled Facilities**

- 5½ miles northeast of Helmsley on the A170
- Tetleys, Black Sheep
- 12-2 & 6-8.30
- 4 en suite rooms
- Quiz night Tuesdays, music once a month at weekends
- Parking, courtyard patio
- All the major cards
- Sun-Thurs 12-12; Fri & Sat midday-1 a.m.

In the centre of the lovely town of Kirkby Moorside, a charming and ancient market town of fine Georgian houses, narrow twisting lanes and cobbled marketplace, The Black Swan is a 17th-century coaching inn with many original features. Welcoming with a strikingly handsome interior, this convivial inn boasts great food, drink and hospitality. Real ales vie with lagers, wines, spirits, cider, stout and soft drinks to tempt the tastebuds, while the menu and specials board boasts hearty portions of home-cooked favourites served at lunch and dinner. The bar and lounge are comfortable and cosy, while outdoors there's a lovely beer garden, just the place to enjoy a quiet and relaxing drink or meal on fine days.

15 The Blacksmiths Arms

Lastingham, North Yorkshire YO62 6TL
☎ 01751 417247
e-mail: peter.hils@blacksmithslastingham.co.uk
🌐 www.blacksmithslastingham.co.uk

Real Ales, Bar Food, Restaurant Menu,
Accommodation, No Smoking Area

- ☛ Off the A170 6 miles northeast of Helmsley
- 🍺 Theakstons Best and 2 guest ales
- 🍴 12-2 & 7-9
- 🛏 3 en suite rooms
- 🎵 Jam session, food themed nights
- ⚓ Beer garden, small function room
- 💳 All major cards
- 🏆 *The Good Pub Guide, The Good Beer Guide*
- 🚫 No smoking in restaurant
- 🕐 Nov-April Mon-Thurs 12-2 & 6-close, Tues 6-close, Fri-Sun all day; May1-Oct all day every day
- 🏛 St Mary's Church, Lastingham; North Yorks Moors National Park, Helmsley Castle, Duncombe Park, Rievaulx Abbey

A late 17th-century stonebuilt coaching inn well hidden in the North Yorks Moors National Park, The Blacksmiths Arms is well worth seeking out for its real ales, great home-cooked food and superb accommodation.

Handsome and welcoming, this impressive inn has a wealth of traditional features such as the exposed beamwork, and is comfortable and cosy all year round.

Owners Peter and Hilary Trafford and their friendly, attentive staff offer all guests a high standard of service and quality. Real ales include Theakstons Best and changing guest ales, while there's also a good selection of lagers, wines, spirits, soft drinks, cider and stout to quench every thirst. To eat, there's a very good choice of dishes from the menu or specials board, all home-cooked to order and featuring traditional favourites such as steak and ale or lamb and mint pie, Yorkshire hot pot, roast of the day, jumbo crispy cod and more.

This fine establishment also boasts three very comfortable guest bedrooms, attractively furnished and decorated and perfect as a base while exploring the many sights and attractions – not least Lastingham's own village church of St Mary's, which has a Norman crypt and shrine of St Cedd built in 1078 on the site of a Celtic monastery – as well as Duncombe Park, Rievaulx Abbey and the North Yorks Moors National Park.

17 Blacksmiths Arms

89 Main Street, Cayton, Scarborough,
North Yorkshire YO11 3RP
Tel: 01723 582272

Real Ales, Bar Food, Restaurant Menu,
No Smoking Area, Disabled Facilities

See panel below

18 Blacksmith's Arms Inn

High Street, Cloughton, Scarborough,
North Yorkshire YO13 0AE
Tel: 01723 870244

Bar Food, Restaurant Menu, Accommodation,
No Smoking Area, Disabled Facilities

19 The Blue Ball

14 Newbiggin, Malton, North Yorkshire YO17 7JF
Tel: 01653 692236

Real Ales, Bar Food, Restaurant Menu,
No Smoking Area, Disabled Facilities

20 The Blue Bell Inn

Weaverthorpe, Malton, North Yorkshire YO17 8EX
Tel: 01944 738204

Real Ales, Bar Food, Restaurant Menu,
Accommodation, No Smoking Area, Disabled Facilities

21 Board Inn

Lealholm, Whitby, North Yorkshire YO21 2AJ
Tel: 01947 897279

Real Ales, Bar Food, Restaurant Menu,
Accommodation, No Smoking Area

22 Bonhommes

Royal Crescent Court, The Crescent, Filey,
North Yorkshire YO14 9JH
Tel: 01723 512034

Real Ales

23 The Bridge Inn

High Street, Ruswarp, Whitby,
North Yorkshire YO21 1NH
Tel: 01947 602780

Real Ales, Disabled Facilities

17 Blacksmiths Arms

Main Street, Cayton, North Yorkshire YO11 3RP
☎ 01723 582272

Real Ales, Bar Food, Restaurant Menu, No Smoking Area, Disabled Facilities

- 20 miles southeast of Whitby on the B1261
- John Smiths, Tetleys
- Mon-Sat 12-2 & 6-9; Sun 12-3
- Quiz night Weds, karaoke Friday night
- Parking, beer garden, patio, disabled access
- No smoking in restaurant
- Mon-Thurs & Sun 12-12; Fri & Sat 12-1 a.m.
- Cayton, East Ayton, Filey, Scarborough, Hunmanby

Dating back to the 15th century, Black smiths Arms began life as a coaching inn and retains many original features. Added onto in the early 1900s, this warm and convivial establishment is the perfect place to seek out for a relaxing drink or excellent meal while exploring the North Yorks coast. Tempting dishes using the freshest local ingredients are served at lunch and dinner every day, and include hot and cold baguettes, pies and Cumberland sausages at lunch to salmon steak, pork stroganoff, beef bourgignon, mixed grills and a selection of home-made pizzas and vegetarian dishes for dinner. Booking advised for the superb Sunday carvery. To drink there's a range of real ales, lagers, cider, stout, wines, spirits and soft drinks, and the atmosphere at this welcoming pub is always relaxed and friendly.

35 The Cresswell Arms

Appleton le Street, Malton,
North Yorkshire YO17 6PG
☎ 01653 693647

Real Ales, Bar Food, Restaurant Menu, Accommodation, No Smoking Area, Disabled Facilities

- 🚗 On the B1257 off the A64 west of Malton
- 🍺 John Smiths, guest ale
- 🍴 Mon-Sat 12-2 & 6-9, Sun 12-8.30
- 🛏 10 en suite rooms in purpose-built block
- ⛴ Car park, disabled access, beer garden
- 💳 All major cards
- 🚫 No smoking in restaurant or bedrooms
- 🕐 12-2 & 6-1 a.m.
- 🏛 Castle Howard, Malton, York, Easingwold

The Cresswell Arms is a classic stonebuilt roadside inn, with an accent firmly on great food, drink and accommodation. The interior is warm and welcoming, with a wealth of burnished wood and very comfortable seating and a décor that is tasteful and a relaxed ambience. To drink there are real ales complemented by a good range of lagers, wines, spirits, cider, stout and soft drinks. The menus are expertly crafted and use the freshest ingredients to create dishes such as fillet of salmon, roast duckling, grilled lamb, pesto vegetable tart and sirloin steaks. The accommodation comprises exquisite traditional rooms where attention has been paid to every detail to enhance guests' comfort. The décor and furnishings are simply superb.

37 The Crown

Hutton le Hole, North Yorkshire YO62 6UA
☎ 01751 417343

Real Ales, Bar Food, Restaurant Menu, No Smoking Area, Disabled Facilities

- 🚗 7 miles northwest of Pickering off the A170
- 🍺 Black Sheep, Tetleys
- 🛏 Caravan site behind the pub
- ⛴ Car park, disabled access
- 💳 All major cards
- 🕐 Summer: 10.30-11; Winter 11.30-2.30 & 6-11
- 🏛 Rosedale Abbey, Pickering, Helmsley, Malton

A handsome village pub set on the edge of the National Park and in a very pretty little village not far off the A170, The Crown makes an ideal base for exploring the moors or heading off to the coast. Cosy and welcoming, the interior features open fires and comfortable seating. A fine example of the better Yorkshire inn, there's fine food and drink on offer with real ales complemented by a good range of wines, spirits, soft drinks, lagers and more, and a daily menu and specials board of hearty and tempting dishes including roast beef, chicken, pasta and a selection of vegetarian options. Owner Phillip Mintoft has been here some 20 years, and has a wealth of experience not just of the trade but of the region and can advise guests on the many sights and attractions nearby.

24 Bryherstones Inn

Newlands Road, Cloughton, Scarborough,
North Yorkshire YO13 0AR
Tel: 01723 870744

Real Ales, Bar Food, Restaurant Menu,
No Smoking Area

25 Buck Hotel

Chestnut Avenue, Thornton Dale, Pickering,
North Yorkshire YO18 7RW
Tel: 01751 474212

Real Ales, Bar Food, Restaurant Menu,
Accommodation, No Smoking Area

26 Buck Inn

Cliffe Road, Wrelton, Pickering,
North Yorkshire YO18 8PG
Tel: 01751 477144

Bar Food, Restaurant Menu

27 Burton Arms

Bridlington Road, Burton Fleming, Driffield,
North Humberside YO25 3PE
Tel: 01262 470292

Real Ales, Bar Food, Restaurant Menu,
Accommodation, No Smoking Area

28 The Byways

Station Road, Crossgates, Scarborough,
North Yorkshire YO12 4LT
Tel: 01723 863254

Real Ales, Bar Food, Restaurant Menu,
No Smoking Area, Disabled Facilities

29 The Cayley Arms

Allerston, Pickering, North Yorkshire YO18 7PJ
Tel: 01723 859338

Real Ales, Bar Food, Restaurant Menu,
Accommodation, No Smoking Area

30 Coach & Horses

1 Scarborough Road, Rillington, Malton,
North Yorkshire YO17 8LH
Tel: 01944 758373

Real Ales, Bar Food, Restaurant Menu,
No Smoking Area

31 The Coach House

Rosedale Abbey, Pickering,
North Yorkshire YO18 8SD
Tel: 01751 417208

Real Ales, Bar Food, Restaurant Menu,
No Smoking Area, Disabled Facilities

32 Coachman Inn

Pickering Road West, Snainton, Scarborough,
North Yorkshire YO13 9PL
Tel: 01723 859231

Real Ales, Restaurant Menu, Accommodation,
No Smoking Area

33 Copper Horse

Main Street, Seamer, Scarborough,
North Yorkshire YO12 4PS
Tel: 01723 862029

Real Ales, Bar Food, Restaurant Menu,
No Smoking Area

34 The Cottage Inn

23-25 Cross Hill, Hunmanby, Filey,
North Yorkshire YO14 0JT
Tel: 01723 892475

35 **The Cresswell Arms**

Le Street, Appleton-le-Street, Malton,
North Yorkshire YO17 6PG
Tel: 01653 693647

Real Ales, Bar Food, Restaurant Menu,
Accommodation, No Smoking Area, Disabled Facilities

See panel opposite

36 Cross Keys Hotel

47 Wheelgate, Malton, North Yorkshire YO17 7HT
Tel: 01653 692676

Real Ales, Bar Food, Restaurant Menu,
No Smoking Area, Disabled Facilities

37 **The Crown**

Hutton-le-Hole, York, Yorkshire YO62 6UA
Tel: 01751 417343

Real Ales, Bar Food, Restaurant Menu,
No Smoking Area, Disabled Facilities

See panel opposite

40 The Derwent Arms

26 Church Street, Norton, Malton,
North Yorkshire YO17 9HS
☎ 01653 693631

Real Ales, Bar Food, No Smoking Area, Disabled Facilities

☛ On the main street in Norton, reached off the A19 18 miles from York

🍺 Tetleys and John Smiths

🍴 Mon-Fri 12-3 & 5-8.30; Sat & Sun 12-7; all-day sandwiches

♫ Occasional live music, Weds night quiz and disco

⚓ Car park, disabled access, small front patio

💳 All major cards

🚫 No smoking areas

🕐 11-close

🏛 York, Castle Howard, Scarborough

Having recently undergone a major

several pubs in the area but now the Derwent Arms is their only establishment. Popular with locals and visitors alike, the pub features real ales together with a comprehensive range of lagers, wines, spirits, cider, stout and soft drinks – something to quench every thirst. In summer guests can partake of a drink or meal at the seating area to the front of the pub. Bernie their cook, who has been with them for 27 years has created an excellent reputation for home cooked food and the pub is well known for its good quality food at reasonable prices. A huge choice of dishes at lunch and dinner, include hearty steaks, home-made pies, curries, pasta, vegetarian dishes and much more. In addition to this there are freshly made sandwiches and light snacks served all day long.

The pub is the perfect place to enjoy a drink or meal while exploring the many sights and attractions of the region, which include Norton's own church of St Mary Magdalene.

refurbishment The Derwent Arms now combines the best of traditional comforts with modern quality and styling. Located in the main street in Norton – eight miles from Castle Howard and the Pickering to Grosmont Steam Train and 2 miles from Scarborough and the East Coast –it is a welcoming and convivial pub with great food and drink.

The pub is owned by the Rushworth family and run by eldest son Warren. The Rushworths have been licencees for 30 years, running

38 Dawnay Arms

West Heslerton, Malton,
North Yorkshire YO17 8RQ
Tel: 01944 728203

Real Ales, Bar Food, Restaurant Menu,
No Smoking Area, Disabled Facilities

39 Denison Arms

40 Main Street, East Ayton, Scarborough,
North Yorkshire YO13 9HL
Tel: 01723 862131

Real Ales, Restaurant Menu, No Smoking Area

40 **The Derwent Arms**

26 Church Street, Norton, Malton,
North Yorkshire YO17 9HS
Tel: 01653 693631

Real Ales, Bar Food, No Smoking Area,
Disabled Facilities

See panel opposite

41 The Dolphin

Robin Hood's Bay, Whitby, Yorkshire YO21 4SH
Tel: 01947 880337

Real Ales, Bar Food, Restaurant Menu

42 Dotterel Inn

Reighton, Filey, North Yorkshire YO14 9RU
Tel: 01723 890300

Real Ales, Bar Food, Restaurant Menu,
Accommodation, Disabled Facilities

43 Downe Arms Hotel

Main Road, Wykeham, Scarborough,
North Yorkshire YO13 9QB
Tel: 01723 862471

Real Ales, Bar Food, Restaurant Menu,
Accommodation, No Smoking Area, Disabled Facilities

44 The Downe Arms Inn

3 High Street, Castleton, Whitby,
North Yorkshire YO21 2EE
Tel: 01287 660223

Real Ales, Bar Food, Restaurant Menu,
Accommodation, No Smoking Area, Disabled Facilities

45 The Duchess

152 Hovingham Drive, Scarborough,
North Yorkshire YO12 5DT
Tel: 01723 351884

Real Ales

46 Duke Of Wellington

2 West Lane, Danby, Whitby,
North Yorkshire YO21 2LY
Tel: 01287 660351

Real Ales

47 Dunsley Hall

Dunsley, Whitby, North Yorkshire YO21 3TL
Tel: 01947 893437

Real Ales, Bar Food, Restaurant Menu,
Accommodation, No Smoking Area, Disabled Facilities

48 East Riding Hotel

St Hildas Street, Sherburn, Malton,
North Yorkshire YO17 8PG
Tel: 01944 710386

Real Ales, Bar Food, Restaurant Menu,
No Smoking Area, Disabled Facilities

49 The Eastfield

Manham Hill, Eastfield, Scarborough,
North Yorkshire YO11 3LA
Tel: 01723 583437

No Smoking Area

50 English Rose Hotels

St Nicholas Street, Scarborough,
North Yorkshire YO11 2HE
Tel: 01723 364333

Bar Food, Restaurant Menu, Accommodation,
No Smoking Area, Disabled Facilities

51 **The Eskdale Inn**

Castleton, Whitby, North Yorkshire YO21 2EU
Tel: 01287 660234

Real Ales, Bar Food, Restaurant Menu,
No Smoking Area, Disabled Facilities

See panel on page 77

60 The Fox & Hounds Inn

Sinnington, North Yorkshire YO62 6SQ
☎ 01751 431577

🌐 www.thefoxandhoundsinn.co.uk

Real Ales, Bar Food, Restaurant Menu, Accommodation, No Smoking Area, Disabled Facilities

☞ On the A170 between Kirkbymoorside and Pickering

🍺 Theakstons Best, Black Sheep

🍴 12-2 & 6.30-9

🛏 10 en suite rooms

🎵 Occasional live music

🅿 Car park, beer garden, disabled access

💳 All major cards

🏆 AA Rosette, *Which Good Food Guide*, Silver Award ETC

🚫 No smoking in restaurant, lounge or bedrooms

🕐 12-2 & 6.30-close

🏛 North Yorks Moors National Park, Pickering, Dalby Forest Drive, Hutton-le-Hole

The Fox & Hounds Inn is a perfect example of a truly top-class Yorkshire inn. Owned

and run by Andrew and Catherine Stephens, it has been a labour of love that offers superlative food, drink and accommodation to all guests. Catherine and Andrew are perfectionists – the entire inn is their creation over many painstaking months and years, and their dedication has paid off: it's far and away one of the best little inns in all of Yorkshire, from the traditional bar to the elegant restaurant and gracious, luxurious guest bedrooms, some of which are large and spacious enough to count as suites.

The décor and furnishings throughout are tasteful and classic, with warm burnished woods and a wealth of brass ornaments. There are large open fireplaces, intimate lighting and overall a warm and relaxed ambience at this charming 18th-century inn. In the stunning restaurant, only the freshest ingredients are combined by head chef Mark and his creative team, David and Calvin, to create a varied and delicious menu encompassing new and unique tastes.

Hand in hand with their kitchen team, the Stephens have, over a period of several years, extensively refurbished the restaurant to create a relaxed, smoke-free, comfortable ambience in which to enjoy the best in cuisine. Just a small sample from the evening menu includes roast fillet of pork with apple, homemade pie with mash, slow braised faggot and buttered spinach, slow-cooked shoulder of lamb, roast root vegetables on a rosemary and garlic mash, and chargrilled sirloin steak with hand-cut chips and a grilled field mushroom, sautéed onions and green salad. The accommodation boasts beautifully appointed en suite guest bedrooms, each with a quiet elegance and furnished and decorated with impeccable taste and style. As the starting points for the famous Riverside and Woodland walks, it is an ideal base for exploring the many sights and attractions of North Yorkshire.

51 The Eskdale Inn

Station Road, Castleton, Whitby,
North Yorkshire YO21 2EU
☎ 01287 660234

Real Ales, Bar Food, Restaurant Menu, Accommodation, No Smoking Area, Disabled Facilities

- ☛ Off the A171 10 miles west of Whitby
- 🍺 Tetleys, Black Sheep, guest ales
- 🍴 Mon-Sat 12-9; Sun 12-8
- 🛏 2 en suite rooms
- 🎵 Sun night quiz
- ⛏ Car park, disabled access, garden
- 💳 All major cards
- 🏆 Best Village Pub (Northern Region) 2004; Best Railway Pub 2005
- 🕐 Mon-Sat 11-11; Sun 12-12
- 🏛 Esk Valley Railway, Church of St Michael and St George, The Moors Centre, Arncliffe Woods

Built in 1840, The Eskdale Inn is a sandstone traditional village inn that has won awards for its quality and service. All home-cooked food includes the excellent rabbit pie, mince or steak pie, Whitby scampi, curry and lasagna. Real ales include changing guest ales. The accommodation is cosy and comfortable.

52 Everley Hotel

Hackness, Scarborough, North Yorkshire YO13 0BT
Tel: 01723 882202

Real Ales, Bar Food, Restaurant Menu, Accommodation, No Smoking Area

53 Falcon Inn

Whitby Road, Cloughton, Scarborough,
North Yorkshire YO13 0DY
Tel: 01723 870717

Real Ales, Bar Food, Restaurant Menu, Accommodation, No Smoking Area

54 The Falling Stone

Main Street, Thwing, Driffield,
North Humberside YO25 3DS
Tel: 01262 470403

Real Ales, Restaurant Menu, No Smoking Area

55 Flaneburg Hotel & Restaurant

North Marine Road, Flamborough, Bridlington,
North Humberside YO15 1LF
Tel: 01262 850284

Bar Food, Restaurant Menu, Accommodation,
No Smoking Area

56 Flask Inn

Robin Hoods Bay, Fylingdales, Whitby,
North Yorkshire YO22 4QH
Tel: 01947 880305

Real Ales, Bar Food, Accommodation,
No Smoking Area

57 Fleece Inn

Westgate, Rillington, Malton,
North Yorkshire YO17 8LN
Tel: 01944 758464

Real Ales, Bar Food, Restaurant Menu,
No Smoking Area

58 Fox & Hounds

45 Brook Lane, Ainthorpe, Whitby,
North Yorkshire YO21 2LD
Tel: 01287 660218

Real Ales, Bar Food, Restaurant Menu,
Accommodation, No Smoking Area

59 Fox & Hounds

Goldsborough, Whitby, North Yorkshire YO21 3RX
Tel: 01947 893372

Real Ales, No Smoking Area

60 The Fox & Hounds Inn

Main Street, Sinnington, York, Yorkshire YO62 6SQ
Tel: 01751 431577

Real Ales, Bar Food, Restaurant Menu,
Accommodation, No Smoking Area, Disabled Facilities

See panel opposite

61 The Fox & Rabbit Inn

Whitby Road, Lockton, Pickering,
North Yorkshire YO18 7NQ
Tel: 01751 460213

Real Ales, Bar Food, Restaurant Menu,
No Smoking Area, Disabled Facilities

62 Fox Hound Inn

Main Street, Flixton, Scarborough,
North Yorkshire YO11 3UB
Tel: 01723 890301

Real Ales, Bar Food, Restaurant Menu,
No Smoking Area

63 Foxholm Hotel

Main Street, Ebberston, Scarborough,
North Yorkshire YO13 9NJ
Tel: 01723 859550

Accommodation, No Smoking Area, Disabled Facilities

64 Fylingdales Inn

Thorpe Lane, Fylingthorpe, Whitby,
North Yorkshire YO22 4TH
Tel: 01947 880433

Real Ales, Bar Food, Restaurant Menu,
Accommodation, No Smoking Area

65 Ganton Greyhound

Main Road, Ganton, Scarborough,
North Yorkshire YO12 4NX
Tel: 01944 710116

Real Ales, Bar Food, Restaurant Menu,
Accommodation, No Smoking Area, Disabled Facilities

66 George & Dragon Hotel

17 Market Place, Kirkbymoorside, York,
Yorkshire YO62 6AA
Tel: 01751 433334

Real Ales, Bar Food, Restaurant Menu,
Accommodation, No Smoking Area, Disabled Facilities

67 The Golden Lion

Golden Lion Bank, Whitby,
North Yorkshire YO21 3BS
Tel: 01947 602106

Real Ales, Bar Food, Disabled Facilities

See panel adjacent

68 Golden Lion

21 Market Place, Malton,
North Yorkshire YO17 7LP
Tel: 01653 692364

No Smoking Area

67 The Golden Lion

Golden Lion Bank, Whitby,
North Yorkshire YO21 3BS
☎ 01947 602106

Real Ales, Bar Food, Disabled Facilities

 In the centre of Whitby

 Tetleys Cask

all day 7 days a week

 Disabled access

 10-30 to close (can be up to 2am)

Captain Cook Memorial Museum, Victorian Jet Works, Whitby Abbey, Robin Hood's Bay

Dating back to 1607, The Golden Lion is a picturesque little pub brimming with character and set just opposite the bridge that crosses the river that splits the centre of Whitby. Quick and tasty, very reasonably priced food accompanies the good range of ale, lagers, wines, spirits and soft drinks.

69 Golden Lion

Great Barugh, Malton, North Yorkshire YO17 6UZ
Tel: 01653 668242

Real Ales, Bar Food, Restaurant Menu,
Accommodation, No Smoking Area, Disabled Facilities

70 Grainary Hotel

Keasbeck Hill Farm, Harwood Dale, Scarborough,
North Yorkshire YO13 0DT
Tel: 01723 870026

Bar Food, Restaurant Menu, Accommodation,
No Smoking Area, Disabled Facilities

71 The Grapes Inn

Ebberston, Scarborough, North Yorkshire YO13 9PA
Tel: 01723 859273

Real Ales, Bar Food, Restaurant Menu,
Accommodation, No Smoking Area, Disabled Facilities

72 Grapes Inn

Great Habton, Malton, North Yorkshire YO17 6TU
Tel: 01653 669166

Real Ales, Bar Food, Restaurant Menu,
No Smoking Area

73 Grapes Inn
Railway Street, Slingsby, York, Yorkshire YO62 4AL
Tel: 01653 628229

Real Ales, Bar Food, Restaurant Menu,
No Smoking Area

74 Grosvenor Hotel
Station Road, Robin Hoods Bay, Whitby,
North Yorkshire YO22 4RA
Tel: 01947 880320

Real Ales, Bar Food, Restaurant Menu,
Accommodation, No Smoking Area, Disabled Facilities

75 Hackness Grange Hotel
Hackness, Scarborough,
North Yorkshire YO13 0JW
Tel: 01723 882345

Bar Food, Restaurant Menu, Accommodation,
No Smoking Area

76 Ham & Cheese Inn
Scagglethorpe, Malton, North Yorkshire YO17 8DY
Tel: 01944 758249

Real Ales, Bar Food, Restaurant Menu,
Accommodation, No Smoking Area, Disabled Facilities

77 Hare & Hounds Inn
High Hawsker, Whitby, North Yorkshire YO22 4LH
Tel: 01947 880453

Real Ales, Bar Food, Restaurant Menu,
No Smoking Area

78 Hart Inn
East Row, Sandsend, Whitby,
North Yorkshire YO21 3SU
Tel: 01947 893304

Real Ales, Bar Food, Restaurant Menu,
No Smoking Area, Disabled Facilities

79 Hayburn Wyke Inn
Newlands Road, Cloughton, Scarborough,
North Yorkshire YO13 0AR
Tel: 01723 870202

Real Ales, Bar Food, Restaurant Menu,
Accommodation, No Smoking Area

80 Heatherdene Hotel
Goathland, Whitby, North Yorkshire YO22 5AN
Tel: 01947 896334

Restaurant Menu, Accommodation, No Smoking Area

81 Honey Pot Inn
Flamborough Road, Speeton, Filey,
North Yorkshire YO14 9TA
Tel: 01723 891783

Real Ales, Bar Food, Restaurant Menu,
No Smoking Area

82 Horse Shoe Inn
89 Stonegate, Hunmanby, Filey,
North Yorkshire YO14 0PU
Tel: 01723 890419

Real Ales, Bar Food, Disabled Facilities

83 The Horseshoe Inn
4 Hall Garth, Pickering,
North Yorkshire YO18 7AW
Tel: 01751 472856

84 Horseshoe Inn
Main Street, Levisham, Pickering,
North Yorkshire YO18 7NL
Tel: 01751 460240

Real Ales, Bar Food, Restaurant Menu,
Accommodation, No Smoking Area, Disabled Facilities

85 Huntsman Inn
Main Road, Aislaby, Whitby,
North Yorkshire YO21 1SW
Tel: 01947 810637

Real Ales, Bar Food, Restaurant Menu,
Accommodation, No Smoking Area, Disabled Facilities

86 The Imperial
Hope Street, Filey, North Yorkshire YO14 9DL
Tel: 01723 512185

Real Ales

87 Kings Head Hotel
5 Market Place, Malton, North Yorkshire YO17 7LP
Tel: 01653 692289

Real Ales, Bar Food, Restaurant Menu,
Accommodation, No Smoking Area, Disabled Facilities

88 Kings Head Hotel

5 High Market Place, Kirkbymoorside, York,
Yorkshire YO62 6AT
Tel: 01751 431340

Real Ales, Bar Food, Restaurant Menu,
Accommodation, No Smoking Area, Disabled Facilities

89 Lastingham Grange

High Street, Lastingham, York, Yorkshire YO62 6TH
Tel: 01751 417402

Bar Food, Restaurant Menu, Accommodation,
No Smoking Area, Disabled Facilities

90 The Lettered Board

8 Smiddy Hill, Pickering, North Yorkshire YO18 7AN
Tel: 01751 472282

Real Ales

91 Londesborough Arms

24 Main Street, Seamer, Scarborough,
North Yorkshire YO12 4PS
Tel: 01723 863230

Real Ales, Bar Food, Accommodation

92 Mallyan Spout Hotel

Goathland, Whitby, North Yorkshire YO22 5AN
Tel: 01947 896486

Real Ales, Bar Food, Restaurant Menu,
Accommodation, No Smoking Area

93 Milburn Arms Hotel

Rosedale Abbey, Pickering,
North Yorkshire YO18 8RA
Tel: 01751 417312

Real Ales, Bar Food, Restaurant Menu,
Accommodation, No Smoking Area

94 The Moorcock Inn

Langdale End, Scarborough,
North Yorkshire YO13 0BN
Tel: 01723 882268

Real Ales, Bar Food, Restaurant Menu, No Smoking Area

95 Nags Head Inn

High Street, Scalby, Scarborough,
North Yorkshire YO13 0PT
Tel: 01723 373229

Real Ales, Bar Food

96 New Globe Inn

1-5 Yorkersgate, Malton,
North Yorkshire YO17 7AA
Tel: 01653 692395

Real Ales, Bar Food, Restaurant Menu,
Accommodation, No Smoking Area

97 New Inn

Thornton Dale, Pickering,
North Yorkshire YO18 7LJ
Tel: 01751 474226

Real Ales, Bar Food, Restaurant Menu,
Accommodation

98 New Inn

Cropton, Pickering, North Yorkshire YO18 8HH
Tel: 01751 417330

Real Ales, Bar Food, Restaurant Menu,
Accommodation, No Smoking Area

99 Oakwheel

17-19 Coastal Road, Burniston, Scarborough,
North Yorkshire YO13 0HR
Tel: 01723 870230

Real Ales, Bar Food, Accommodation

100 Old Lodge Hotel

Old Maltongate, Malton,
North Yorkshire YO17 7EG
Tel: 01653 690570

Real Ales, Bar Food, Restaurant Menu

101 Ox Pasture Hall Country Hotel

Throxenby, Scarborough,
North Yorkshire YO12 5TD
Tel: 01723 365295

Bar Food, Restaurant Menu, Accommodation,
No Smoking Area, Disabled Facilities

102 The Peacock Hotel

66 High Street, Snainton, Scarborough,
North Yorkshire YO13 9AJ
Tel: 01723 859257

Bar Food, Restaurant Menu, Accommodation,
No Smoking Area, Disabled Facilities

103 The Plough Inn
21-23 High Street, Scalby, Scarborough,
North Yorkshire YO13 0PT
Tel: 01723 362622

Real Ales, Bar Food, No Smoking Area

104 Plough Inn
180 Coach Road, Sleights, Whitby,
North Yorkshire YO22 5EN
Tel: 01947 810412

Real Ales, Bar Food, Restaurant Menu,
No Smoking Area

105 Postgate Inn
Egton Bridge, Whitby, North Yorkshire YO21 1UX
Tel: 01947 895241

Real Ales, Bar Food, Restaurant Menu,
Accommodation, No Smoking Area

106 The Providence Inn
Yedingham, Malton, North Yorkshire YO17 8SL
Tel: 01944 728093

Real Ales, Bar Food, No Smoking Area

107 The Queen's Head
High Street, Amotherby, Malton,
North Yorkshire YO17 6TL
Tel: 01653 693630

Real Ales, Restaurant Menu, No Smoking Area,
Disabled Facilities

See panel adjacent

108 Railway Tavern
65 Sands Lane, Hunmanby, Filey,
North Yorkshire YO14 0LT
Tel: 01723 890878

Real Ales, Bar Food

109 Raven Hall Hotel
Ravenscar, Scarborough, North Yorkshire YO13 0ET
Tel: 01723 870353

Real Ales, Bar Food, Restaurant Menu,
Accommodation, No Smoking Area

107 The Queen's Head
High Street, Amotherby, Malton,
North Yorkshire YO17 6TL
☎ 01653 693630

Real Ales, Restaurant Menu, No Smoking Area,
Disabled Facilities

On the B1257 Helmsley Road, off the A64
and 3 miles northwest of Malton

Tetleys Cask, Copper Dragon and changing
guest ale

5-11

Car park, disabled access, beer garden,
children's play area

All major cards

No smoking in restaurant

5-11

Malton, Kirkham Priory, Castle Howard, York

Authentic Cantonese cuisine is on the menu at The Queen's Head, a spacious and welcoming inn in the tranquil village of Amotherby. This Free House has an elegant restaurant where guests can sample one of the best Chinese meals available in the area, including special seafood dishes added to the menu on Wednesdays and Thursdays. Takeaway meals also available.

110 Red Lion
28 High Street, Cloughton, Scarborough,
North Yorkshire YO13 0AE
Tel: 01723 870702

Real Ales, Bar Food, Restaurant Menu,
Accommodation, No Smoking Area

111 Red Lion Inn
High Street, Lythe, Whitby,
North Yorkshire YO21 3RT
Tel: 01947 893300

Bar Food, Restaurant Menu, Accommodation,
Disabled Facilities

112 The Rose Inn
Bridge Street, Pickering,
North Yorkshire YO18 8DT
Tel: 01751 475366

Real Ales, Bar Food, Restaurant Menu

113 The Rosette Inn

Newby Bridge Lane, Scarborough,
North Yorkshire YO12 6UD
Tel: 01723 507214

Real Ales, Bar Food, Restaurant Menu,
No Smoking Area, Disabled Facilities

114 Royal Crescent Vaults

South Crescent Road, Filey, North Yorkshire YO14 9JJ
Tel: 01723 513058

Real Ales, Bar Food, Restaurant Menu, No Smoking
Area

115 Royal Dog & Duck

Dog & Duck Square, Flamborough, Bridlington,
North Humberside YO15 1NB
Tel: 01262 850206

Real Ales, Bar Food, Restaurant Menu,
No Smoking Area

116 Royal Oak

26 Market Place, Malton, North Yorkshire YO17 7LX
Tel: 01653 692122

Real Ales

117 The Royal Oak

Eastgate, Pickering, North Yorkshire YO18 7DW
Tel: 01751 472718

Real Ales, Bar Food, No Smoking Area,
Disabled Facilities

See panel below

118 Royal Oak Hotel

Royal Oak, Filey, North Yorkshire YO14 9QE
Tel: 01723 513586

Real Ales, Bar Food, Restaurant Menu,
Accommodation, No Smoking Area, Disabled Facilities

119 Royal Oak Inn

Main Street, Gillamoor, York, Yorkshire YO62 7HX
Tel: 01751 431414

Real Ales, Bar Food, Restaurant Menu,
No Smoking Area, Disabled Facilities

120 Russells

20 Market Place, Pickering, North Yorkshire YO18 7AE
Tel: 01751 472749

Real Ales, Bar Food, Restaurant Menu,
No Smoking Area, Disabled Facilities

117 The Royal Oak

Eastgate, Pickering, North Yorkshire YO18 7DW
☎ 01751 472718

**Real Ales, Bar Food, No Smoking Area, Disabled
Facilities**

- On the A170 east of Pickering
- John Smiths, guest ales
- 12-2 & 6-9
- Beer garden, heated patio area
- 12-11
- Pickering, Thornton le Dale, Brompton, East Ayton, Scarborough

The Royal Oak is a tidy and compact inn that is very spacious inside and boasts open fires and other traditional comforts. Steve Kennedy is the very 'hand's on' owner here, overseeing everything from the bar to the kitchen and offering, along with his friendly staff, a warm welcome and great service to all his guests. The changing menu features all home-cooked dishes including hearty favourites from steaks to curries, home-made pies and more. Recently refurbished to offer every modern comfort while retaining its many charming original features, this very pleasant roadside inn is the perfect place to stop for a relaxing drink and meal while exploring the region. Handy for Pickering, the North York Moors and the coast around Scarborough and Robin Hood's Bay.

121 The Salmon Leap

6 Coach Road, Sleights, Whitby,
North Yorkshire YO22 5AA
Tel: 01947 810233

Real Ales, Bar Food, Restaurant Menu,
Accommodation, No Smoking Area, Disabled Facilities

122 Seabirds

Tower Street, Flamborough, Bridlington,
North Humberside YO15 1PD
Tel: 01262 850242

Real Ales, Bar Food, Restaurant Menu, No Smoking
Area

123 Ship Inn & Restaurant

Post Office Street, Flamborough, Bridlington,
North Humberside YO15 1NA
Tel: 01262 850454

Real Ales, Bar Food, Restaurant Menu,
Accommodation, No Smoking Area

124 Snooty Fox Hotel

Scarborough Road, East Heslerton, Malton,
North Yorkshire YO17 8EN
Tel: 01944 710554

Bar Food, Restaurant Menu, Accommodation,
No Smoking Area

125 Southdown Hotel

7-8 The Beach, Filey, North Yorkshire YO14 9LA
Tel: 01723 513392

Real Ales, Bar Food, Restaurant Menu,
Accommodation, Disabled Facilities

126 Spotted Cow

Cattle Market, Malton, North Yorkshire YO17 7JN
Tel: 01653 692100

Real Ales

127 Star Inn

Weaverthorpe, Malton, North Yorkshire YO17 8EX
Tel: 01944 738273

Real Ales, Bar Food, Restaurant Menu,
Accommodation, No Smoking Area, Disabled Facilities

128 Star Inn

88 Main Street, Cayton, Scarborough,
North Yorkshire YO11 3RP
Tel: 01723 582395

Real Ales, Disabled Facilities

129 The Station

15 Church Street, Filey, North Yorkshire YO14 9ED
Tel: 01723 512236

Bar Food, Restaurant Menu, Accommodation,
No Smoking Area

130 The Station Tavern

Front Street, Grosmont, Whitby,
North Yorkshire YO22 5PA
Tel: 01947 895060

Real Ales, Bar Food, Accommodation, No Smoking
Area, Disabled Facilities

See Panel below

---

130 The Station Tavern

Front Street, Grosmont, Whitby,
North Yorkshire YO22 5PA
☎ 01947 895060

**Real Ales, Bar Food, Accommodation, No Smoking
Area, Disabled Facilities**

- Next to Grosmont Station, off the A169/
  A171 16½ miles southeast of Great Ayton
- John Smiths Cask, Camerons Strongarm, Guest
  Ales
- 12-2.30 & 7-8.45
- 4 guest bedrooms
- Weekly live music
- Parking, disabled access
- All major cards
- No-smoking room
- 11-11 (summer); 7-11pm (winter)
- North Yorkshire Moors Railway, Arncliffe
  Woods, Egton Bridge, Grosmont, Beck Hole,
  Goathland

Adjoining Grosmont Railway Station and
dating back to 1836, the excellent Station
Tavern boasts real ales and delicious home-
cooked food. This charming traditional inn has
very comfortable accommodation and has
been featured on a couple of occasions in
ITV's *Heartbeat*. The NYMR locomotive sheds
are nearby.

131 The Strongwood Hotel

Eastway, Eastfield, Scarborough,
North Yorkshire YO11 3LT
Tel: 01723 582635

No Smoking Area

132 The Sun Inn

136 Westgate, Pickering, North Yorkshire YO18 8BB
Tel: 01751 472797

Real Ales

133 The Sun Inn

Normanby, Sinnington, York, Yorkshire YO62 6RH
Tel: 01751 431051

Real Ales, Bar Food, Restaurant Menu,
No Smoking Area, Disabled Facilities

134 The Talbot Hotel

Yorkersgate, Malton, North Yorkshire YO17 7AJ
Tel: 01653 694031

Restaurant Menu, Accommodation, No Smoking Area

135 Three Tuns

Murray Street, Filey, North Yorkshire YO14 9DG
Tel: 01723 512183

Bar Food, Accommodation, No Smoking Area,
Disabled Facilities

136 Ugthorpe Lodge Hotel

Guisborough Road, Ugthorpe, Whitby,
North Yorkshire YO21 2BE
Tel: 01947 840111

Real Ales, Bar Food, Accommodation,
No Smoking Area

See panel adjacent

137 Union Inn

46 Commercial Street, Norton, Malton,
North Yorkshire YO17 9ES
Tel: 01653 692945

Real Ales, Accommodation

138 Victoria Hotel

Station Road, Robin Hoods Bay, Whitby,
North Yorkshire YO22 4RL
Tel: 01947 880205

Real Ales, Bar Food, Restaurant Menu,
Accommodation, No Smoking Area

136 Ugthorpe Lodge Hotel

Guisborough Road, Ugthorpe, Whitby,
North Yorkshire YO21 2BE
☎ 01947 840111

Real Ales, Bar Food, Accommodation, No Smoking
Area

- Off the A171 8 miles west of Whitby
- Rotating guest ales
- 12-2.30 & 6-9
- 3 en suite rooms
- Weekend music in summer
- Parking, disabled access, beer garden
- All major cards
- No smoking areas
- Mon-Thurs 12-3 & 7-11, Fri-Sun 12-11 (summer); Mon-Weds & Fri 7-11, Sat & Sun 12-3 & 7-11 (winter)
- Whitby, Robin Hood's Bay, Grosmont, Goathland, Castleton

Dating back to 1605, this stonebuilt country house hotel and pub enjoys a well-deserved reputation. The menu boasts hearty favourites such as the Ugthorpe mixed grill, steak and kidney pudding, beef and ale pie, Mediterranean vegetable bake and more. The accommodation is comfortable and makes a good base from which to explore this beautiful region.

139 Wentworth Arms Hotel

Town Street, Old Malton, Malton,
North Yorkshire YO17 7HD
Tel: 01653 692618

Real Ales, Bar Food, Restaurant Menu,
Accommodation, No Smoking Area, Disabled Facilities

140 Wheatsheaf Inn

Egton, Whitby, North Yorkshire YO21 1TZ
Tel: 01947 895271

Real Ales, Bar Food, Restaurant Menu,
Accommodation, No Smoking Area

141 White Horse Farm Hotel

Rosedale Abbey, Pickering, North Yorkshire YO18 8SE
Tel: 01751 417239

Real Ales, Bar Food, Restaurant Menu,
Accommodation, No Smoking Area, Disabled Facilities

142 White Horse Hotel
5 Market Place, Kirkbymoorside, York,
Yorkshire YO62 6AB
Tel: 01751 431296

Real Ales, Bar Food, Restaurant Menu,
Accommodation, No Smoking Area, Disabled Facilities

143 The White Horse Inn
30 High Street, Bempton, Bridlington,
North Humberside YO15 1HB
Tel: 01262 850266

Real Ales, Bar Food, No Smoking Area

144 White House Hotel
Upgang Lane, Whitby, North Yorkshire YO21 3JJ
Tel: 01947 600469

Real Ales, Bar Food, Restaurant Menu,
Accommodation, No Smoking Area

145 The White Swan
1 Church Hill, Hunmanby, Filey,
North Yorkshire YO14 0JU
Tel: 01723 890232

Real Ales, Bar Food, Restaurant Menu,
Accommodation, No Smoking Area

146 The White Swan Hotel
Newton-on-Rawcliffe, Pickering,
North Yorkshire YO18 8QA
Tel: 01751 472505

Real Ales, Bar Food, Accommodation,
No Smoking Area

147 White Swan Hotel
Market Place, Pickering, North Yorkshire YO18 7AA
Tel: 01751 472288

Real Ales, Bar Food, Restaurant Menu,
Accommodation, No Smoking Area, Disabled Facilities

148 White Swan Inn
Old Maltongate, Malton,
North Yorkshire YO17 7EH
Tel: 01653 694424

Real Ales

149 Wilson Arms
Beacon Way, Sneaton, Whitby,
North Yorkshire YO22 5HS
Tel: 01947 602552

Real Ales, Bar Food, Restaurant Menu,
Accommodation, No Smoking Area

150 Ye Horseshoe Inn
Egton, Whitby, North Yorkshire YO21 1TZ
Tel: 01947 895274

Real Ales, Bar Food, Restaurant Menu,
Accommodation, No Smoking Area

151 Ye Olde Forge Valley
Pickering Road, West Ayton, Scarborough,
North Yorkshire YO13 9JE
Tel: 01723 862146

Real Ales, Restaurant Menu, Accommodation,
No Smoking Area

See panel below

151 Ye Olde Forge Valley
West Ayton, Scarborough, North Yorkshire YO13 9JE
☎ 01723 862146

Real Ales, Restaurant Menu, Accommodation, No Smoking Area

- On the A170 southwest of Scarborough
- Tetleys, John Smiths, Black Sheep, guest ale
- Tues-Sun 12-2; Tues-Sat 6-8
- 2 guest bedrooms
- Live music at weekends; blues night Tues; folk night Thurs; quiz night Sun
- Car park, beer garden, function suite
- All major cards
- Mon-Thurs & Sun 11 a.m.-1 a.m.; Fri & Sat 11 a.m.-2 a.m.
- Ryedale, Pickering, Scarborough

Dating back to 1788, Ye Olde Forge Valley Inn is a traditional coaching inn with great food, drink and accommodation. Simple, hearty fare is the byword here, with a range of home-cooked favourite dishes. Handy for the North Yorks Moors National Park and the coast, it makes an ideal touring base.

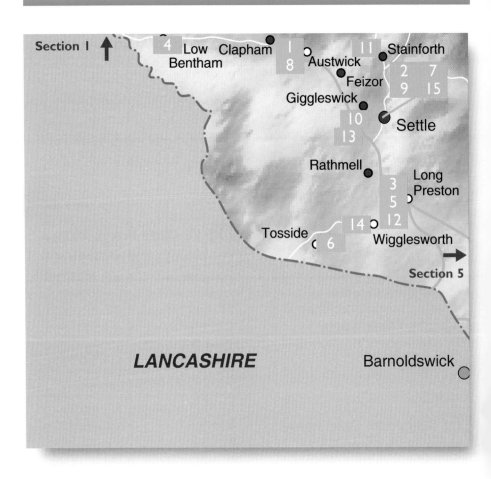

Section I

Low Clapham
Bentham

4

Austwick
1
8

Stainforth
11

2   7
9   15

Feizor

Giggleswick

10
13

Settle

Rathmell

Long
Preston

3
5

Tosside

14

12

6

Wigglesworth

Section 5

LANCASHIRE

Barnoldswick

11   Pub or Inn Reference Number - Detailed Information

12   Pub or Inn Reference Number - Summary Entry

● ■   Place of interest mentioned in the chapter introduction

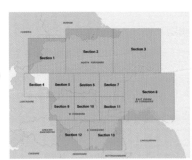

SECTION 4

Clapham

By far the largest building in the village is **Ingleborough Hall**, once the home of the Farrer family and now a centre for outdoor education. One member of the family, Reginald Farrer, was an internationally renowned botanist and he was responsible for introducing many new plant species into the country. Many examples of his finds still exist in the older gardens of the village and in the hall's grounds, and there is a particularly pleasant walk, the **Reginald Farrer Nature Trail**, which leads from Clapham to nearby **Ingleborough Cave**.

Feizor

The village dates back to monastic times when it lay on the route from Kilnsey to the Lake District, which was much used by the monks of Fountains Abbey. The **Yorkshire Dales Falconry and Conservation Centre** boasts demonstration flights held throughout the day.

Giggleswick

This ancient village, which lies below the limestone scar that is part of the Craven fault, is home to several interesting places including the 15th-century **Church of St Alkelda** and the well-known **Giggleswick School**. Just to the north of Giggleswick can be found the famous **Ebbing and Flowing Well**. Also on the edge of town is the **Yorkshire Dales Falconry & Conservation Centre**, home to a wide variety of birds of prey from around the world.

Rathmell

From this small village, set beside the River Ribble, there are many footpaths along the riverbanks through the nearby woods and up to Whelpstone Crag.

Settle

Settle is best known because of the famous **Settle-Carlisle Railway**, a proudly preserved memento of the glorious age of steam. The trains thunder over 21

Packhorse Bridge, Clapham

viaducts, through 14 tunnels and over numerous bridges. Settle town itself is dominated by one of these huge viaducts as well as the towering limestone cliffs of **Castleberg Crag**, which offer spectacular views over the town.

Stainforth

This sheltered sheep-farming village owes its existence to the Cistercian monks who

brought those animals to this area. The monks were also responsible for building the 14th-century stone packhorse bridge which carries the road over the local beck, a tributary of the River Ribble. **Catrigg Force**, found along a track known as Goat Scar Lane, is a fine waterfall which drops some 60 feet into a wooded pool, while to the west is **Stainforth Force** flowing over a series of rock shelves.

1 The Austwick Country House Hotel & Restaurant
Austwick, Lancaster, Yorkshire LA2 8BY
Tel: 01524 251224
Restaurant Menu, Accommodation, No Smoking Area, Disabled Facilities

2 Black Horse
Church Street, Giggleswick, Settle, North Yorkshire BD24 0BE
Tel: 01729 822506
Real Ales, Bar Food, Restaurant Menu, Accommodation, No Smoking Area, Disabled Facilities

3 Boars Head
Main Street, Long Preston, Skipton, North Yorkshire BD23 4ND
Tel: 01729 840217
Real Ales, Bar Food, Restaurant Menu, Accommodation, No Smoking Area

4 Coach House Hotel
Main Street, Bentham, High Bentham, Lancaster LA2 7HF
Tel: 01524 262305
Real Ales, Bar Food, Restaurant Menu, Accommodation, No Smoking Area

5 The Country House Hotel
Church Street, Long Preston, Skipton, North Yorkshire BD23 4NJ
Tel: 01729 840246
Real Ales, Bar Food, Restaurant Menu, Accommodation, No Smoking Area, Disabled Facilities

6 Crow Trees Inn
Tosside, Skipton, North Yorkshire BD23 4SD
Tel: 01729 840591
Real Ales, Bar Food, No Smoking Area, Disabled Facilities

7 Falcon Manor Hotel
Skipton Road, Settle, North Yorkshire BD24 9BD
Tel: 01729 823814
Real Ales, Bar Food, Restaurant Menu, Accommodation, No Smoking Area, Disabled Facilities

8 Game Cock
Austwick, Lancaster, Yorkshire LA2 8BB
Tel: 01524 251226
Real Ales, Bar Food, Restaurant Menu, No Smoking Area, Disabled Facilities

9 Golden Lion Hotel

Duke Street, Settle, North Yorkshire BD24 9DU
Tel: 01729 822203

Real Ales, Bar Food, Restaurant Menu,
Accommodation, No Smoking Area

10 Harts Head Hotel

Belle Hill, Giggleswick, Settle,
North Yorkshire BD24 0BA
Tel: 01729 822086

Real Ales, Bar Food, Restaurant Menu,
Accommodation, No Smoking Area

11 Helwith Bridge

Helwith Bridge, Horton-in-Ribblesdale, Settle,
North Yorkshire BD24 0EY
Tel: 01729 860220

Real Ales, Bar Food, Restaurant Menu,
Disabled Facilities

12 Maypole Inn

Maypole Green, Long Preston, Skipton,
North Yorkshire BD23 4PJ
Tel: 01729 840219

Real Ales, Bar Food, Restaurant Menu,
Accommodation, No Smoking Area, Disabled Facilities

13 The Old Station

Giggleswick, Settle, North Yorkshire BD24 0EA
Tel: 01729 823623

Real Ales, Bar Food, Restaurant Menu,
Accommodation, No Smoking Area

14 Plough Inn

Wigglesworth, Skipton, North Yorkshire BD23 4RJ
Tel: 01729 840243

Real Ales, Bar Food, Restaurant Menu,
Accommodation, No Smoking Area, Disabled Facilities

15 The Talbot Arms Hotel

High Street, Settle, North Yorkshire BD24 9EX
Tel: 01729 823566

Real Ales, Bar Food, Restaurant Menu,
Accommodation

NORTH YORKSHIRE

Section 1

Section 2

45

Kilnsey

6 26
31 36

Pateley Bridge

68

9 Wilsill

10
46 Malham
62
74

Threshfield
54

Grassington
H 14 en

52

65 5

78

Bewerley

32
Burnsall
23

48
25
61 17
53

2

Appletreewick

Section 4

15

Embsay

Bolton
Abbey

Blubberhouses

69

40

Section 6

56 Gargrave
1
50
72 19 29
12

51

24

18 21
30 66
70

Broughton
20

11

Skipton

Addingham

73

71 42

67 Silsden

Ilkley

7

Elslack

Thornton in Craven

59
76

8 44
58 60
63

64

16 34

Earby

37

57 75 35

39 lenston

28

43 55

77

13 33

4 3

Section 8 Riddleoden...

22 49

27 38 47 41

11	Pub or Inn Reference Number - Detailed Information
12	Pub or Inn Reference Number - Summary Entry
● ■	Place of interest mentioned in the chapter introduction

SECTION 5

Appletreewick

This peaceful village, which is known locally as Aptrick, lies between the banks of the River Wharfe and the bleak moorland and is overlooked by the craggy expanse of **Simon's Seat**, one of Wharfedale's best-loved hilltops. Just to the north of Appletreewick lie **Parcevall Hall Gardens**, a wonderful woodland garden which includes many varieties of unusual plants and shrubs. Though the 16-acre gardens are high above sea level (which provides the visitor with splendid views), many of the plants still flourish in these beautiful surroundings.

Bewerley

Recorded as *Bevrelie* (a clearing inhabited by badgers) in the *Domesday Book*, this is Nidderdale's oldest settlement. It was also the site of the earliest and most important of Fountains Abbey's many granges. Not only were they farming here but lead was being extracted from the nearby moor. The recently restored Chapel, built here by one of the last abbots, Marmaduke Huby, acted for many years as the village school.

Bolton Abbey

The village is actually a collection of small hamlets which have all been part of the estate of the Dukes of Devonshire since 1748. **Bolton Abbey** itself lies on the banks of the River Wharfe while the hamlets of Storiths, Hazelwood, Deerstones, and Halton East lie higher up. The main attraction in the village is the substantial ruin of **Bolton Priory**, an Augustinian house that was founded in 1155 by monks from Embsay. In an idyllic situation on the banks of the River Wharfe, the ruins are well preserved while the nave of the priory church, first built in 1220, is now incorporated into the parish church. In and around this beautiful village there are some 80 miles of footpaths and nature trails, skirting the riverbanks and climbing up onto the high moorland. Upstream from the priory lies one of the most visited natural features in Wharfedale, a point where the wide river suddenly narrows into a confined channel of black rock through which the water thunders. This spectacular gorge is known as **The Strid** because, over the centuries, many heroic (or foolhardy) types have attempted to leap across it as a test of bravery.

Broughton

Broughton Hall dates back to 1597. Enlarged in the 18th and 19th centuries, the hall is open to the public on Bank Holidays when guided tours are conducted around this interesting building. Those lucky enough to visit on the last Sunday in June will also be witness to the Broughton Hall Game Fair, a well-attended event which covers all manner of country sports and pursuits.

Burnsall

The village is very dramatically situated on a bend in the River Wharfe with the slopes of Burnsall Fell as a backdrop. Of ancient origins it is thought that, prior to the 8th century, Wilfrid Bishop of York founded a wooden church on the site of which now stands the village's 12th-century church. However, it is not this sturdy Dales' church which draws visitors, but its bridge, which has five stone arches.

Elslack

Overlooking the village is the 1,274-foot high Pinhaw Beacon from which there are some fine panoramic views over the heather-covered moorland. During the Napoleonic Wars in the early 19th century, when there was great fear of an invasion from France, the beacon, one in a countrywide chain of communication beacons, was manned 24 hours a day.

Embsay

The village is home to the **Embsay Steam Railway** which is based at the small country station. As well as taking a scenic steam train journey to the end of the line, a couple of miles away, there are over 20 locomotives, both steam and diesel, on display together with railway carriages. Special events are arranged throughout the year and opening times vary though the trains run every Sunday. Those choosing to walk over the moor to the north of the village should take care as the area is peppered with old coal pits and disused shafts. However, the view from **Embsay Crag** (1,217 feet high) is well worth the effort of climbing.

Grassington

One of the best-loved villages within the Yorkshire Dales National Park, Grassington

Linton Falls, Grassington

in many ways typifies the Dales' settlement with its characteristic market square. Known as the capital of Upper Wharfedale, the historically important valley roads meet here and the ancient monastic route from Malham to Fountains Abbey passes through the village.

Hebden

From this quiet hamlet it is only a short distance to the wonderful 500,000-year-old cave at **Stump Cross Caverns**. This large show cave holds a fantastic collection of stalactites and stalagmites which make it one of the most visited underground attractions in the area.

Ilkley

Originally an Iron Age settlement, Ilkley was eventually occupied by the Romans who

92

built a camp here to protect their crossing of the River Wharfe. One of the most famous West Yorkshire attractions has to be **Ilkley Moor**, immortalised in the well-known song. Like any of the Yorkshire moors, Ilkley Moor can look inviting and attractive on a sunny day but ominous and forbidding when the weather takes a turn for the worse. The River Wharfe runs along the edge of the moor and through the town of Ilkley which is clustered within a narrow section of the valley in the midst of heather moorland, craggy gritstone and wooded hillside.

Kilnsey

This small hamlet, on the opposite bank of the River Wharfe from Conistone, is a great place from which many anglers fly fish. This quiet and peaceful place is overlooked by the now uninhabited Old Hall which was originally built as a grange for the monks of Fountains Abbey. The striking outline of **Kilnsey Crag** is unmistakable as one side of this limestone hill was gouged out by a passing glacier during the Ice Age. One of the most spectacular natural features in the Dales, the crag has a huge 'lip' or overhang which presents an irresistible challenge to adventurous climbers.

Linton

This delightful and unspoilt village, that is more correctly called Linton-in-Craven, has grown up around its village green through which runs a small beck. This flat area of land was once a lake and around its edge was grown

flax which the villagers spun into linen. The village is also the home of the **Church of St Michael and All Angels**, a wonderful building that is a fine example of rural medieval architecture.

Malham

This pretty village of farms and cottages is one of the most visited places in the Yorkshire Dales. To the north of the village lies the ancient glacial grandeur of **Malham Cove**. Access is from the Langcliffe road beyond the last buildings of the village, down a path alongside the beck that leads through a scattering of trees. The 300-foot limestone amphitheatre is the most spectacular section of the mid-Craven fault. A steep path leads to the limestone pavement at the top, with its characteristic clints and grykes, where water has carved a distinctive natural sculpture through the weaknesses in the limestone. From here it is not too far to reach the equally inspiring **Gordale Scar**, a huge gorge carved by glacial melt water with an impressive waterfall leaping, in two stages, from a fissure in its face. Further on still is another

Kilnsey Crag

waterfall known as Janet's Foss. Three miles north of the scar is **Malham Tarn**, a glacial lake which by way of an underground stream is the source of the River Aire.

Pateley Bridge

Considered one of the prettiest towns in the Dales, Pateley Bridge straggles up the hillside from its elegant 18th-century bridge over the Nidd. A town of quaint and pretty buildings, the oldest is St Mary's Church, a lovely ruin dating from 1320 from which there are some fine panoramic views. Another excellent vista can be viewed from the aptly named **Panorama Walk**, part of the main medieval route from Ripon to Skipton.

Riddlesden

Parts of **East Riddlesden Hall**, now a National Trust property, date back to Saxon times. The main building, however, was constructed in the 1630s by James Murgatroyd, a wealthy Halifax clothier and merchant. A fine example of a 17th-century manor house, the gabled hall is built of dark stone with mullioned windows, and it retains its original centre hall, superb period fireplaces, oak panelling, and plaster ceilings.

Skipton

Often called the 'Gateway to the Dales', Skipton's origins can be traced to the 7th century when Anglian farmers christened it Sheeptown. **Skipton Castle** was begun in 1090 and the powerful stone structure seen today was devised in 1310 by Robert de Clifford, the 1st Earl of Skipton.

Thornton-in-Craven

This attractive village stands on the Pennine Way and from here there are magnificent views of Airedale and, towards, the west, Pendle Forest in Lancashire. Now a quiet place, during the Civil War the manor house was ruined by Royalist soldiers shortly after Cromwell had stayed here to attend a local wedding. The present house is situated opposite the original site. Past parish records associated with the 12th-century Church of St Mary are lost as they were accidentally burnt by the local rector.

Wilsill

About two miles east of Wilsill are **Brimham Rocks** (National Trust), an extraordinary natural sculpture park. Formed into fantastic shapes by years of erosion, these great millstone grit boulders lie atop a steep hill amidst some 400 acres of heathland.

Skipton Castle

1 The Anchor Inn

Hellifield Road, Gargrave, Skipton,
North Yorkshire BD23 3NB
Tel: 01756 749666

Bar Food, Restaurant Menu, No Smoking Area,
Disabled Facilities

2 Angel

Hetton, Skipton, North Yorkshire BD23 6LT
Tel: 01756 730263

Real Ales, Bar Food, Restaurant Menu,
Accommodation, No Smoking Area, Disabled Facilities

3 The Bay Horse Inn

Ellers Road, Sutton-in-Craven, Keighley,
West Yorkshire BD20 7LY
Tel: 01535 632219

Real Ales

4 Bay Horse Inn

Keighley Road, Cowling, Keighley,
West Yorkshire BD22 0AH
Tel: 01535 632797

Real Ales

5 Birch Tree Inn

Wilsill, Harrogate, North Yorkshire HG3 5EA
Tel: 01423 711131

Real Ales, Bar Food, Restaurant Menu,
Accommodation, No Smoking Area, Disabled Facilities

6 The Black Horse

2 Garrs Lane, Grassington, Skipton,
North Yorkshire BD23 5AT
Tel: 01756 752770

Real Ales, Bar Food, Restaurant Menu,
Accommodation, No Smoking Area, Disabled Facilities

7 The Black Horse Hotel

Askwith, Otley, West Yorkshire LS21 2JQ
Tel: 01943 461074

Real Ales, Bar Food, Restaurant Menu,
No Smoking Area

8 Bridge Inn

Keighley Road, Silsden, Keighley,
West Yorkshire BD20 0EA
Tel: 01535 653144

Real Ales, Accommodation, No Smoking Area

9 Bridge Inn

Low Wath Road, Pateley Bridge, Harrogate,
North Yorkshire HG3 5HL
Tel: 01423 711484

Real Ales, Bar Food, Restaurant Menu,
Accommodation, No Smoking Area, Disabled Facilities

10 Buck Inn

Malham, Skipton, North Yorkshire BD23 4DA
Tel: 01729 830317

Real Ales, Bar Food, Restaurant Menu,
Accommodation, No Smoking Area, Disabled Facilities

11 The Bull Inn

Broughton, Skipton, North Yorkshire BD23 3AE
Tel: 01756 792065

Real Ales, Bar Food, Restaurant Menu,
No Smoking Area, Disabled Facilities

12 Cavendish Arms

Skipton Road, Embsay, Skipton, North Yorkshire
BD23 6QT
Tel: 01756 793980

Real Ales, Bar Food, Restaurant Menu,
No Smoking Area, Disabled Facilities

13 Chevin Inn

West Chevin Road, Menston, Ilkley,
West Yorkshire LS29 6BE
Tel: 01943 873841

Real Ales, Bar Food, Disabled Facilities

14 Clarendon Hotel

Grassington, Hebden, Skipton,
North Yorkshire BD23 5DE
Tel: 01756 752446

Real Ales, Bar Food, Restaurant Menu,
Accommodation, No Smoking Area, Disabled Facilities

15 Coniston Hall
Coniston Cold, Skipton,
North Yorkshire BD23 4EB
Tel: 01756 748080

Real Ales, Bar Food, Restaurant Menu,
Accommodation, No Smoking Area, Disabled Facilities

16 Cow & Calf Hotel
Hangingstone Road, Ey, Ilkley,
West Yorkshire LS29 8BT
Tel: 01943 607335

Real Ales, Bar Food, Restaurant Menu,
Accommodation, No Smoking Area, Disabled Facilities

17 Craven Arms
Appletreewick, Skipton,
North Yorkshire BD23 6DA
Tel: 01756 720270

Real Ales, Bar Food, Restaurant Menu,
Accommodation, No Smoking Area, Disabled Facilities

18 Craven Heifer Inn
Main Street, Addingham, Ilkley,
West Yorkshire LS29 0PL
Tel: 01943 830106

Real Ales, Bar Food, Restaurant Menu,
Accommodation, No Smoking Area

19 Craven Heifer Inn
Grassington Road, Skipton,
North Yorkshire BD23 3LA
Tel: 01756 792521

Real Ales, Bar Food, Restaurant Menu,
No Smoking Area, Disabled Facilities

20 The Cross Keys
East Marton, Skipton, North Yorkshire BD23 3LP
Tel: 01282 844326

Real Ales, Bar Food, Restaurant Menu

21 Crown Inn
Main Street, Addingham, Ilkley,
West Yorkshire LS29 0NS
Tel: 01943 830278

Real Ales, Accommodation, No Smoking Area

22 Dalesgate Hotel & Restaurant
406 Skipton Road, Keighley,
West Yorkshire BD20 6HP
Tel: 01535 664930

Real Ales, Bar Food, Restaurant Menu,
Accommodation, No Smoking Area

23 Devonshire Arms
Grassington Road, Cracoe, Skipton,
North Yorkshire BD23 6LA
Tel: 01756 730237

Real Ales, Bar Food, Restaurant Menu,
Accommodation, No Smoking Area, Disabled Facilities

24 Devonshire Arms Country House Hotel
Bolton Abbey, Skipton, North Yorkshire BD23 6AJ
Tel: 01756 718111

Real Ales, Bar Food, Restaurant Menu,
Accommodation, No Smoking Area, Disabled Facilities

25 Devonshire Fell
Burnsall, Skipton, North Yorkshire BD23 6BT
Tel: 01756 729000

Real Ales, Bar Food, Restaurant Menu,
Accommodation, No Smoking Area, Disabled Facilities

26 The Devonshire Hotel
25-27 Main Street, Grassington, Skipton,
North Yorkshire BD23 5AD
Tel: 01756 752525

Real Ales, Bar Food, Restaurant Menu,
Accommodation, No Smoking Area

27 Dick Hudsons
Otley Road, Bingley, West Yorkshire BD16 3BA
Tel: 01274 552121

Real Ales, Bar Food, No Smoking Area

28 The Dog & Gun Inn
Malsis, Sutton-in-Craven, Keighley,
West Yorkshire BD20 8DS
Tel: 01535 633855

Real Ales, Bar Food, Restaurant Menu,
No Smoking Area, Disabled Facilities

29 Elm Tree Inn
5 Elm Tree Square, Embsay, Skipton,
North Yorkshire BD23 6RB
Tel: 01756 790717

Real Ales, Bar Food, Restaurant Menu,
Accommodation, No Smoking Area

30 Fleece Inn
152-154 Main Street, Addingham, Ilkley,
West Yorkshire LS29 0LY
Tel: 01943 830491

Bar Food, Restaurant Menu, No Smoking Area

31 Forrester Arms
20 Main Street, Grassington, Skipton,
North Yorkshire BD23 5AA
Tel: 01756 752349

Real Ales, Bar Food, Restaurant Menu,
Accommodation, No Smoking Area

32 Fountaine Inn
Linton, Skipton, North Yorkshire BD23 5HJ
Tel: 01756 752210

Real Ales, Bar Food, Restaurant Menu,
No Smoking Area

33 Fox Beefeater
Bradford Road, Menston, Ilkley,
West Yorkshire LS29 6EB
Tel: 01943 873024

Real Ales, Bar Food, Restaurant Menu,
No Smoking Area, Disabled Facilities

34 The Generous Pioneer
Main Street, Burley In Wharfedale, Ilkley,
West Yorkshire LS29 7BT
Tel: 01943 865316

Real Ales, Bar Food, Restaurant Menu,
No Smoking Area, Disabled Facilities

35 Goats Head
2 Skipton Road, Steeton, Keighley,
West Yorkshire BD20 6NR
Tel: 01535 653266

Real Ales

36 Grassington Hotel
The Square, Grassington, Skipton,
North Yorkshire BD23 5AQ
Tel: 01756 752406

Real Ales, Bar Food, Restaurant Menu,
Accommodation, Disabled Facilities

37 Hare & Hounds
Lothersdale, Keighley, West Yorkshire BD20 8EL
Tel: 01535 630977

Real Ales, Bar Food, No Smoking Area

38 Hare & Hounds
Bradford Road, Menston, Ilkley,
West Yorkshire LS29 6BU
Tel: 01943 873998

Real Ales, Bar Food, Restaurant Menu,
No Smoking Area, Disabled Facilities

39 The Hermit
Moor Road, Burley Woodhead, Ilkley,
Yorkshire LS29 7AS
Tel: 01943 863204

Real Ales, Bar Food, Restaurant Menu,
No Smoking Area

40 Hopper Lane Hotel
Skipton Road, Blubberhouses, Otley,
West Yorkshire LS21 2NZ
Tel: 01943 880246

Real Ales, Bar Food, Restaurant Menu,
Accommodation, No Smoking Area, Disabled Facilities

41 Ings Hotel
45 Ings Lane, Guiseley, Leeds, Yorkshire LS20 9HR
Tel: 01943 873315

Real Ales, Disabled Facilities

42 King Henry VIII
Keighley Road, Lp On, Skipton,
North Yorkshire BD23 2TA
Tel: 01756 796428

Real Ales, Bar Food

43 The Kings Arms

High Street, Sutton-in-Craven, Keighley,
West Yorkshire BD20 7LP
Tel: 01535 632332

Real Ales

44 The Kings Arms

Bolton Road, Silsden, Keighley,
West Yorkshire BD20 0JY
Tel: 01535 653216

Real Ales, Bar Food, Restaurant Menu,
No Smoking Area

45 The Kings Head Hotel

The Green, Kilnsey, Skipton,
North Yorkshire BD23 5PW
Tel: 01756 760242

Real Ales, Bar Food, Restaurant Menu,
Accommodation, No Smoking Area

46 Listers Arms Hotel

Malham, Skipton, North Yorkshire BD23 4DB
Tel: 01729 830330

Real Ales, Bar Food, Accommodation,
No Smoking Area, Disabled Facilities

47 The Malt Shovel

32 Main Street, Menston, Ilkley,
West Yorkshire LS29 6LL
Tel: 01943 873882

Bar Food, Restaurant Menu, Disabled Facilities

48 Manor House Hotel

Main Street, Burnsall, Skipton,
North Yorkshire BD23 6BW
Tel: 01756 720231

Real Ales, Bar Food, Restaurant Menu,
Accommodation, No Smoking Area, Disabled Facilities

49 The Marquis Of Granby

1 Hospital Road, Riddlesden, Keighley,
West Yorkshire BD20 5EP
Tel: 01535 607164

Real Ales, Disabled Facilities

50 The Masons Arms

Marton Road, Gargrave, Skipton,
North Yorkshire BD23 3NL
Tel: 01756 749304

Real Ales, Bar Food, Restaurant Menu,
No Smoking Area, Disabled Facilities

51 Masons Arms Inn

Barden Road, Eastby, Skipton,
North Yorkshire BD23 6SN
Tel: 01756 792754

Real Ales, Bar Food, Restaurant Menu,
No Smoking Area, Disabled Facilities

52 Miners Arms

Pateley Bridge, Greenhow Hill, Harrogate,
North Yorkshire HG3 5JQ
Tel: 01423 711227

Real Ales, Bar Food, Restaurant Menu,
Accommodation, No Smoking Area, Disabled Facilities

53 New Inn

Appletreewick, Skipton,
North Yorkshire BD23 6DA
Tel: 01756 720252

Real Ales, Bar Food, Restaurant Menu,
Accommodation, No Smoking Area, Disabled Facilities

54 Old Hall Inn

Grassington, Threshfield, Skipton,
North Yorkshire BD23 5HB
Tel: 01756 752441

Real Ales, Bar Food, Restaurant Menu,
Accommodation, No Smoking Area, Disabled Facilities

55 Old Star Inn

Skipton Road, Steeton, Keighley,
West Yorkshire BD20 6SD
Tel: 01535 652246

Real Ales

56 Old Swan Inn

High Street, Gargrave, Skipton,
North Yorkshire BD23 3RB
Tel: 01756 749232

Real Ales, Bar Food, Restaurant Menu,
Accommodation, No Smoking Area, Disabled Facilities

57 Old White Bear

Keighley Road, Cross Hills, Keighley,
West Yorkshire BD20 7RN
Tel: 01535 632115

Real Ales, Bar Food, Restaurant Menu

58 The Punch Bowl Inn

Bridge Road, Silsden, Keighley,
West Yorkshire BD20 9ND
Tel: 01535 652360

Real Ales, Bar Food

59 The Railway

Main Street, Cononley, Keighley,
West Yorkshire BD20 8LS
Tel: 01535 633238

Real Ales, Bar Food, Restaurant Menu,
No Smoking Area

60 The Red Lion

47 Kirkgate, Silsden, Keighley,
West Yorkshire BD20 0AQ
Tel: 01535 655393

Real Ales

61 Red Lion Hotel

Burnsall, Skipton, North Yorkshire BD23 6BU
Tel: 01756 720204

Real Ales, Bar Food, Restaurant Menu,
Accommodation, No Smoking Area, Disabled Facilities

62 River House Hotel

Malham, Skipton, North Yorkshire BD23 4DA
Tel: 01729 830315

Real Ales, Bar Food, Restaurant Menu,
Accommodation, No Smoking Area, Disabled Facilities

63 The Robin Hood Inn

Kirkgate, Silsden, Keighley, West Yorkshire BD20 0AJ
Tel: 01535 652163

Real Ales

64 Rombalds Hotel

11 West View, Ilkley, West Yorkshire LS29 9JG
Tel: 01943 603201

Bar Food, Restaurant Menu, Accommodation,
No Smoking Area, Disabled Facilities

65 The Royal Oak

Bridgehouse Gate, Pateley Bridge, Harrogate,
North Yorkshire HG3 5HG
Tel: 01423 711577

Real Ales, Bar Food, Restaurant Menu,
No Smoking Area, Disabled Facilities

66 The Sailor

Main Street, Addingham, Ilkley,
West Yorkshire LS29 0PD
Tel: 01943 830216

Real Ales, Bar Food, Restaurant Menu,
No Smoking Area, Disabled Facilities

67 Slaters Arms

Crag Lane, Bradley, Keighley,
West Yorkshire BD20 9DE
Tel: 01535 632179

Real Ales, Bar Food, No Smoking Area

68 Sportsmans Arms Hotel

Wath, Harrogate, North Yorkshire HG3 5PP
Tel: 01423 711306

Real Ales, Bar Food, Restaurant Menu,
No Smoking Area, Disabled Facilities

69 The Stone House Inn

Thruscross, Harrogate, North Yorkshire HG3 4AH
Tel: 01943 880325

Real Ales, Bar Food, Restaurant Menu,
No Smoking Area, Disabled Facilities

70 The Swan

106 Main Street, Addingham, Ilkley,
West Yorkshire LS29 0NS
Tel: 01943 830375

Real Ales, Bar Food, No Smoking Area

71 The Swan

Main Street, Carleton, Skipton,
North Yorkshire BD23 3DR
Tel: 01756 794282

Real Ales, Bar Food, Restaurant Menu,
No Smoking Area

76 The White Lion Hotel

Priest Bank Road, Kildwick, Skipton,
West Yorkshire BD20 9BH
☎ 01535 632265
🌐 www.thewhitelionatkildwick.co.uk

Real Ales, Bar Food, Restaurant Menu, Accommodation, No Smoking Area

☛	Off the A629 (main Skipton-Keighley road)
🍺	Tetleys Cask, Tetleys Mild, Timothy Taylor Landlord, guest ales
🍴	Mon-Weds 12-2 & 6-8.30; Fri & Sat 12-2.30 & 6-9; Sun 12-6
🛏	3 en suite rooms
🅿	Parking
💳	All major cards
🚫	No smoking in restaurant or bar areas
🕐	Mon-Weds 10 a.m.-11 p.m.; Fri & Sat 10-midnight; Sun 11-10.30
🏛	Keighley, Skipton, Ilkley

The White Lion Hotel is an impressive inn opposite the church in this picturesque

village on the north bank of the River Aire. Duncan and Elaine Jamieson, ably assisted by their son Andrew, are welcoming hosts who have between them a wealth of experience in offering guests good ales, great food and genuine hospitality.

Behind the handsome stone frontage, the look is charmingly traditional, with beamwork, exposed stone, dark wood panelling and rustic furniture all contributing to the inviting atmosphere. A minimum of three ales are available along with a choice of draught keg lagers, cider, stout, wines, spirits and soft drinks. And the food here is simply excellent. In the restaurant, where horse brasses, pewter tankards and old prints adorn the walls, diners have a plentiful choice of dishes. The main menu is supplemented by the daily specials board, and the chef's specialities include his tempting fresh fish dishes. Booking is advised for Friday, Saturday and Sunday. Children welcome.

For anyone looking for a base from which to explore the many scenic man-made and natural delights of the region, the inn offers three en suite guest bedrooms that are cosy and comfortable. The village church of St Andrew dates mainly from the 14th and 15th centuries and the village lies on the River Aire and on the Leeds & Liverpool Canal, no longer used commercially but popular with pleasure craft and with walkers.

72 Tarn House

Stirton, Skipton, North Yorkshire BD23 3LQ
Tel: 01756 794891

Bar Food, Restaurant Menu, Accommodation,
No Smoking Area, Disabled Facilities

73 Tempest Arms

Elslack, Skipton, North Yorkshire BD23 3AY
Tel: 01282 842450

Real Ales, Bar Food, Restaurant Menu,
Accommodation, No Smoking Area, Disabled Facilities

74 The Victoria Inn

Kirkby Malham, Skipton,
North Yorkshire BD23 4BS
Tel: 01729 830499

Real Ales, Bar Food, Restaurant Menu,
Accommodation, No Smoking Area, Disabled Facilities

75 White Bear Inn

Main Road, Eastburn, Keighley,
West Yorkshire BD20 7SN
Tel: 01535 653000

Real Ales, Bar Food, No Smoking Area

76 **The White Lion Hotel**

Priest Bank Road, Kildwick, Skipton,
West Yorkshire BD20 9BH
Tel: 01535 632265

Real Ales, Bar Food, Restaurant Menu,
Accommodation, No Smoking Area

See panel opposite

77 The Willow Tree Inn

Ilkley Road, Riddlesden, Keighley,
West Yorkshire BD20 5PN
Tel: 01535 210487

Real Ales

78 Ye Olde Oak

Low Laithe, Harrogate, North Yorkshire HG3 4DD
Tel: 01423 780247

Real Ales, Bar Food, Restaurant Menu

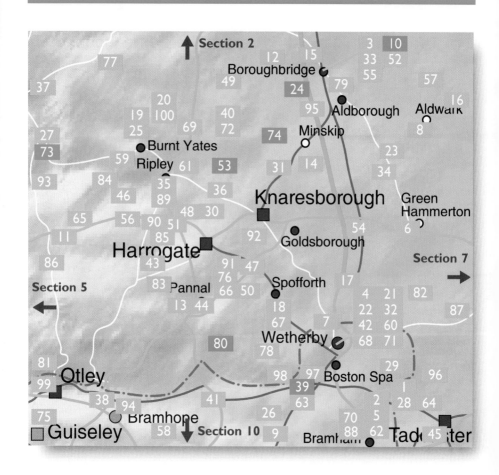

77

37

Section 2

12 15

Boroughbridge

3 10
33 52
55

57

49

24

79

16

20
19 100
25   69
27
73   59

40
72

95

Aldborough

Aldwark

74

Minskip

8

23

Burnt Yates

Ripley 61   53

31   14

34

93

84

35

36

Knaresborough

Green
Hammerton

46

89

6

65

56

90 51

48 30

92

Goldsborough

54

11

85

Harrogate

43

91 47

Section 7

86

76

83 Pannal

66 50

Spofforth

17

Section 5

13 44

18

4   21   82

Section 5

67

7

22   32

87

42   60

80

Wetherby

68   71

78

81

98   97 Boston Spa

29

96

99 Otley

39

1

38 94

41

63

2   28   64

75

26

70   5

Guiseley

58   Section 10

Bramhope

9

Bramham

88   62 Tad 45 ter

11 Pub or Inn Reference Number - Detailed Information

12 Pub or Inn Reference Number - Summary Entry

● ■ Place of interest mentioned in the chapter introduction

SECTION 6

Aldborough

The ancient Roman town of Isurium Brigantum, or Aldborough, as it is known today, was once the home of the 9th Legion, who wrested it from the Celtic Brigantian tribe. The **Aldborough Roman Museum** houses relics of the town's past. The **Church of St Andrew** was built in 1330 on the site of a Norman church that was burnt down by the Scots in 1318. One ancient relic that is still preserved in the church's grounds is an Anglo-Saxon sundial known as the Ulph Stone.

Boroughbridge

This attractive and historic town dates from the reign of William the Conqueror though it was once on a main thoroughfare used by both the Celts of Brigantia and, later, the Romans. The bridge over the River Ure, from which the village takes its name, was built in 1562 and it formed part of an important road link between Edinburgh and London. The great **Devil's Arrows**, three massive Bronze Age monoliths, stand like guardians close to the new road and form Yorkshire's most famous ancient monument: thought to date from around 2000 BC, the tallest is 30 feet high.

Boston Spa

Set beside the broad-flowing River Wharfe, this attractive little town enjoyed many years of prosperity after a Mr John Shires discovered a mineral spring here in 1744. The spa activities have long since ceased.

There's a pleasant riverside walk which can be continued along the track of a dismantled railway as far as Tadcaster in one direction, Wetherby in the other. The town's impressive 19th-century church is notable for its stately tower and the 36 stone angels supporting the nave and aisles.

Bramham

Bramham Park is one of Yorkshire's most exquisite country houses and has gardens modelled on Louis XIV's Versailles.

Burnt Yates

Located at one of the highest points in Nidderdale, Burnt Yates enjoys some fine views of the surrounding hills and moors. Its tiny village school of 1750 still stands. Its original endowment provided for 30 poor boys to be taught the three Rs and for an equivalent number of poor girls to learns the skills of needlework and spinning.

Goldsborough

This rather special village was an estate village from the time of the Norman Conquest until the 1950s when it was sold by the Earl of Harewood to pay enormous death duties. The charming 12th-century **Church of St Mary** has some interesting features including a Norman doorhead and an effigy of a knight. It is also a 'green man church' and the image of the Celtic god of fertility, with his oak-leafed head, is well hidden on one of the many Goldsborough family tombs.

Harrogate

One of England's most attractive towns and a frequent winner of Britain in Bloom, Harrogate features acres of gardens that offer an array of colour throughout the year, open spaces, and broad tree lined boulevards. The **Royal Pump Room Museum** was built in 1842 to enclose the Old Sulphur Well and this major watering

Royal Pump Room Museum, Harrogate

place for spa visitors has been painstakingly restored to illustrate all the aspects of Harrogate's history. Beneath the building the sulphur water still rises to the surface and can be sampled. At the **Turkish Baths** visitors can enjoy a sauna, beauty treatment and massage. The **Mercer Art Gallery** is housed in the oldest of the town's surviving spa buildings, originally built in 1806. Another attractive aspect of the town is **The Stray**, which is unique to Harrogate and virtually encircles the town centre. The 215 acres of open space include spacious lawns, are at their most picturesque during the spring when edged with crocus and daffodils. Another of Harrogate's major visitor attractions is the **RHS Harlow Carr Botanical Gardens**, just over a mile from the town centre.

Knaresborough

This ancient town of pantiled cottages and Georgian houses is precariously balanced on

a hillside by the River Nidd. A stately railway viaduct, 90 feet high and 338 feet long, completed in 1851, spans the gorge. There are many unusual and attractive features in the town, among them a maze of steep stepped narrow streets leading down to the river and numerous alleyways. In addition to boating on the river, there are many enjoyable riverside walks. The town is dominated by the ruins of **Knaresborough Castle**, built high on a crag overlooking the River Nidd. A mile or so to the south of Knaresborough, **Plumpton Rocks** provide an ideal picnic spot. There's an idyllic lake surrounded by dramatic millstone grit rocks and woodland paths that were laid out in the 18th century.

Otley

Otley has retained its distinctive character, still boasting a busy cobbled marketplace with a maypole standing on the site of the old market cross, many little alleyways and courtyards. An attractive feature of the town is **Chevin Forest Park**, a forested ridge above the town which can be reached by a delightful walk that starts alongside the River Wharfe.

Ripley

Magnificent **Ripley Castle** has been home to the Ingilby family for nearly 700 years. The castle is open to the public and is set in an outstanding Capability Brown landscape, with lakes, a deer park, and an avenue of tall beeches over which the attractive towers only just seem to peek. Its tranquillity belies the events that took place here after the battle at Marston Moor, when Cromwell, exhausted after his day's slaughter, camped his Roundheads here and chose to rest in the castle.

Spofforth

This ancient village, situated on the tiny River Crimple, is home to the

Ripley Castle

splendid Palladian mansion, **Stockeld Park**, built between 1758 and 1763 by Paine. Containing some excellent furniture and a fine picture collection, the house is surrounded by extensive parkland which offers garden walks. Though privately owned, the house is open by appointment. **Spofforth Castle** (English Heritage) is another place of note, an historic building whose sight stirs the imagination, despite its ruined state.

Tadcaster

The lovely magnesian limestone used in so many fine Yorkshire churches came from

the quarries established here in Roman times. Their name for Tadcaster was simply 'Calcaria' – limestone. By 1341, however brewing had become the town's major industry, using water from River Wharfe. Three major breweries are still based in Tadcaster: Samuel Smiths, established in 1758 and the oldest in Yorkshire; John Smith's, whose bitter is the best-selling ale in Britain; and Coors Tower Brewery. Also worth visiting is **The Ark**, the oldest building in Tadcaster dating back to the 1490s. Tadcaster also offers some attractive riverside walks, one of which takes you across the 'Virgin Viaduct' over the River

Wharfe, built in 1849 by the great railway entrepreneur George Hudson.

Wetherby

Situated on the Great North Road, at a point midway between Edinburgh and London, Wetherby has remained unspoilt and has a quaint appearance with a central marketplace that was first granted to the Knights Templar. Many of the houses in the town are Georgian, Regency, or early Victorian. About five miles south of Wetherby, **Bramham Park** is noted for its magnificent gardens, 66 acres of them, and its pleasure grounds which cover a further 100 acres. They are the only example of a formal, early 18th-century landscape in Britain. Temples, ornamental ponds, cascades, a 2-mile long avenue of beech trees and one of the best wildflower gardens in the country are just some of the attractions. In early June, the park hosts the Bramham Horse Trials. The house itself, an attractive Queen Anne building, is open to groups of six or more by appointment only.

1 The Admiral Hawke
252 High Street, Boston Spa, Wetherby,
West Yorkshire LS23 6AJ
Tel: 01937 842170

Real Ales, Bar Food, No Smoking Area

2 Albion
Chapel Lane, Clifford, Wetherby,
West Yorkshire LS23 6HU
Tel: 01937 842093

Real Ales, Bar Food, No Smoking Area,
Disabled Facilities

3 Anchor Inn
Langthorpe, Boroughbridge, York YO51 9BP
Tel: 01423 323675

Real Ales, Bar Food, No Smoking Area,
Disabled Facilities

4 Angel Public House
High Street, Wetherby, West Yorkshire LS22 6LT
Tel: 01937 581422

Real Ales, Bar Food, No Smoking Area,
Disabled Facilities

5 The Bay Horse Inn
High Street, Clifford, Wetherby,
West Yorkshire LS23 6HR
Tel: 01937 842542

Real Ales

6 Bay Horse Inn
York Road, Green Hammerton, York,
Yorkshire YO26 8BN
Tel: 01423 330338

Real Ales, Bar Food, Restaurant Menu,
Accommodation, No Smoking Area, Disabled Facilities

7 Bay Horse Inn
Main Street, Kirk Deighton, Wetherby,
West Yorkshire LS22 4DZ
Tel: 01937 582443

Real Ales, Bar Food, Restaurant Menu,
No Smoking Area, Disabled Facilities

8 Bay Horse Inn
, Aldwark, York YO61 1UB
Tel: 01347 838324

Real Ales, Bar Food, Restaurant Menu,
No Smoking Area, Disabled Facilities

9 Bingley Arms
37 Church Lane, Bardsey, Leeds, Yorkshire LS17 9DR
Tel: 01937 572462

Real Ales, Bar Food, Restaurant Menu,
No Smoking Area

10 The Black Bull Inn
6 St. James Square, Boroughbridge, York,
Yorkshire YO51 9AR
Tel: 01423 322413

Real Ales, Restaurant Menu, Accommodation,
No Smoking Area, Disabled Facilities

See panel below

10 The Black Bull Inn
6 St James Square, Boroughbridge,
North Yorkshire YO51 9AR
☎ 01423 322413

Real Ales, Restaurant Menu, Accommodation, No Smoking Area, Disabled Facilities

☛ From J48 of the A1/M1, Boroughbridge is just off the B6265

🍺 Theakstons, John Smiths Cask, guest ale

🍴 12-2 & 6-9.30

🛏 6 en suite rooms

♫ Tuesday night quiz

🅿 Car park, disabled access

🚫 No smoking areas

🕐 11-11

🏛 Fountains Abbey, Studley Royal Gardens, Ripon, Harrogate, Thirsk

In the heart of Boroughbridge, The Black Bull Inn boasts great real ales, home-made food and comfortable accommodation. This historic premises dates back to 1262. Lots of traditional features remain inside, complemented by an up-to-date décor and furnishings. The tasty home-cooked dishes served include steaks and grills, fresh fish, duck breast, lamb cutlets and more, expertly prepared and presented by professional chefs.

24 The Crown at Roecliffe

Roecliffe, Boroughbridge, North Yorkshire YO51 9LY
☎ 01423 322578

🌐 www.thecrowninnroecliffe.co.uk

Real Ales, Bar Food, Restaurant Menu, Accommodation, No Smoking Area, Disabled Facilitiex

- ☛ Off J48 of the A1/M1
- 🍺 John Smiths, Black Sheep, Timothy Taylor Landlord, guest ales
- 🍴 12-2.30 (Sun 12-3.30) & 6-9.30
- ⊨ 7 en suite rooms
- 🎵 Licenced for civil weddings
- 🏕 Car park, disabled access, patio area
- 💳 All major cards
- ♟ 3 Diamonds AA, RAC and ETC
- 🚫 No smoking in restaurant or bedrooms
- 🕐 M-Th 12-3 & 6-11; F-S 12-11 (Sun and Bank Holidays to 10.30)
- 🏛 Devil's Arrows, Boroughbridge

Dating back to the 16th century, The Crown is a lovely coaching inn situated in the heart of the pleasant and picturesque village of Roecliffe. Open fires in the bar add to the comfortable and welcoming ambience, and the public bar – also known as 'the tap room' – is the ideal place to enjoy the range of real ales, lagers, cider, wines, spirits or soft drinks served here. The elegant restaurant boasts an excellent menu of classic dishes such as pan-seared or roast breast of chicken, roast sirloin of beef, medallions of fillet steak, roast loin of pork or salmon steak alongside imaginative creations such as breast of French duck glazed with sweet red onion marmalade and Mediterranean vegetable tart tartin topped with glazed goat's cheese, all expertly prepared and presented. Daily specials can include breaded wholetail scampi, spicy king prawns and beef, mushroom and ale pie. Owned and run by Charlotte and Mark Penrose, Mark is also the chef, creating all dishes using the best and freshest local produce. If you've only time for a light bite, do ask at the bar about that day's 'quick snack', which can include tempting dishes such as Stilton and mushroom crepes, duck liver pate or pan-cooked langoustines in garlic butter. The restaurant seats 40 in great style and comfort. The traditional coach house now doubles as a function suite, perfect for conferences as well as family celebrations – and as The Crown holds a licence for civil weddings, both the ceremony and the festivities afterwards can be held at this handsome and impressive facility. The menu for functions includes fillet of Beef Wellington, paupiettes of Sole or pan-seared loin of lamb. The accommodation here is made up of seven en suite guest bedrooms including two doubles, two family rooms and a room with a marvellous four-poster bed. A few yards away from the inn can be found 'The Devil's Arrows', three fascinating large monoliths dating back to prehistoric times. The inn is also ideally placed for exploring Boroughbridge and the surrounding area.

11 The Black Bull

Skipton Road, Felliscliffe, Harrogate,
North Yorkshire HG3 2LP
Tel: 01423 770233

Real Ales, Bar Food, Restaurant Menu,
No Smoking Area, Disabled Facilities

12 The Black Lion

Skelton-on-Ure, Ripon, North Yorkshire HG4 5AJ
Tel: 01423 322516

Real Ales, Bar Food, Restaurant Menu,
No Smoking Area, Disabled Facilities

13 The Black Swan At Burn Bridge

Burn Bridge Road, Burn Bridge, Harrogate,
North Yorkshire HG3 1PB
Tel: 01423 871031

Real Ales, Bar Food, Restaurant Menu,
No Smoking Area

14 Blue Bell Inn

Moor Lane, Arkendale, Knaresborough,
North Yorkshire HG5 0QT
Tel: 01423 340222

Real Ales, Bar Food, Restaurant Menu,
No Smoking Area, Disabled Facilities

15 Blue Bell Inn

Kirby Hill, Boroughbridge, York, Yorkshire YO51 9DN
Tel: 01423 324180

Real Ales, Bar Food, Restaurant Menu,
No Smoking Area, Disabled Facilities

16 Bluebell Inn

Main Street, Alne, York, Yorkshire YO61 1RR
Tel: 01347 838331

Real Ales, Bar Food, Restaurant Menu,
No Smoking Area, Disabled Facilities

17 The Bridge Inn Hotel

Walshford, Wetherby, West Yorkshire LS22 5HS
Tel: 01937 580115

Real Ales, Bar Food, Restaurant Menu,
Accommodation, No Smoking Area, Disabled Facilities

18 The Castle Inn

High Street, Spofforth, Harrogate,
North Yorkshire HG3 1BQ
Tel: 01937 590200

Real Ales, Bar Food, Restaurant Menu,
No Smoking Area, Disabled Facilities

19 The Chequers Inn & Restaurant

Bishop Thornton, Harrogate,
North Yorkshire HG3 3JN
Tel: 01423 771544

Restaurant Menu, Accommodation, Disabled Facilities

20 Cross Keys Inn

High Street, Markington, Harrogate,
North Yorkshire HG3 3NR
Tel: 01765 677555

Real Ales, Bar Food, Restaurant Menu

21 Crown Hotel

128 High Street, Boston Spa, Wetherby,
West Yorkshire LS23 6BW
Tel: 01937 842608

Real Ales, Bar Food, Restaurant Menu,
Accommodation

22 The Crown Inn

25 High Street, Wetherby, West Yorkshire LS22 6LR
Tel: 01937 584402

Real Ales, Bar Food, Restaurant Menu

23 Crown Inn

Main Street, Great Ouseburn,
York, Yorkshire YO26 9RF
Tel: 01423 330430

Real Ales, Bar Food, Restaurant Menu,
No Smoking Area, Disabled Facilities

24 The Crown at Roecliffe

Roecliffe, York, Yorkshire YO51 9LY
Tel: 01423 322578

Real Ales, Bar Food, Restaurant Menu,
Accommodation, No Smoking Area, Disabled Facilities

See panel opposite

25 The Drovers Inn

Bishop Thornton, Harrogate,
North Yorkshire HG3 3JN
Tel: 01262 420259

Real Ales, Bar Food, Restaurant Menu,
No Smoking Area, Disabled Facilities

26 The Duke Of Wellington

Main Street, East Keswick, Leeds,
Yorkshire LS17 9DB
Tel: 01274 832482

Real Ales, Bar Food, Restaurant Menu,
No Smoking Area, Disabled Facilities

27 Flying Dutchman Inn

Summerbridge, Harrogate,
North Yorkshire HG3 4HP
Tel: 01423 780321

Real Ales, Bar Food, Accommodation

28 The Fox & Hounds

288 High Street, Boston Spa, Wetherby, West
Yorkshire LS23 6AJ
Tel: 01937 842185

Real Ales, Bar Food, Restaurant Menu

29 Fox & Hounds

Main Street, Walton, Wetherby,
West Yorkshire LS23 7DJ
Tel: 01937 842192

Real Ales, Bar Food, Restaurant Menu,
No Smoking Area, Disabled Facilities

30 Gardeners Arms

Bilton Lane, Harrogate, North Yorkshire HG1 4DH
Tel: 01423 506051

Real Ales, No Smoking Area, Disabled Facilities

31 General Tarleton

Boroughbridge Road, Ferrensby, Knaresborough,
North Yorkshire HG5 0PZ
Tel: 01423 340284

Real Ales, Bar Food, Restaurant Menu,
Accommodation, No Smoking Area, Disabled Facilities

32 George & Dragon

8 High Street, Wetherby, West Yorkshire LS22 6LT
Tel: 01937 582888

Real Ales, Bar Food, No Smoking Area,
Disabled Facilities

33 The Grantham Arms Hotel

Milby, Boroughbridge, York, Yorkshire YO51 9BW
Tel: 01423 322261

Real Ales, Bar Food, Accommodation,
No Smoking Area, Disabled Facilities

34 Green Tree Inn

Boroughbridge Road, Little Ouseburn, York,
Yorkshire YO26 9TJ
Tel: 01423 330930

Real Ales, Bar Food, Restaurant Menu,
No Smoking Area

35 The Greyhound Inn

Ripon Road, Killinghall, Harrogate,
North Yorkshire HG3 2DG
Tel: 01423 506356

Real Ales, Bar Food, Restaurant Menu,
No Smoking Area, Disabled Facilities

36 Guy Fawkes Arms

Main Street, Scotton, Knaresborough,
North Yorkshire HG5 9HU
Tel: 01423 862598

Real Ales, Bar Food, Restaurant Menu,
No Smoking Area

37 Half Moon Inn

Pateley Bridge, Fellbeck, Harrogate,
North Yorkshire HG3 5ET
Tel: 01423 711560

Real Ales, Bar Food, Restaurant Menu,
Accommodation, No Smoking Area

39 The Half Moon

Harewood Road, Collingham, Wetherby,
West Yorkshire LS22 5BL .

☎ 01937 572641

🌐 www.the-half-moon-collingham.co.uk

Real Ales, Bar Food, Restaurant Menu, No Smoking Area

- ☛ Off the A1 1½ miles from Wetherby
- 🍺 Abbot Ale, Black Sheep, John Smiths Cask
- 🍽 12-3 & 6-9.30; all-day light bites
- 🅿 Parking, disabled access, beer garden, patio, children's play area
- 💳 All major cards
- 🚫 No smoking in restaurant
- 🕐 12-11
- 🏛 Wetherby, Bramham Park, Pontefract, Lotherton Estate and Gardens (Aberford)

Stylish and elegant, The Half Moon at Collingham is a marvellous place to enjoy a relaxing drink or meal. The accent is firmly on the best quality freshest food, with creations ranging from traditional dishes such as roast Norfolk turkey and roast loin of pork to gateau of Mediterranean vegetables and seared salmon fillet, all expertly prepared and presented. To drink there are several real ales complemented by a great range of lagers, a good wine list, cider, stout, spirits and soft drinks. Owned and personally run by Jeremy Beasley and Julie Fletcher, this distinctive place offers all guests a memorable dining experience amid bucolic surroundings.

---

38 Half Moon Inn

Main Street, Pool In Wharfedale, Otley,
West Yorkshire LS21 1LH
Tel: 01132 842878

Real Ales, Bar Food, Restaurant Menu,
Accommodation, No Smoking Area

39 The Half Moon

Harewood Road, Collingham, Wetherby,
West Yorkshire LS22 5BL
Tel: 01937 572641

Real Ales, Bar Food, Restaurant Menu,
No Smoking Area

See panel above

40 Hare & Hounds

Mill Lane, Burton Leonard, Harrogate,
North Yorkshire HG3 3SH
Tel: 01765 677355

Real Ales, Bar Food, Restaurant Menu, No Smoking
Area, Disabled Facilities

41 Harewood Arms Hotel

Harrogate Road, Harewood, Leeds,
Yorkshire LS17 9LH
Tel: 01132 886566

Real Ales, Bar Food, Restaurant Menu,
Accommodation, No Smoking Area, Disabled Facilities

42 Harris's Bar & Restaurant

22 High Street, Wetherby,
West Yorkshire LS22 6LT
Tel: 01937 582008

Real Ales, Restaurant Menu, No Smoking Area,
Disabled Facilities

43 The Harrogate Arms

Crag Lane, Beckwithshaw, Harrogate,
North Yorkshire HG3 1QA
Tel: 01423 502434

Bar Food, Restaurant Menu, No Smoking Area,
Disabled Facilities

53 The Malt Shovel

Brearton, Harrogate, North Yorkshire HG3 3BX
☎ 01423 862929

Real Ales, Bar Food, Restaurant Menu, No Smoking Area

- ☛ Off the B6165 north of Knaresborough
- 🍺 Daleside, Black Sheep, Theakstons, two guest ales
- 🍴 Tues-Sun 11.45-2 & Tues-Sat 6.45-9
- 🎵 Occasional quiz night
- 🅿️ Car park, disabled access, heated rear patio
- 💳 All major cards
- 🏵 *The Good Pub Guide, Harden's* (Remy Martin) *Restaurant Guide*
- 🚫 Separate no-smoking room
- 🕐 Tues-Sun 11.45-3 & 6.45-close
- 🏛 Knaresborough, Harrogate, Ripley

The Malt Shovel is well worth seeking out. The accent is firmly on excellent food and

drink at this spacious and pristine country pub, which dates back to 1570 and boasts many original features. The exposed beamwork, low ceilings and casement windows add to the cosy and genuine 16th-century feel of the place, while the service and comfort are bang up to date. On cold days there's a roaring fire going at this traditional coaching inn, which adds to the welcoming ambience.

The staff play their part in making guests welcome, offering a high standard of service and quality in everything they do. Owners Jamie and Hayley Stewart bring enthusiasm and commitment to providing the best in food, drink and hospitality. Jamie is the chef, using the freshest ingredients to create a wide range of dishes that are expertly prepared and presented. A small sample from the menu and specials board includes chicken with tarragon, steak and (local) ale pie, fragrant lamb curry, steaks, sausage and mash and beef lasagna – a selection of traditional and more innovative dishes to satisfy every palate.

To drink there are several real ales together with a good choice of lagers, cider, stout, wines, spirits and soft drinks. The inn is justly popular with locals and with those exploring or sightseeing in the region, which includes sights and attractions such as Harrogate with its Royal Pump Room Museum, Royal Baths Assembly Rooms, Mercer Art Gallery and Harlow Carr Botanical Garden, Knaresborough Castle, Aldborough Roman Museum, the Devil's Arrows, Ripley Castle and Wetherby.

44 The Harwood

Station Road, Pannal, Harrogate,
North Yorkshire HG3 1JJ
Tel: 01423 872570

Real Ales, Bar Food, Restaurant Menu,
No Smoking Area, Disabled Facilities

45 Jackdaw Inn

Holly Tree Walk, Tadcaster,
North Yorkshire LS24 9HT
Tel: 01937 835407

46 The Joiners Arms

High Street, Hampsthwaite, Harrogate,
North Yorkshire HG3 2EU
Tel: 01423 771673

Real Ales, Bar Food, Restaurant Menu,
No Smoking Area, Disabled Facilities

47 The Kestrel

Wetherby Road, Plompton, Knaresborough,
North Yorkshire HG5 8LY
Tel: 01423 797979

Real Ales, Bar Food, Restaurant Menu,
Accommodation, No Smoking Area, Disabled Facilities

48 Knox Arms

Knox Lane, Harrogate, North Yorkshire HG1 3AP
Tel: 01423 525284

Real Ales, Bar Food, Disabled Facilities

49 The Lamb & Flag Inn

Boroughbridge Road, Bishop Monkton, Harrogate,
North Yorkshire HG3 3QN
Tel: 01765 677322

Real Ales, Bar Food, Restaurant Menu,
Accommodation, No Smoking Area, Disabled Facilities

50 The Lascelles Arms

Main Street, Follifoot, Harrogate,
North Yorkshire HG3 1DU
Tel: 01423 871212

Real Ales, Bar Food, No Smoking Area,
Disabled Facilities

51 The Little Wonder

Ripon Road, Harrogate, North Yorkshire HG1 2BY
Tel: 01423 505352

Accommodation

52 The Malt Shovel

St James Square, Boroughbridge, York,
Yorkshire YO51 9AR
Tel: 01423 322158

Real Ales, Bar Food, No Smoking Area,
Disabled Facilities

53 **The Malt Shovel**

Brearton, Harrogate, North Yorkshire HG3 3BX
Tel: 01423 862929

Real Ales, Bar Food, Restaurant Menu,
No Smoking Area

See panel opposite

54 Masons Arms

Hopperton, Knaresborough,
North Yorkshire HG5 8NX
Tel: 01423 330442

Real Ales, Bar Food, Restaurant Menu,
No Smoking Area, Disabled Facilities

55 The Musketeer

Horsefair, Boroughbridge, York,
Yorkshire YO51 9AA
Tel: 01423 322511

Real Ales, Bar Food, Restaurant Menu,
No Smoking Area, Disabled Facilities

56 The Nelson Inn

Skipton Road, Killinghall, Harrogate,
North Yorkshire HG3 2BU
Tel: 01423 500340

Real Ales, Bar Food, Restaurant Menu,
No Smoking Area, Disabled Facilities

57 The New Inn

Tholthorpe, York, Yorkshire YO61 1SL
Tel: 01347 838329

Bar Food, Restaurant Menu, Accommodation,
No Smoking Area, Disabled Facilities

73 **The Royal Oak**

Oak Lane, Dacre Banks, Harrogate, North
Yorkshire HG3 4EN

🌐 www.the-royaloak-dacre.co.uk

☎ 01423 780200

**Real Ales, Bar Food, Restaurant Menu, Accommo-
dation, No Smoking Area, Disabled Facilities**

🖝 On the B6451 6 miles northwest of
Harrogate and 3 miles north of the A59

🍺 Rudgate, Tetleys, Theakstons, guest ale

🍴 1130-2 & 6-9

🛏 3 en suite rooms

♿ Disabled access, carpark, beer garden, games
room, boules, petanque

💳 All the major cards

🏆 4 Diamonds ETC; featured in *2005 Good Pub
Guide, Good Beer Guide 2005, AA Best Inns
and Pubs*

🚭 No-smoking areas

🕐 11-3 & 5-11 (Closed Christmas Day)

🏛 Harrogate, Pateley Bridge, Otley, Nidderdale,
Leeds

Built in 1752 and clad with rich red ivy, The
Royal Oak Inn is a fine example of a
traditional Yorkshire alehouse. Bringing to life all
that is best about distinctive and venerable
coaching
inns, the
interior
features a
cosy bar
with open
fires, low
timber
beams, stone
floors and exposed stone walls, while the
atmosphere is always relaxed and welcoming.
The accent here is on great food, with two
chefs preparing a range of tempting dishes
using local produce, including a wide choice of
creative meat, fish, steak and vegetarian dishes
served at lunch and evening every day. The
extensive menu changes with the seasons and
can include whole lemon sole, monkfish
medallions, Thai green king prawn curry, goat's
cheese, sundried tomato and vegetable filo

parcel, herb-crusted rack of lamb, Nidderdale
pigeon breasts, pork, mozzarella and black
pudding parcel and roast rib of prime Yorkshire
beef. There is also an excellent selection of
snacks such as salads, bruschetta, ciabattas,
sandwiches, burgers, giant Yorkshire puddings
and more. Meals are served in the dining
room, Eric's Pantry (no smoking) and in Dale
View (a ventilated smoking area). Booking
essential at weekends. The dining room seats
40 in comfort and can also be booked for
special occasions. And to drink? This Free
House boasts four real ales on tap including
Yorkshire Dales bitter and Nidderdale best
bitter, together with a good choice of lagers,
cider, stout, wines, spirits and soft drinks as
well as a selection of malt whiskies and
expertly prepared cocktails. Family-owned and
-run by Steve and Anna and Anna's mum, Pat,
personal service and hospitality are ensured.
The interior is decorated with numerous
quotations and old sayings to do with food and
drink painted on the beams and oak panels,
while to the rear of the inn there's a lovely
garden with plenty of seating commanding
views over lower Nidderdale. The comfortable
and cosy accommodation comprises two
twins and one double room, all well-appointed
and awarded a
4-Diamond
rating by the
English Tourism
Council. The
tariff includes a
delicious hearty
breakfast.

58 The New Inn

Eccup Lane, Leeds, Yorkshire LS16 8AU
Tel: 01132 886335

Real Ales, Bar Food, No Smoking Area

59 New Inn

Pateley Bridge Road, Burnt Yates, Harrogate,
North Yorkshire HG3 3EG
Tel: 01423 771070

Real Ales, Bar Food, Restaurant Menu,
Accommodation, No Smoking Area

60 New Inn

18 Westgate, Wetherby, West Yorkshire LS22 6LL
Tel: 01937 584713

Real Ales, Bar Food, Restaurant Menu,
No Smoking Area, Disabled Facilities

61 Nidd Hall Country House

Nidd, Harrogate, North Yorkshire HG3 3BN
Tel: 01423 771598

Real Ales, Bar Food, Restaurant Menu,
Accommodation, No Smoking Area, Disabled Facilities

62 The Old Star Inn

High Street, Clifford, Wetherby,
West Yorkshire LS23 6HR
Tel: 01937 842486

Real Ales

63 The Old Star Inn

Leeds Road, Collingham, Wetherby,
West Yorkshire LS22 5AP
Tel: 01937 579310

Restaurant Menu, No Smoking Area,
Disabled Facilities

64 The Pax

The Village, Thorp Arch, Wetherby,
West Yorkshire LS23 7AR
Tel: 01937 843183

Real Ales, Bar Food, Restaurant Menu

65 Queens Head Inn

Kettlesing, Harrogate, North Yorkshire HG3 2LB
Tel: 01423 770263

Real Ales, Bar Food, Restaurant Menu,
Accommodation, No Smoking Area, Disabled Facilities

66 The Radcliffe Arms

Pannal Road, Follifoot, Harrogate,
North Yorkshire HG3 1DR
Tel: 01423 871417

Restaurant Menu, No Smoking Area

67 The Railway Inn

Park Terrace, Spofforth, Harrogate,
North Yorkshire HG3 1BW
Tel: 01937 590257

68 The Red Lion

19 High Street, Wetherby, West Yorkshire LS22 6LR
Tel: 01937 582136

Real Ales, Bar Food, Restaurant Menu

69 The Red Lion

Ripon Road, South Stainley, Harrogate,
North Yorkshire HG3 3ND
Tel: 01423 770132

Real Ales, Bar Food, Restaurant Menu,
No Smoking Area, Disabled Facilities

70 The Red Lion

The Square, Bramham, Wetherby,
West Yorkshire LS23 6QU
Tel: 01937 843524

Real Ales, Bar Food, Restaurant Menu,
No Smoking Area, Disabled Facilities

71 Royal Oak

60 North Street, Wetherby,
West Yorkshire LS22 6NR
Tel: 01937 580508

Real Ales

72 The Royal Oak

Copgrove Road, Burton Leonard, Harrogate,
North Yorkshire HG3 3SJ
Tel: 01765 677332

Real Ales, Bar Food, Restaurant Menu,
No Smoking Area, Disabled Facilities

74 The Royal Oak

Main Street, Staveley, Knaresborough,
North Yorkshire HG5 9LD
☎ 01423 340267

Real Ales, Bar Food, Restaurant Menu, Accommodation, No Smoking Area, Disabled Facilities

☛ Off J48 of the A1(M) or the A59 a few miles northwest of Knaresborough

🍺 Black Sheep, Rudgate, Timothy Taylor Landlord, Tetleys and a rotating guest ale

🍴 Tues-Sat 12-2 & 6-9 (Sun 12-8)

🎵 Quiz night Weds

⛺ Car park, disabled access, front patio, beer garden

💳 All major cards

🏆 *Good Beer Guide*

🕐 12-2.30 & 5-11 (Sun and Bank Holidays 12-10.30)

🏛 Knaresborough, Harrogate, Ripley, Ripon, Sion Hill, Thirsk

In the heart of the picture-postcard village of Staveley, The Royal Oak takes its name from the huge tree to the front, a venerable oak that complements the traditional frontage and

welcoming bright red door. The interior is cosy and comfortable, guaranteed to warm the cockles – open brick fires, exposed beamwork, rich wood panelling and a tasteful selection of traditional brass and china ornaments. The accent is firmly on great food here, with bar meals include tempting sandwiches and hot and cold snacks, and a very good selection of delicious home-cooked dishes. Daily specials change with the seasons, making the most of the freshest local produce, and include tempting delights such as lamb shank with Port and rosemary, creamy curried chicken and bacon, pork fillet topped with salami and tomato, duck breast, pork medallions, strips of beef fillet, chicken wrapped in bacon with a

Port and Stilton sauce, and many other hearty and filling dishes, including vegetarian ones, all expertly prepared and presented. Guests can dine throughout the inn, or, when the weather is fine, on the front patio or the small beer garden.

This superb inn, which has featured in *The Good Beer Guide*, offers a good choice of real ales together with lagers, cider, stout, wines, spirits and soft drinks, makes an excellent place to stop for a quiet and relaxing drink or meal in good company while you are exploring the many sights and attractions of the region. These include the Yorkshire spa towns of Knaresborough, Ripley and Harrogate; Knaresborough boasts several draws including its Castle, the Old Courthouse Museum and Ye Oldest Chymists' Shoppe, Ripley boasts a Castle of its own, dating back to the 1300s, while Harrogate has the Royal Baths Assembly Room, Royal Pump Room Museum and acres of gardens that offer myriad colours throughout the year. And of course this is a region of great natural beauty, with numerous walks and drives available that allow you to discover for yourself the riches on offer.

73 The Royal Oak

Oak Lane, Dacre Banks, Harrogate,
North Yorkshire HG3 4EN
Tel: 01423 780200

Real Ales, Bar Food, Restaurant Menu,
Accommodation, No Smoking Area, Disabled Facilities

See panel on page 114

74 The Royal Oak

Main Street, Staveley, Knaresborough,
North Yorkshire HG5 9LD
Tel: 01423 340267

Real Ales, Bar Food, Restaurant Menu,
No Smoking Area, Disabled Facilities

See panel opposite

75 Royalty Inn

Yorkgate, Otley, West Yorkshire LS21 3DG
Tel: 01943 461156

Real Ales, Bar Food, Restaurant Menu,
No Smoking Area

76 Rudding Park Hotel & Golf

Rudding Park, Follifoot, Harrogate,
North Yorkshire HG3 1JH
Tel: 01423 871350

Bar Food, Restaurant Menu, Accommodation,
No Smoking Area, Disabled Facilities

77 Sawley Arms

Fountains Abbey, Sawley, Ripon,
North Yorkshire HG4 3EQ
Tel: 01765 620642

Bar Food, Accommodation, No Smoking Area,
Disabled Facilities

78 The Scotts Arms

Main Street, Sicklinghall, Wetherby,
West Yorkshire LS22 4BD
Tel: 01937 582100

Real Ales, Bar Food, Restaurant Menu,
Accommodation, No Smoking Area, Disabled Facilities

79 The Ship Inn

Low Road, Westow, Aldborough, York YO60 7LX
Tel: 01423 322749

Real Ales, Bar Food, Restaurant Menu,
Accommodation, No Smoking Area, Disabled Facilities

80 The Shoulder Of Mutton Inn

Main Street, Kirkby Overblow, Harrogate,
North Yorkshire HG3 1HD
Tel: 01423 871205

Real Ales, Bar Food, Restaurant Menu,
Accommodation, Disabled Facilities

See panel 0n page 118

81 The Spite Inn

Roebuck Terrace, Newall With Clifton, Otley,
West Yorkshire LS21 2EY
Tel: 01943 463063

Real Ales, Bar Food, Restaurant Menu,
No Smoking Area

82 Spotted Ox

Westfield Road, Tockwith, York, Yorkshire YO26 7PY
Tel: 01423 358387

Real Ales, Bar Food, No Smoking Area,
Disabled Facilities

83 The Squinting Cat

Whinney Lane, Lund House Green, Harrogate,
North Yorkshire HG3 1QF
Tel: 01423 565650

Real Ales, Bar Food, Restaurant Menu

84 Station Hotel

Birstwith, Harrogate, North Yorkshire HG3 3AG
Tel: 01423 770254

Real Ales, Bar Food, Restaurant Menu,
No Smoking Area

85 The Stone Beck

Grantley Drive, Harrogate,
North Yorkshire HG3 2XS
Tel: 01423 503971

Real Ales

80 The Shoulder of Mutton Inn

Main Street, Kirkby Overblow, Harrogate,
North Yorkshire HG3 1HD
☎ 01423 871205

Real Ales, Bar Food, Restaurant Menu, Accommodation, Disabled Facilities

- Off the A61 south of Harrogate
- Timothy Taylor Landlord, Black Sheep, Tetleys
- Tues-Sun 12-2 & Tues-Sat 6-9
- Self-catering accommodation next to the pub
- Quiz night on Sunday
- Parking, beer garden, disabled access
- All major cards
- No smoking area
- Tues-Sat 11.30-3 & 6-11; Sun 12-3
- Harrogate, Bolton Abbey, Leeds

David and Kate Deacon offer all their guests a warm welcome at The Shoulder

of Mutton Inn, a true gem of a village inn. The stonebuilt façade is bedecked with ivy and plants in pots, and when you step inside it's the epitome of the best of Yorkshire: cosy and comfortable, with a homely feel that makes you feel immediately welcome.

Excellent food and drink are the bywords here, with a range of real ales together with lagers, cider, stout, wines, spirits and soft drinks to quench every thirst. Food is served at lunch six days a week and at dinner five evenings, and the menu and specials board boasts a selection of home-made Yorkshire cuisine. David is the chef, creating a wide choice of delicious dishes from the freshest ingredients, including tempting options such as braised shoulder of lamb, chicken and leek pie, fresh fish and chips, grilled fillet of salmon, steak and onion pie and deep-fried scampi.

Next to the pub there is terrific self-catering accommodation available in The Stables, a well-appointed and comfortable unit that makes a perfect base for exploring the many attractions of the region, which include the spa town of Harrogate, Ripley Castle, Knaresborough, Spofforth Castle, Harewood House and Ripon Cathedral. Slightly further afield are the draws at Bolton Abbey and the city of Leeds.

86 Sun Inn

Norwood, Harrogate, North Yorkshire HG3 1SZ
Tel: 01943 880220

Real Ales, Bar Food, Restaurant Menu, No Smoking Area

87 The Sun Inn

York Road, Long Marston, York, Yorkshire YO26 7PG
Tel: 01904 738258

Real Ales, Bar Food, Restaurant Menu,
No Smoking Area, Disabled Facilities

88 The Swan

Town Hill, Bramham, Wetherby,
West Yorkshire LS23 6QA
Tel: 01937 843570

Real Ales

89 Three Horseshoes

Ripon Road, Killinghall, Harrogate,
North Yorkshire HG3 2DH
Tel: 01423 506302

Real Ales, Bar Food, Restaurant Menu,
No Smoking Area

90 Travellers Rest

Otley Road, Killinghall, Harrogate,
North Yorkshire HG3 2AP
Tel: 01423 503518

Real Ales, Bar Food, Disabled Facilities

91 Travellers Rest

Crimple Lane, Follifoot, Harrogate,
North Yorkshire HG3 1DF
Tel: 01423 883960

Real Ales, Bar Food, Restaurant Menu,
No Smoking Area, Disabled Facilities

92 The Union

Thistle Hill, Knaresborough, North Yorkshire HG5 8JL
Tel: 01423 862084

Real Ales, Bar Food, Restaurant Menu,
No Smoking Area, Disabled Facilities

93 The Wellington Inn

Darley, Harrogate, North Yorkshire HG3 2QQ
Tel: 01423 780362

Real Ales, Bar Food, Restaurant Menu,
Accommodation, No Smoking Area, Disabled Facilities

94 The Wharfedale Inn & Restuarant

Arthington Lane, Arthington, Otley,
West Yorkshire LS21 1NL
Tel: 01132 842921

Real Ales, Bar Food, Restaurant Menu,
Accommodation, No Smoking Area, Disabled Facilities

95 White Swan

Minskip, York, Yorkshire YO51 9JF
Tel: 01423 322598

Real Ales, Bar Food, Accommodation,
No Smoking Area, Disabled Facilities

96 White Swan Inn

Main Street, Wighill, Tadcaster,
North Yorkshire LS24 8BQ
Tel: 01937 832217

Real Ales, Bar Food, Restaurant Menu,
No Smoking Area, Disabled Facilities

97 Windmill Inn

Main Street, Linton, Wetherby,
West Yorkshire LS22 4HT
Tel: 01937 582209

Real Ales, Bar Food, Restaurant Menu,
No Smoking Area, Disabled Facilities

98 Wood Hall

Trip Lane, Linton, Wetherby,
West Yorkshire LS22 4JA
Tel: 01937 587271

Real Ales, Bar Food, Restaurant Menu,
Accommodation, No Smoking Area, Disabled Facilities

99 Yew Tree Inn

Newall Carr Road, Otley, West Yorkshire LS21 2AU
Tel: 01943 461330

Real Ales, Bar Food, No Smoking Area

100 Yorkshire Hussar Inn

High Street, Markington, Harrogate,
North Yorkshire HG3 3NR
Tel: 01765 677715

Real Ales, Disabled Facilities

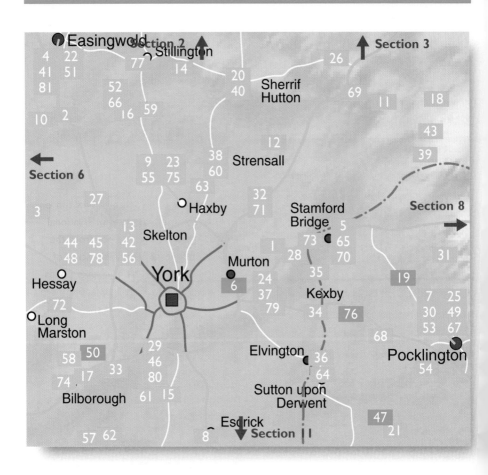

Easingwold
Section 2
Stillington
4   22
41 51   77   14
81   20   Sherrif
      52   40   Hutton
      66   Section 3
         16 59   26
10   2   69   11   18
                                                                              43
Section 6   39
      27   9   23   38   Strensall
                55 75   60
                     63   12
3   32   Stamford
         13   Haxby   71   Bridge   Section 8
             Skelton   5
      44 45 42   73 65
      48 78 56   1   28   70   31
                        Murton
Hessay   York   24   35   19
                        6   37   Kexby
      72   79   34   76   7   25
Long   30 49
Marston   53 67
                        29   68
      58 50   Elvington 36   Pocklington
      74 17 33   46   64   54
         80
      Bilborough   61 15   Sutton upon
                              Derwent
                     Escrick   47
      57 62   8   ▼ Section 11   21

- 🔵 Pub or Inn Reference Number - Detailed Information
- 🟦 Pub or Inn Reference Number - Summary Entry
- ●■ Place of interest mentioned in the chapter introduction

SECTION 7

Easingwold

This agreeable market town at the foot of the Howardian Hills was once surrounded by the Forest of Galtres, a vast hunting preserve of Norman kings. A little to the south of Easingwold, on the B1363, is **Sutton Park**, a noble mansion built in 1730 by Thomas Atkinson and containing some fine examples of Sheraton and Chippendale furniture, and much admired decorative plasterwork by the Italian maestro in this craft, Cortese. The ubiquitous Capability Brown designed the lovely gardens and parkland in which you'll find a Georgian ice-house, well-signposted woodland walks and a nature trail.

Elvington

During the Second World War RAF Elvington was the base for British, Canadian and French bomber crews flying missions to occupied Europe. With virtually all its original buildings still intact, the base now provides an authentic setting for the **Yorkshire Air Museum** and is the largest Second World War Bomber Command Station open to the public in the UK.

Murton

Although a small village, Murton is an important, modern livestock centre and it is also home to the **Yorkshire Museum of Farming**, found at Murton Park. As well as wandering around the fields and pens, visitors can also see reconstructions of a Roman fort, a Danelaw village from the Dark Ages and Celtic Roundhouses. Other attractions at the park include the Derwent Valley Light Railway.

Newton-on-Ouse

About a mile to the south of Newton on Ouse is **Beningbrough Hall** (National Trust), a baroque masterpiece from the early 18th century with seven acres of gardens, wilderness play area, pike ponds and scenic walks. A major attraction here is the permanent exhibition of more than 100 portraits on loan from the National Portrait Gallery.

Pocklington

Set amidst rich agricultural land with the Wolds rising to the east, Pocklington is a lively market town with an unusual layout of twisting alleys running off the marketplace. Its splendid church, mostly 15th century but with fragments of an earlier Norman building, certainly justifies its title as the Cathedral of the Wolds. William Wilberforce went to the old grammar school here and, a more dubious claim to fame, the last burning of a witch in England took place in Pocklington in 1630. **Burnby Hall and Gardens** comprise eight acres of gardens world-famous for the rare collection of water-lilies planted in the two large lakes. A mile outside the town is **Kilnwick Percy Hall**, a magnificent Georgian mansion of 1784. A few miles of Pocklington is **Londesborough Park**, a 400-acre estate once owned by the legendary railway entrepreneur, George Hudson. He had the York-to-Market Weighton railway diverted here so that he could build himself a comfortable private station. The railway has now disappeared, but part of its route is included in the

York Minster and Gate House

popular long-distance footpath, the Wolds Way.

Stamford Bridge

Everyone knows that 1066 was the year of the Battle of Hastings but, just a few days before that battle, King Harold had clashed at Stamford Bridge with his half-brother Tostig and Hardrada, King of Norway who between them had mustered some 60,000 men. On a rise near the corn mill is a stone commemorating the event with an inscription in English and Danish.

York

'The history of York is the history of England,' said the Duke of York, later George VI. One of the grandest cityscapes in the country opens up as you walk along the old city walls towards **York Minster**, a sublime expression of medieval faith while, in Coppergate, the story of York during the years of Danish rule is imaginatively told in the many displays at the **Jorvik Centre**. Other sights include the **National Railway Museum** and the **Yorkshire Museum & Gardens**.

1 The Agar Arms
Warthill, York, Yorkshire YO19 5XW
Tel: 01904 488142
Real Ales, Bar Food, Restaurant Menu

2 Aldwark Manor Hotel
Aldwark, Alne, Yorkshire YO61 1RA
Tel: 01347 838146
Bar Food, Restaurant Menu, Accommodation,
No Smoking Area, Disabled Facilities

3 Alice Hawthorn Inn
The Green, Nun Monkton, York,
Yorkshire YO26 8EW
Tel: 01423 330303
Real Ales, Bar Food, No Smoking Area

4 Angel Inn
Market Place, Easingwold, York,
Yorkshire YO61 3AA
Tel: 01347 821605
Real Ales, Bar Food, No Smoking Area

5 Bay Horse Inn
6 Main Street, Stamford Bridge, York,
Yorkshire YO41 1AB
Tel: 01759 371320
Real Ales

6 The Bay Horse
Murton, York, Yorkshire YO19 5UQ
Tel: 01904 489684
Real Ales, Bar Food, Restaurant Menu
See panel below

7 Black Bull
18 Market Place, Pocklington, York,
Yorkshire YO42 2AR
Tel: 01759 302649
Real Ales, Bar Food, Restaurant Menu,
No Smoking Area

8 Black Bull Inn
Main Street, Escrick, York, Yorkshire YO19 6JP
Tel: 01904 728245
Real Ales, Bar Food, Restaurant Menu,
Accommodation, No Smoking Area

6 The Bay Horse
Murton, East Yorkshire YO19 5UQ
☎ 01904 489684

Real Ales, Bar Food, Restaurant Menu

- 3 miles east of York off the A64
- Black Sheep, John Smiths Cask, guest ale
- Tues-Sat 12-2 & 6-9, Sun 12-2.30; all-day snacks
- Quiz night Weds, occasional live music Sat night
- Parking, disabled access, beer garden
- All major cards
- Mon 5-12, Tues-Sun 12-12
- Yorkshire Museum of Farming (Murton), Yorkshire Air Museum (Elvington), Pocklington, Stamford Bridge

Dating back to the 1800s, The Bay Horse is a classic village inn set back from a quiet country lane. Murton is home to the Yorkshire Museum of Farming, and this inn makes an excellent place to enjoy a relaxing drink or meal while exploring the sights and excellent walking in the region. Owned and run by Paul Gallagher, this traditional inn has a range of real ales together with lagers, cider, stout, wines, spirits and soft drinks. Paul also oversees the kitchen, where he creates simple and hearty traditional meals such as steak and ale pie. The décor and ambience are attractive and welcoming, and the service always of a high standard.

19 The Carpenters Arms

Fangoss, East Yorkshire YO41 5QG
☎ 01759 368222

Real Ales, Bar Food, Restaurant Menu

- ☛ Off the A166 below Full Sutton
- 🍺 John Smiths Cask and three changing guest ales
- 🍴 Mon-Thurs 12-2 & 5.30-9; Fri & Sat 12-3 & 6-9; Sun 12-6; all-day snacks
- 🎵 Sunday night quiz
- ⛱ Parking, beer garden, children's play area, disabled access
- 💳 All major cards
- 🕐 11.30-3 & 5.30-11
- 🏛 York, Sutton Park, Murton, Elvington

Dating back to the late 1700s, The Carpenters Arms is a traditional Georgian pub with every modern comfort. A

seeking out. Along with several real ales there's a good range of lagers, wines, spirits, soft drinks, cider and stout. All-day snacks are complemented by an excellent range of hearty and delicious dishes such as Carpenters Chicken (pan-fried chicken breast with a vegetable risotto and herb and wine sauce), home-made pie of the day and Whitby scampi alongside a selection of a la carte dishes and daily specials using the freshest local ingredients. Jon is the chef and takes justified pride in creating a choice of excellent dishes at lunch and dinner.

The décor and furnishings are comfortable and impressive throughout, and the inn is the perfect place to stop and enjoy a relaxing drink or meal while exploring the many sights and attractions – natural and man-made – of the region.

true picture postcard pub, as you step inside on cold days you feel the roaring fire and notice everywhere around you the gracious elegance of a bygone age: buttoned leather seats, exposed beamwork on the ceilings and other traditional features that enhance the warm and cosy ambience.

Owned and run by Jon and Emma Szpakowski, who bring a wealth of enthusiasm to offering all their guests the best in food, drink and hospitality, this fine inn is well worth

9 Black Horse

42-44 The Village, Wigginton, York,
Yorkshire YO32 2PJ
Tel: 01904 758473

Real Ales, Bar Food, Restaurant Menu

10 Black Horse Inn

Newton Road, Tollerton, York, Yorkshire YO61 1QT
Tel: 01347 838280

Real Ales, Bar Food, Restaurant Menu,
No Smoking Area, Disabled Facilities

11 Blacksmith Arms

Main Street, Westow, York, Yorkshire YO60 7NE
Tel: 01653 618365

Real Ales, Bar Food, Restaurant Menu,
Accommodation, No Smoking Area

12 Blacksmith Arms

Flaxton, York, Yorkshire YO60 7RJ
Tel: 01904 468210

Real Ales, Bar Food, Restaurant Menu,
No Smoking Area, Disabled Facilities

13 The Blacksmiths Arms

Shipton Road, Skelton, York, Yorkshire YO30 1XW
Tel: 01904 471902

14 Blacksmiths Arms

Farlington, York, Yorkshire YO61 1NW
Tel: 01347 810581

Real Ales, Bar Food, No Smoking Area

15 Blacksmiths Arms

Main Street, Naburn, York, Yorkshire YO19 4PN
Tel: 01904 623464

Real Ales, Bar Food, Restaurant Menu,
Accommodation, No Smoking Area, Disabled Facilities

16 Blackwell Ox

Huby Road, Sutton-on-The-Forest, York,
Yorkshire YO61 1DT
Tel: 01347 810328

Real Ales, Bar Food, Restaurant Menu,
No Smoking Area, Disabled Facilities

17 The Buckles Inn

Tadcaster Road, Bilbrough, York,
Yorkshire YO23 3PW
Tel: 01904 706377

Real Ales, Bar Food, Restaurant Menu

18 Burythorpe House Hotel

Burythorpe, Malton, North Yorkshire YO17 9LB
Tel: 01653 658200

Real Ales, Bar Food, Restaurant Menu,
Accommodation, No Smoking Area

19 **The Carpenters Arms**

Fangfoss, York, Yorkshire YO41 5QG
Tel: 01759 368222

Real Ales, Bar Food, Restaurant Menu

See panel opposite

20 The Castle Inn

Sheriff Hutton, York, Yorkshire YO60 6ST
Tel: 01347 878335

Real Ales, Bar Food, Restaurant Menu,
No Smoking Area, Disabled Facilities

21 The College Arms

Bielby, York, Yorkshire YO42 4JW
Tel: 01759 318361

Real Ales, Bar Food, Disabled Facilities

22 The Commercial Inn

Market Place, Easingwold, York,
Yorkshire YO61 3AN
Tel: 01347 821252

Real Ales

23 The Cottage Inn

115 The Village, Haxby, York, Yorkshire YO32 2JH
Tel: 01904 763949

Real Ales, Bar Food, No Smoking Area,
Disabled Facilities

24 The Cross Keys

Common Road, Dunnington, York,
Yorkshire YO19 5NG
Tel: 01904 488847

Real Ales, Bar Food, Restaurant Menu,
No Smoking Area

47 The Melborne Arms

Melborne, York, East Yorkshire YO42 4QJ
☎ 01759 318257

Bar Food, Restaurant Menu, No Smoking Area, Disabled Facilities

- ☞ Off the A1079 east of York
- 🍺 Speckled Hen, John Smiths Cask
- 🍴 Tues-Sat 12-2 & 6-9.30, Sun 12-2
- 🎵 Quiz night Weds
- ⚓ Parking, patio, disabled access, small private function room
- 💳 All major cards
- 🚫 No smoking in restaurant
- 🕐 Tues-Thurs 12-2.30 & 5-11, Fri 12-2.30 & 5-11, Sat & Sun 12-11
- 🏛 York, Beverley, Malton, the coast

The Melborne Arms is a very impressive country inn with many handsome

France, New Zealand, Australia, Italy, Argentina, Chile, California and Spain, together with a selection of champagnes and sparkling wines such as Veuve Cliquot Yellow Label NV, Dom Perignon 1996 and Laurent Perrier Rosé NV. The menu and specials board are equally impressive, with a wonderful choice of tempting dishes at lunch and dinner. Chef Chris is hugely talented and uses the freshest local ingredients to create traditional and innovative dishes that will appeal to every palate. The menus change with the seasons to offer the freshest seasonal produce.

The inn is well worth seeking out while exploring the sights and attractions of York and the surrounding area, or as a destination on its own.

traditional features. The interior is redolent of days gone by, pristine and attractive with stone slab and polished wood flooring, solid pine furniture, a stylish brickbuilt bar and subdued lighting. The inn manages to be modern while not sacrificing any traditional comfort.

Spacious and airy, it is a very pleasant place to enjoy a relaxing drink or meal. The accent is firmly on quality and a high standard of service here, with a truly marvellous wine list of over 30 reds, whites and rosés including wines from

25 Cross Keys Hotel
89 Market Street, Pocklington, York,
Yorkshire YO42 2AE
Tel: 01759 302179

Real Ales, Bar Food, Restaurant Menu,
No Smoking Area

26 Crown & Cushion
Welburn, York, Yorkshire YO60 7DZ
Tel: 01653 618304

Real Ales, Bar Food, Restaurant Menu

27 The Dawnay Arms
Main Street, Shipton By Beningbrough, York,
Yorkshire YO30 1AB
Tel: 01904 470334

Real Ales, Bar Food, Restaurant Menu,
No Smoking Area, Disabled Facilities

28 Duke Of York Inn
Gate Helmsley, York, Yorkshire YO41 1JS
Tel: 01759 373698

Real Ales, Bar Food, Restaurant Menu,
No Smoking Area, Disabled Facilities

29 The Ebor Inn
Main Street, Bishopthorpe, York, Yorkshire YO23 2RB
Tel: 01904 706190

Real Ales, Bar Food, Restaurant Menu,
No Smoking Area

30 Feathers Hotel
Market Place, Pocklington, York, Yorkshire YO42 2AH
Tel: 01759 303155

Real Ales, Bar Food, Restaurant Menu

31 The Fleece Inn
Main Street, Bishop Wilton, York, Yorkshire YO42 1RU
Tel: 01759 368251

Real Ales, Bar Food, Restaurant Menu,
No Smoking Area

32 The Four Ails Inn
Malton Road, Kirkbymoorside, York,
Yorkshire YO62 6NT
Tel: 01904 468233

Real Ales, Bar Food, Restaurant Menu,
No Smoking Area, Disabled Facilities

33 Fox & Hounds
39 Top Lane, Copmanthorpe, York,
Yorkshire YO23 3UH
Tel: 01904 706395

Real Ales

34 Gateway To York Hotel
Hull Road, Kexby, York YO41 5LD
Tel: 01759 388223

Real Ales, Restaurant Menu, Accommodation,
No Smoking Area, Disabled Facilities

35 Gold Cup Inn
Low Catton, York, Yorkshire YO41 1EA
Tel: 01759 371354

Real Ales, Bar Food, Restaurant Menu,
No Smoking Area

36 Grey Horse Inn
Main Street, Elvington, York, Yorkshire YO41 4AG
Tel: 01904 608335

Real Ales, Bar Food, Restaurant Menu

37 The Greyhound
York Street, Dunnington, York, Yorkshire YO19 5PN
Tel: 01904 488018

Real Ales

38 The Half Moon
3 The Village, Strensall, York, Yorkshire YO32 5XS
Tel: 01904 492919

No Smoking Area, Disabled Facilities

39 Half Moon Inn
Acklam, Malton, North Yorkshire YO17 9RG
Tel: 01653 658323

Real Ales

40 Highwayman Inn
The Square, Sheriff Hutton, York, Yorkshire YO60 6QZ
Tel: 01347 878328

Bar Food, No Smoking Area, Disabled Facilities

41 Horseshoe
Long Street, Easingwold, York, Yorkshire YO61 3JB
Tel: 01347 821134

Bar Food, No Smoking Area, Disabled Facilities

50 The Nags Head Inn

Askham Bryan, York, North Yorkshire YO23 3QS
☎ 01904 706953

Real Ales, Bar Food, No Smoking Area, Disabled
Facilities

- ☛ Off the A1237 on the outskirts of York
- 🍺 Black Sheep, John Smiths Cask, Tetleys Cask
- 🍴 Mon-Sat 12.30-2 & 5.30-9; all day Sunday0
- 🅿 Parking, disabled access, beer garden
- 💳 All major cards
- 🚫 No smoking areas
- 🕐 11.30-3 & 5.30-11
- 🏛 York, Castle Howard, Sutton Park

Built in 1778, The Nags Head Inn began life as three cottages and occupies a substantial site in the extremely picturesque

simple Yorkshire fare to superb cuisine dishes and superb daily fish menus. A small sample of the culinary delights at this fine pub include mixed grills and steaks, roast chicken, baked salmon, roast of the day, tuna and mozzarella fish cakes, whole trout, halibut steak and poached haddock. All dishes are cooked fresh to order using the best local produce. The décor is charming, with exposed beamwork, brickbuilt fires and other original features.

The village and the inn make a perfect place to stop for a relaxing drink or meal while exploring the attractions of York – York Minster, the Yorvik Viking Centre, York Castle Museum, The Shambles and the National Railway Museum, to name just a few – as well as the surrounding region, which include Castle Howard, Beningbrough Hall, Easingwold, Sutton Park and the Yorkshire Air Museum.

village of Askham Bryan on the outskirts of York. Several comfortable rooms brimming with character mark this inn out as special, with roaring open fires from late November onwards adding to the warm and welcoming atmosphere. Owner Karen Hirst and her friendly, experienced staff offer a high standard of service and hospitality to all their guests.

The menu and specials boards offer a huge choice of excellent dishes, from

42 Jarvis International Hotel

Shipton Road, Skelton, York, Yorkshire YO30 1XW
Tel: 01904 670222

Bar Food, Restaurant Menu, Accommodation,
No Smoking Area, Disabled Facilities

43 Jolly Farmer Inn

Main Street, Leavening, Malton, Yorkshire YO17 9SA
Tel: 01653 658276

Real Ales, Bar Food, Restaurant Menu,
Accommodation, No Smoking Area, Disabled Facilities

44 Lord Collingwood Inn

Hodgson Lane, Upper Poppleton, York,
Yorkshire YO26 6EA
Tel: 01904 794388

Real Ales, Bar Food, No Smoking Area

45 The Lord Nelson Inn

9 Main Street, Nether Poppleton, York,
Yorkshire YO26 6HS
Tel: 01904 794320

Real Ales, Bar Food

46 The Marcia

29 Main Street, Bishopthorpe, York,
Yorkshire YO23 2RA
Tel: 01904 706185

Real Ales, Bar Food, Restaurant Menu,
No Smoking Area

47 **The Melborne Arms**

Melborne, York, Yorkshire YO42 4QJ
Tel: 01759 318257

Bar Food, Restaurant Menu, No Smoking Area,
Disabled Facilities

See panel on page 126

48 The Moor's Inn

Appleton-le-Moors, York, Yorkshire YO62 6TF
Tel: 01751 417435

Real Ales, Bar Food, Restaurant Menu,
Accommodation, No Smoking Area

49 The Mount Royale Hotel

Pocklington, York, Yorkshire YO24 1GU
Tel: 01904 628856

Real Ales, Restaurant Menu, Accommodation,
No Smoking Area

50 **The Nags Head Inn**

Main Street, Askham Bryan, York,
Yorkshire YO23 3QS
Tel: 01904 706953

Real Ales, Bar Food, No Smoking Area,
Disabled Facilities

See panel opposite

51 New Inn

62-66 Long Street, Easingwold, York,
Yorkshire YO61 3HT
Tel: 01347 822093

Real Ales, Bar Food, No Smoking Area, Disabled Facilities

52 New Inn Motel

Main Street, Huby, York, Yorkshire YO61 1HQ
Tel: 01347 810219

Real Ales, Bar Food, Restaurant Menu,
Accommodation, No Smoking Area, Disabled Facilities

53 Oddfellows Arms

12 Union Street, Pocklington, York, Yorkshire YO42 2JL
Tel: 01759 302283

Real Ales, Bar Food, Disabled Facilities

54 Plough Inn

PO Box 221, Allerthorpe, York, Yorkshire YO42 4WY
Tel: 01759 302349

Real Ales, Bar Food, Restaurant Menu,
No Smoking Area, Disabled Facilities

55 The Red Lion

52 The Village, Haxby, York, Yorkshire YO32 2HX
Tel: 01904 752811

Bar Food, Disabled Facilities

56 Riverside Farm

Shipton Road, Skelton, York, Yorkshire YO30 1XJ
Tel: 01904 642525

Bar Food, Restaurant Menu, No Smoking Area,
Disabled Facilities

57 Roebuck Inn

Main Street, Appleton Roebuck, York,
Yorkshire YO23 7DG
Tel: 01904 744351

Real Ales, Bar Food, Restaurant Menu,
No Smoking Area, Disabled Facilities

58 The Rose & Crown

Main Street, Askham Richard, York, Yorkshire YO23 3PT
Tel: 01904 707501

Real Ales, Bar Food, Restaurant Menu,
No Smoking Area, Disabled Facilities

59 Rose & Crown

Main Street, Sutton-on-The-Forest, York,
Yorkshire YO61 1DP
Tel: 01347 811333

Real Ales, Bar Food, Restaurant Menu,
No Smoking Area, Disabled Facilities

60 Ship Inn

23 The Village, Strensall, York, Yorkshire YO32 5XS
Tel: 01904 490302

Real Ales, Bar Food, No Smoking Area

61 The Ship Inn

Moor End, Acaster Malbis, York, Yorkshire YO23 2UH
Tel: 01904 703888

Real Ales, Bar Food, Restaurant Menu,
Accommodation, No Smoking Area, Disabled Facilities

62 Shoulder Of Mutton

Chapel Green, Appleton Roebuck, York,
Yorkshire YO23 7DP
Tel: 01904 744227

Real Ales, Bar Food, Restaurant Menu

63 The Six Bells

Oxcarr Lane, Strensall, York, Yorkshire YO32 5TD
Tel: 01904 490715

Real Ales, Bar Food, Restaurant Menu,
No Smoking Area, Disabled Facilities

64 St Vincent Arms

Main Street, Sutton On Derwent, York
Yorkshire YO41 4BN
Tel: 01904 608349

Real Ales, Bar Food, Restaurant Menu, No Smoking Area

65 The Stamford

5 The Square, Stamford Bridge, York,
Yorkshire YO41 1AG
Tel: 01759 371338

Real Ales

66 Star Inn

Main Street, Huby, York, Yorkshire YO61 1HS
Tel: 01347 810382

67 The Station Hotel

Pavement, Pocklington, York, Yorkshire YO42 2AU
Tel: 01759 307916

Disabled Facilities

68 Steer Inn

Hull Road, Wilberfoss, York, Yorkshire YO41 5PF
Tel: 01759 380600

Real Ales, Bar Food, Restaurant Menu

69 Stone Trough Inn

Kirkham Abbey, York, Yorkshire YO60 7JS
Tel: 01653 618713

Real Ales, Bar Food, Restaurant Menu,
No Smoking Area, Disabled Facilities

70 Swordsman Inn

The Square, Stamford Bridge, York,
Yorkshire YO41 1AF
Tel: 01759 371307

Real Ales, Bar Food, Restaurant Menu

71 Tanglewood

Malton Road, York, Yorkshire YO32 9TW
Tel: 01904 468611

Bar Food, Restaurant Menu, No Smoking Area,
Disabled Facilities

72 The Tankard Inn

Wetherby Road, Rufforth, York,
Yorkshire YO23 3QF
Tel: 01904 738621

Real Ales, Bar Food, Restaurant Menu,
No Smoking Area, Disabled Facilities

73 Three Cups

York Road, Stamford Bridge, York,
Yorkshire YO41 1AX
Tel: 01759 375901

Real Ales, Bar Food, Restaurant Menu,
No Smoking Area, Disabled Facilities

74 Three Hares Inn

Main Street, Bilbrough, York, Yorkshire YO23 3PH
Tel: 01937 832128

Real Ales, Bar Food, Restaurant Menu,
No Smoking Area, Disabled Facilities

75 The Tiger Inn

29 The Village, Haxby, York, Yorkshire YO32 3HS
Tel: 01904 768355

Real Ales, Bar Food, No Smoking Area

76 The Village Inn

Main Street, Wilberfoss, York, Yorkshire YO41 5NN
Tel: 01759 380268

Real Ales, Bar Food, Restaurant Menu

See panel below

77 The White Bear Inn

Main Street, Stillington, York, Yorkshire YO61 1JU
Tel: 01347 810338

Real Ales, Bar Food, Restaurant Menu,
No Smoking Area, Disabled Facilities

78 White Horse Inn

The Green, Upper Poppleton, York,
Yorkshire YO26 6DF
Tel: 01904 606921

Real Ales, Bar Food, Restaurant Menu,
No Smoking Area, Disabled Facilities

79 The Windmill

Hull Road, Dunnington, York, Yorkshire YO19 5LP
Tel: 01904 481898

Real Ales, Bar Food, Restaurant Menu,
No Smoking Area, Disabled Facilities

80 The Woodman Inn

18 Main Street, Bishopthorpe, York,
Yorkshire YO23 2RB
Tel: 01904 706507

Real Ales, Bar Food, No Smoking Area,
Disabled Facilities

81 The York

Market Place, Easingwold, York,
Yorkshire YO61 3AD
Tel: 01347 821235

76 The Village Inn

Wilberfoss, York, East Yorkshire YO41 5NN
☎ 01759 380268
🌐 www.thevillageinnyork.co.uk

Real Ales, Bar Food, Restaurant Menu

- On the A1079 east of York
- John Smiths Cask, Tetleys, guest ales
- Mon-Sat 12-2 & 6-9, Sundays 12-3
- Quiz night Weds, occasional live music
- Parking, patio, disabled access
- All major cards
- 12-11
- York, Pocklington, Yorkshire Museum of Farming (Murton), Yorkshire Air Museum (Elvington)

Dating back to the mid-18th century, The Village Inn is a large and attractive place with home-cooked food, real ales and genuine hospitality. This family-run pub is a convivial and welcoming place to enjoy a quiet meal and drink while exploring this part of Yorkshire. All dishes are made with the freshest and finest local produce, with an extensive menu and daily specials board featuring several speciality dishes. Booking advised for the Sunday carvery, and early bird menus, steak nights and other theme nights are a regular feature. To drink there's a very good wine list together with a range of real ales, lagers, cider, stout, wines, spirits and soft drinks.

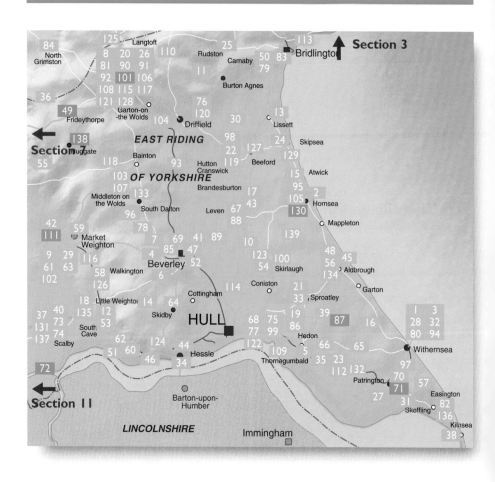

84
North Grimston
125 Langtoft
8 20 26 110
81 90 91
92 101 106
108 115 117
121 128
Rudston
Carnaby
11
25
50 83
79
113
Bridlington
Section 3
36
49
Frideythorpe
Garton-on-the Wolds 104
76
120 Driffield
30
Burton Agnes
13
Lissett
Section 7
138
Tuggate
55
118
EAST RIDING
Bainton
103 OF YORKSHIRE
Middleton on the Wolds 133
96
107
Hutton Cranswick
93
South Dalton
78
98
22 127
119 Beeford
Brandesburton
17
43
Leven
67
88
24 Skipsea
129
15 Atwick
95
105 2
130 Hornsea
Section 11
Mappleton

42 59
111
9 29 116
61 63
102 126
58 Walkington
18 Little Weighton
37 40 135 12
131 73 53
137 74 South Cave
Scalby
72
Market Weighton
7 69 41 89
85 47
4
Beverley 52
6
14 64
Skidby
62
51 60
46
124
44
34 Hessle
10
123 100
54 Skirlaugh
Coniston
114
Cottingham
139
48
56 45
134 Aldbrough
21
33 Sproatley
Garton

HULL
68 75
77 99
122
86
19 39
87 16
Hedon
66 65
109 5
Thornegumbald 35 23
112 132
Patrington
27
1 3
28 32
80 94
Withernsea
97
70
71 57
31 Easington
Skeffling 82
136
Kilnsea
38

Barton-upon-Humber

LINCOLNSHIRE
Immingham

---

11   Pub or Inn Reference Number - Detailed Information

12   Pub or Inn Reference Number - Summary Entry

● ■   Place of interest mentioned in the chapter introduction

SECTION 8

Beverley

'For those who do not know this town, there is a great surprise in store ... Beverley is made for walking and living in.' Such was the considered opinion of the late Poet Laureate, John Betjeman. In medieval times, Beverley was one of England's most prosperous towns and it remains one of the most gracious. Its greatest glory is the **Minster** whose twin towers, built in glowing magnesian limestone, soar above this, the oldest town in East Yorkshire. Close by is the **North Bar**, the only one of the town's five medieval gatehouses to have survived. From Beverley, serious walkers might care to follow some or all of the 15 mile **Hudson Way**, a level route that follows the track of the old railway from Beverley to Market Weighton.

Bridlington

Bridlington lies at the northern tip of the crescent of hills that form the Wolds. The old town lies a mile inland from the bustling seaside resort with its manifold visitor amusements and attractions, popular since early Victorian

Burton Agnes

The overwhelming attraction in this unspoilt village is the sublime Elizabethan mansion, Burton Agnes Hall, but visitors should not ignore **Burton Agnes Manor House** (English Heritage), a rare example of a Norman house. **Burton Agnes Hall** is for its part an outstanding Elizabethan house, built between 1598 and 1610 and little altered, famous for its splendid Jacobean gatehouse, wondrously decorated ceilings and overmantels carved in oak, plaster and alabaster. It also has a valuable collection of paintings and furniture from between the 17th and 19th centuries.

Foston on the Wolds

If you can't tell a Gloucester Old Spot from a Saddleback, or a Belted Galloway from a Belgian Blue, then take a trip to **Cruckley**

Beverley Minster

Animal Farm where all will become clear. This working farm supports many different varieties of cattle, sheep, pigs, poultry and horses. Some of the animals are endangered – Greyfaced Dartmoor and Whitefaced Woodland Sheep, for example, and the farm also safeguards all seven breeds of rare British pigs.

Great Driffield

Located on the edge of the Wolds, Great Driffield is a busy little market town at the heart of an important corn-growing area. A cattle market is held here every Thursday; a general market on both Thursday and Saturday, and the annual agricultural show has been going strong since 1854. All Saints Parish Church, dating back to the 12th century has one of the highest towers in the county and some lovely stained glass windows portraying local nobility.

Hessle

At Hessle the River Humber narrows and it was here that the Romans maintained a ferry, the *Transitus Maximus*, a vital link in the route between Lincoln and York. The ferry remained in operation for almost 2000 years until it was replaced in 1981 by the **Humber Bridge** whose mighty pylons soar more than 500 feet above the village. **Humber Bridge Country Park** is a well-laid-out park giving visitors a true back-to-nature tour a short distance from one of modern man's greatest feats of engineering. The former chalk quarry has been attractively landscaped, providing a nature trail, extensive walks through woodlands and meadows, picnic and play areas, and picturesque water features.

Hornsea

This small coastal town can boast not only the most popular visitor attraction in Humberside, Hornsea Pottery, but also Yorkshire's largest freshwater lake, **Hornsea Mere**. Two miles long and one mile wide, it provides a refuge for over 170 species of birds and a peaceful setting for many varieties of rare flowers. Hornsea is also the home of the **North Holderness Museum of Village Life.** Here, in a converted 18th-century farmhouse, period rooms have been recreated, and there are collections of agricultural equipment and the tools of long gone local tradesmen. Excellent sands, a church built with cobbles gathered from the shore, well-tended public gardens and a breezy, mile-long promenade all add to the town's popularity. The excellent **Hornsea Museum**, established in 1978, is a folk museum housed in a Grade II listed building and has won numerous national awards over the years.

Huggate

Huggate is tucked away deep in the heart of the Wolds with two long-distance walks, the Minster Way and the Wolds Way, skirting it to the north and south. The village clusters around a large green with a well which is claimed to be the deepest in England.

Hull

During the Second World War Hull was mercilessly battered by the Luftwaffe: 7,000 of its people were killed and 92 per cent of its houses suffered bomb damage. Then in the post-war years its once huge fishing fleet steadily dwindled. But Hull has risen

Hull Marina at Sunset

phoenix-like from those ashes and is today the fastest-growing port in England. Waymarked walks such as the **Maritime Heritage Trail** and the **Fish Pavement Trail** make the most of the city's dramatic waterfront.

Kirkburn

The architectural guru Nikolaus Pevsner considered **St Mary's Church** in Kirkburn to be one of the two best Norman parish churches in the East Riding. Dating from 1119, the church has an unusual tower staircase, a richly carved and decorated Victorian screen, and a spectacular early Norman font covered with carved symbolic figures.

Patrington

Shortly after it was built, **St Patrick's Church** at Patrington was dubbed 'Queen of Holderness', and Queen it remains. This sublime church took more than 100 years to build, from around 1310 to 1420, and it is one of the most glorious examples of the eye-pleasing style known as English Decorated. Its spire soars almost 180 feet into the sky making it the most distinctive feature in the flat plains of Holderness. St Patrick's has the presence and proportions of a cathedral although only enjoying the status of a parish church. Clustering around it, picturesque Dutch-style cottages complete an entrancing picture and just to the east of the village the Dutch theme continues in a fine old windmill.

Paull

Fort Paull's role as a frontier landing and watch point goes back to at least Viking times. Henry VIII built a fortress here in the mid-1500s; a second fort was added at the time of the Napoleonic wars. Today, the spacious 10-acre site offers a wide variety of attractions including historical displays of rare period and contemporary artillery, classic military vehicles, a parade ground where re-enactments take place, an assault course for youngsters, a Bird of Prey Centre, museum, gift shop, bar and restaurant.

Skidby

In the 1800s more than 200 windmills were scattered across the Wolds. Today, **Skidby**

Mill is the only one still grinding grain and producing its own wholemeal flour. At the same location is the **Museum of East Riding Life** where the farming year is chronicled using historic implements and fascinating photographs.

Sledmere

Sledmere House is a noble Georgian mansion built by the Sykes family in the 1750s when this area was still a wilderness infested with packs of marauding wolves. Inside, there is fine furniture by Chippendale and Sheraton, and decorated plasterwork by Joseph Rose. The copy of a naked, and well-endowed, Apollo Belvedere in the landing alcove must have caused many a maidenly blush in Victorian times, and the Turkish Room – inspired by the Sultan's salon in Istanbul's Valideh Mosque – is a dazzling example of oriental opulence. Outside, the gardens and the 220 acres of parkland were landscaped by Capability Brown. Across the road are two remarkable, elaborately detailed, monuments. The **Eleanor Cross** – modelled on those set up by Edward I in memory of his Queen – was erected by Sir Tatton Sykes in 1900; the **Wagoners Memorial** designed by Sir Mark Sykes, commemorates the 1,000-strong company of men he raised from the Wolds during the First World War. Their knowledge of horses was invaluable in their role as members of the Army Service Corps.

South Dalton

The most prominent church in East Yorkshire, **St Mary's Church** has a soaring spire more than 200 feet high, an unmistakable landmark for miles around.

Built in 1861 by Lord Beaumont Hotham, the church was designed by the famous Victorian architect JL Pearson and the elaborate internal and external decorations are well worth looking at.

West Newton

Just outside the village of West Newton is **Burton Constable Hall**, named after Sir John Constable who in 1570 built a stately mansion here which incorporated parts of an even older house, dating back to the reign of King Stephen in the 1100s. The Hall was again remodelled, on Jacobean lines, in the 18th century and contains some fine work by Chippendale, Adam and James Wyatt. In the famous Long Gallery with its 15th-century Flemish stained glass, hangs a remarkable collection of paintings, among them Holbein's portraits of Sir Thomas Cranmer and Sir Thomas More, and Zucchero's Mary, Queen of Scots. Dragons abound in the dazzling Chinese Room, an exercise in oriental exotica that long pre-dates the Prince Regent's similar extravaganza at the Brighton Pavilion. Thomas Chippendale himself designed the fantastical Dragon Chair, fit for a Ming Emperor. Outside, there are extensive parklands designed by Capability Brown, and apparently inspired by the gardens at Versailles.

Wharram Percy

A minor road off the B1248 leads to one of the most haunting sights in the county – the deserted medieval village of **Wharram Percy** (English Heritage; free). There had been a settlement here for some 5,000 years, but by the late 1400s the village stood abandoned. For a while the church continued to serve the surrounding hamlets but in time, that too became a ruin. The manor house of the Percy family who gave the village its name, peasant houses dating back to the 13th century, a corn mill, a cemetery complete with exposed skeletons – these sad memorials of a once-thriving community stand windswept and desolate.

Withernsea

The next place of interest down the Holderness coast is Withernsea. Long, golden sandy beaches stretch for miles both north and south, albeit a mile further inland than they were in the days of William the Conqueror. The old **Lighthouse** is a striking feature of the town and those energetic enough to climb the 127-foot tower are rewarded by some marvellous views from the lamp room. South of Withernsea stretches a desolate spit of flat windswept dunes. This is **Spurn Point** which leads to Spurn Head, the narrow hook of ever-shifting sands that curls around the mouth of the Humber estuary. This bleak but curiously invigorating tag end of Yorkshire is nevertheless heavily populated – by hundreds of species of rare and solitary wild fowl, by playful seals, and also by the small contingent of lifeboatmen who operate the only permanently manned lifeboat station in Britain. Access to Spurn Head is only on foot.

1 The Aima Hotel

34 Queen Street, Withernsea,
North Humberside HU19 2AQ
Tel: 01964 612441

2 The Alexandra

Railway Street, Hornsea,
North Humberside HU18 1PS
Tel: 01964 532710

No Smoking Area, Disabled Facilities

3 Alexandra Hotel

90 Queen Street, Withernsea,
North Humberside HU19 2HB
Tel: 01964 615688

Bar Food, Accommodation, Disabled Facilities

4 Altisidora Inn

York Road, Bishop Burton, Beverley,
North Humberside HU17 8QF
Tel: 01964 550284

Real Ales, Bar Food, Restaurant Menu,
No Smoking Area, Disabled Facilities

5 Barn Farm

Main Road, Camerton, Hull, Yorkshire HU12 9NG
Tel: 01964 600100

Real Ales, Bar Food, Restaurant Menu,
No Smoking Area, Disabled Facilities

6 Barrel Inn

35 East End, Walkington, Beverley,
North Humberside HU17 8RX
Tel: 01482 868494

Real Ales

7 The Bay Horse

Main Street, Cherry Burton, Beverley,
North Humberside HU17 7RF
Tel: 01964 550417

Real Ales, Bar Food, Restaurant Menu,
No Smoking Area

8 Bay Horse Inn

North Street, Driffield,
North Humberside YO25 6AS
Tel: 01377 252292

Bar Food, Restaurant Menu, No Smoking Area

9 Bay Horse Inn

75 Market Place, Market Weighton, York,
Yorkshire YO43 3AN
Tel: 01430 873401

Real Ales, Bar Food, Restaurant Menu,
No Smoking Area

10 The Bay Horse Inn

Black Tup Lane, Arnold, Hull, Yorkshire HU11 5JA
Tel: 01964 562491

Real Ales, Bar Food, Restaurant Menu,
No Smoking Area, Disabled Facilities

11 The Bay Horse Inn

Middle Street, Kilham, Driffield,
North Humberside YO25 4RL
Tel: 01262 420220

Real Ales, Bar Food, Restaurant Menu,
No Smoking Area, Disabled Facilities

12 The Bear Inn

61 Market Place, South Cave, Brough,
North Humberside HU15 2AS
Tel: 01430 422461

Real Ales, Bar Food, Restaurant Menu,
No Smoking Area, Disabled Facilities

13 Black Bull Inn

48 Sands Lane, Barmston, Driffield,
North Humberside YO25 8PG
Tel: 01262 468244

Bar Food, Restaurant Menu, No Smoking Area,
Disabled Facilities

14 Black Horse Inn

38 Old Village Road, Little Weighton, Cottingham,
North Humberside HU20 3US
Tel: 01482 843624

Real Ales, Bar Food, Restaurant Menu,
No Smoking Area

15 Black Horse Inn

Atwick, Driffield, North Humberside YO25 8DQ
Tel: 01964 532691

Real Ales, Bar Food, Restaurant Menu,
No Smoking Area

16 Black Horse Inn
Main Street, Roos, Hull, Yorkshire HU12 0HB
Tel: 01964 670405

Real Ales, Bar Food, Restaurant Menu,
No Smoking Area, Disabled Facilities

17 The Black Swan
74 Main Street, Brandesburton, Driffield,
North Humberside YO25 8RG
Tel: 01964 542376

Bar Food, No Smoking Area

18 The Black Swan
41 Church Street, North Cave, Brough,
North Humberside HU15 2LJ
Tel: 01430 422773

Real Ales, Bar Food, Restaurant Menu,
No Smoking Area, Disabled Facilities

19 Blacksmiths Arms
5 Main Street, Preston, Hull, Yorkshire HU12 8UB
Tel: 01482 897591

Real Ales

20 Blue Bell & Riverside Restaurant
5 Riverhead, Driffield,
North Humberside YO25 6NX
Tel: 01377 253209

Bar Food, Restaurant Menu, Accommodation,
Disabled Facilities

21 Blue Bell Inn
1 Main Road, Sproatley, Hull, Yorkshire HU11 4PA
Tel: 01482 813331

Bar Food, Restaurant Menu, No Smoking Area

22 Blue Post Inn
79 Main Street, North Frodingham, Driffield,
North Humberside YO25 8LG
Tel: 01262 488300

Bar Food, Restaurant Menu, No Smoking Area,
Disabled Facilities

23 Bluebell Inn
Main Street, Keyingham, Hull, Yorkshire HU12 9RE
Tel: 01964 622286

Real Ales, No Smoking Area

24 The Board Inn
Back Street, Skipsea, Driffield,
North Humberside YO25 8SW
Tel: 01262 468342

Real Ales, Bar Food, Restaurant Menu,
No Smoking Area, Disabled Facilities

25 The Bosville Arms
Main Street, Rudston, Driffield,
North Humberside YO25 4UB
Tel: 01262 420259

Real Ales, Bar Food, Restaurant Menu,
Accommodation, No Smoking Area, Disabled Facilities

26 The Buck Hotel
1 Market Place, Driffield,
North Humberside YO25 6AP
Tel: 01377 253748

Bar Food, Accommodation

27 Burns Head
Patrington Haven, Patrington, Hull,
Yorkshire HU12 0QJ
Tel: 01964 630530

Real Ales, Bar Food, Restaurant Menu,
No Smoking Area

28 Butterfly Inn
78 Queen Street, Withernsea,
North Humberside HU19 2HB
Tel: 01964 613846

29 Carpenters Arms
56 Southgate, Market Weighton, York,
Yorkshire YO43 3BQ
Tel: 01430 803321

Real Ales, Bar Food

30 Chestnut Horse Inn
Great Kelk, Driffield,
North Humberside YO25 8HN
Tel: 01262 488263

Real Ales, Bar Food, Restaurant Menu,
No Smoking Area

31 Coach & Horses
Main Street, Welwick, Hull, Yorkshire HU12 0RY
Tel: 01964 630503

No Smoking Area

32 Commercial Hotel
130 Queen Street, Withernsea,
North Humberside HU19 2HB
Tel: 01964 612184

Real Ales, Bar Food, Disabled Facilities

33 Constable Arms
Main Road, Sproatley, Hull, Yorkshire HU11 4PA
Tel: 01482 815276

Restaurant Menu, Disabled Facilities

34 Country Park Inn
Cliff Road, Hessle, North Humberside HU13 0HB
Tel: 01482 640526

Bar Food, Accommodation, Disabled Facilities

35 Crooked Billet
Pitt Lane, Ryehill, Hull, Yorkshire HU12 9NN
Tel: 01964 622303

Real Ales, Bar Food, Restaurant Menu,
No Smoking Area

36 Cross Keys
Thixendale, Malton, North Yorkshire YO17 9TG
Tel: 01377 288272

Real Ales, Bar Food, Accommodation

37 Cross Keys Inn
Main Road, Gilberdyke, Brough,
North Humberside HU15 2SP
Tel: 01430 440310

Real Ales, Bar Food

38 Crown & Anchor
Kilnsea Road, Kilnsea, Hull, Yorkshire HU12 0UB
Tel: 01964 650276

Real Ales, Bar Food, Accommodation,
No Smoking Area, Disabled Facilities

39 Crown & Anchor
Elstronwick, Hull, Yorkshire HU12 9BP
Tel: 01964 670308

Real Ales, Bar Food, Restaurant Menu,
Accommodation, No Smoking Area

40 Crown & Anchor
75 Main Road, Newport, Brough,
North Humberside HU15 2RG
Tel: 01430 449757

Real Ales, Bar Food, Restaurant Menu,
Accommodation, No Smoking Area, Disabled Facilities

41 Crown & Anchor
Weel Road, Tickton, Beverley,
North Humberside HU17 9RY
Tel: 01964 542816

Real Ales, Bar Food, Restaurant Menu,
No Smoking Area, Disabled Facilities

42 Crown Inn
York Road, Shiptonthorpe, Market Weighton,
York YO43 3PF
Tel: 01430 873310

Real Ales, Bar Food, Restaurant Menu,
No Smoking Area, Disabled Facilities

43 Dacre Arms
Main Street, Brandesburton, Driffield, North
Humberside YO25 8RL
Tel: 01964 542392

Real Ales, Bar Food, Restaurant Menu,
No Smoking Area

44 Darleys
312 Boothferry Road, Hessle,
North Humberside HU13 9AR
Tel: 01482 643121

Real Ales, Bar Food, Restaurant Menu,
No Smoking Area, Disabled Facilities

45 The Double Dutch
350 Seaside Road, Aldbrough, Hull,
Yorkshire HU11 4SA
Tel: 01964 527786

Bar Food, Restaurant Menu, No Smoking Area

46 The Duke Of Cumberland
High Street, North Ferriby,
North Humberside HU14 3JP
Tel: 01482 631592

Real Ales, Bar Food, Restaurant Menu,
No Smoking Area, Disabled Facilities

47 The Eager Beaver

5 Highfield Road, Beverley,
North Humberside HU17 9QN
Tel: 01482 861517

Real Ales, Bar Food

48 Elm Tree Inn

High Street, Aldbrough, Hull, Yorkshire HU11 4RP
Tel: 01964 527568

Real Ales

49 **The Farmers Arms**

Main Street, Fridaythorpe, Driffield,
North Humberside YO25 9RT
Tel: 01377 288221

Real Ales, Bar Food, Restaurant Menu,
Accommodation, No Smoking Area, Disabled Facilities

See panel on page 142

50 Ferns Farm Hotel

29 Main Street, Carnaby, Bridlington,
North Humberside YO16 4UJ
Tel: 01262 678961

Real Ales, Bar Food, Restaurant Menu,
Accommodation, No Smoking Area

51 Ferry Inn

Station Road, Brough,
North Humberside HU15 1DY
Tel: 01482 667340

Real Ales, Bar Food, No Smoking Area,
Disabled Facilities

52 Foresters Arms

3 Beckside North, Beverley,
North Humberside HU17 0PR
Tel: 01482 867943

Real Ales, No Smoking Area

53 Fox & Coney Inn

52 Market Place, South Cave, Brough,
North Humberside HU15 2AT
Tel: 01430 422275

Real Ales, Bar Food, Restaurant Menu,
Accommodation, No Smoking Area

54 Gardeners Country Inn

Hull Road, Skirlaugh, Hull, Yorkshire HU11 5AE
Tel: 01964 562625

Real Ales, Bar Food, Accommodation,
No Smoking Area, Disabled Facilities

55 The Gate Inn

Millington, York, Yorkshire YO42 1TX
Tel: 01759 302045

Real Ales, Bar Food, Restaurant Menu,
No Smoking Area, Disabled Facilities

56 The George & Dragon Inn

High Street, Aldbrough, Hull, Yorkshire HU11 4RP
Tel: 01964 527230

No Smoking Area

57 The George & Dragon Inn

Main Road, Holmpton, Withernsea,
North Humberside HU19 2QR
Tel: 01964 630478

Real Ales, Bar Food, Restaurant Menu,
No Smoking Area

58 The Gnu Inn

The Green, North Newbald, York,
Yorkshire YO43 4SA
Tel: 01430 827799

Real Ales, Bar Food, Restaurant Menu,
Accommodation, No Smoking Area, Disabled Facilities

59 The Goodmanham Arms

Goodmanham, York, Yorkshire YO43 3JA
Tel: 01430 873849

Real Ales, Bar Food, No Smoking Area

60 The Green Dragon Hotel

Cowgate, Welton, Brough,
North Humberside HU15 1NB
Tel: 01482 666700

Real Ales, Bar Food, Accommodation,
No Smoking Area, Disabled Facilities

49 The Farmers Arms

Fridaythorpe, Driffield, East Yorkshire YO25 9RT
☎ 01377 288221
🌐 www.thefarmersarms.org.uk

Real Ales, Bar Food, Restaurant Menu, Accommodation, No Smoking Area, Disabled Facilities

☛ On the A166 5 miles west of Driffield

🍺 John Smiths, Black Sheep and 3 guest ales

🍴 12-2.30 & 6-9

🛏 7 chalets

🎵 Monday night quiz

🅿 Car park, beer garden, disabled access

💳 All the major cards

🚫 No smoking in restaurant

🕐 Mon-Fri 11-3 & 5-12; all day at weekends

🏛 Driffield, Burton Agnes, Sledmere, Huggate, Stamford Bridge

Situated in the heart of the Yorkshire Wolds, in the highest village in the region, The

with able assistance from his wife and daughter, has five real ales at all times together with a good choice of wines, spirits, soft drinks, lagers, cider and stout. All-day snacks are complemented by an excellent menu of home-made dishes using the freshest local ingredients. A sample from the menu includes roast duck, smoked haddock, steaks, chicken supreme and trout. The Sunday carvery is justly popular, with a choice of traditional roasts or the fish or vegetarian dish of the day.

Separate from the main building are seven en suite chalets offering comfortable and very pleasant accommodation. All have every modern amenity and comfort guests could expect, and one unit is equipped for guests with disabilities. Sights and attractions of the Yorkshire Wolds include The Wolds Way, which runs through Fridaythorpe, Sledmere House, Burton Agnes Manor House and Driffield.

Farmers Arms dates back to the 18th century and began life as the country retreat of the Duke of Devonshire, and was once owned by George Hudson, the railway king. Extensions to the rear of the original building now form the present bar area. The décor is supremely cosy and comfortable, with deep leather settees, exposed beamwork and other original features.

This family-run pub, owned by Mike Garnett

61 The Griffin Inn
74 Market Place, Market Weighton, York,
Yorkshire YO43 3AW
Tel: 01430 873284

Real Ales

62 The Half Moon
61 Main Street, Elloughton, Brough,
North Humberside HU15 1HU
Tel: 01482 667362

Bar Food, Restaurant Menu, No Smoking Area

63 The Half Moon Inn
39 High Street, Market Weighton, York,
Yorkshire YO43 3AQ
Tel: 01430 872247

Real Ales

64 Half Moon Inn
16 Main Street, Skidby, Cottingham,
North Humberside HU16 5TG
Tel: 01482 843403

Real Ales, Bar Food, No Smoking Area

65 The Halsham Arms
North Road, Halsham, Hull, Yorkshire HU12 0BY
Tel: 01964 671357

Real Ales, Bar Food, Restaurant Menu,
No Smoking Area

66 The Hare & Hounds
Main Street, Burstwick, Hull, Yorkshire HU12 9EA
Tel: 01964 602070

Real Ales, Bar Food, Restaurant Menu,
No Smoking Area, Disabled Facilities

67 Hare & Hounds
1 North Street, Leven, Beverley,
North Humberside HU17 5NF
Tel: 01964 542523

Real Ales, No Smoking Area

68 Haven Arms
Haven Side, Hedon, Hull, Yorkshire HU12 8HH
Tel: 01482 897695

Real Ales, Bar Food, Restaurant Menu,
No Smoking Area, Disabled Facilities

69 The Hayride
Grange Way, Beverley,
North Humberside HU17 9GP
Tel: 01482 861486

Bar Food, No Smoking Area, Disabled Facilities

70 Hildyard Arms
Market Place, Patrington, Hull, Yorkshire HU12 0RA
Tel: 01964 630234

Real Ales, Bar Food, Restaurant Menu,
Accommodation, No Smoking Area, Disabled Facilities

71 The Holderness Inn
High Street, Patrington, Hull, Yorkshire HU12 0RE
Tel: 01964 630091

Real Ales, Bar Food, Disabled Facilities

See panel on page 145

72 The Hope & Anchor
Main Street, Blacktoft, Goole,
North Humberside DN14 7YW
Tel: 01430 440441

Real Ales, Bar Food, Restaurant Menu,
No Smoking Area, Disabled Facilities

See panel on page 144

73 The Jolly Sailor Inn
102 Main Road, Newport, Brough,
North Humberside HU15 2RG
Tel: 01430 449191

Real Ales, Bar Food, Restaurant Menu,
No Smoking Area

74 The Kings Arms
Main Road, Newport, Brough,
North Humberside HU15 2QS
Tel: 01430 440289

75 Kings Head
2 Souttergate, Hedon, Hull, Yorkshire HU12 8JS
Tel: 01482 899314

76 The Kings Head
22 Middle Street, Nafferton, Driffield,
North Humberside YO25 4JS
Tel: 01377 254417

Real Ales, Restaurant Menu, No Smoking Area

72 The Hope & Anchor

Main Street, Blacktoft, East Yorkshire DN14 7YW
☎ 01430 440441

Real Ales, Bar Food, Restaurant Menu, No Smoking Area, Disabled Facilities

☛ From Goole, take the B1228 to the junction with the A63, then the B1230; turn right at Gilberdyke onto the minor road to Blacktoft

🍺 John Smiths, Old Mill Mild, two guest ales

🍴 Tues-Sat 12-2.30 & 6-9, Sun 12-3

🎵 Occasional quiz and theme nights

⚓ Parking, disabled access, beer garden, children's play area

💳 All major cards

🚫 No smoking areas

🕐 11-3 & 6-11

🏛 River Ouse, Goole, Hull, Trans Pennine Trail

Standing adjacent to the River Ouse near the place where it meets the River Trent,

they have made it a big success. They and their friendly, efficient staff offer a high standard of service and genuine hospitality to all their guests. To drink there is a selection of real ales together with lagers, cider, stout, wines, spirits and soft drinks. All-day nibbles including pork, apple and Calvados paté, hot and spicy chicken goujons and nachos with cheese vie with delicious main course such as a range of steaks, haddock, Thai green chicken curry and home-made mushroom stroganoff to tempt the palate. All dishes are made with the freshest local ingredients. There are two distinct restaurant areas in which to enjoy your meal, including the charming conservatory restaurant.

The vistas over the River Ouse from the restaurants and garden are quite superb. Booking is advised at this fine inn, where the food, drink and atmosphere are always of the highest standard.

The Hope & Anchor is a well-hidden pub with a lofty and well-deserved reputation for its food, well worth seeking out while exploring the region. Quaint and cosy behind its smart exterior, the interior boasts a wealth of warm woods, with exposed beams and panelling and extremely comfortable seating, as well as an impressive brickbuilt fire and a warm and welcoming ambience.

This fine Free House has been owned and run by Liz and Eddie Payne since 1999, and

71 The Holderness Inn

High Street, Patrington, East Yorkshire HU12 0RE
☎ 01964 630091

Real Ales, Bar Food, Disabled Facilities

- 🖝 17 miles east of Hull on the B1445
- 🍺 Tetleys Cask
- 🍴 12-8.30
- ⚓ Parking, disabled access, beer garden
- 🕐 12-11
- 🏛 Thornton Abbey, Normanby Hall, Epsworth Rectory, Spurn Point Bird Sanctuary

David and Andrea Hackney offer all their guests a warm welcome at The Holderness Inn, a spacious and convivial pub with great food and drink. The traditional interior will please real pub lovers, while the menu has something to tempt every appetite. Home-made pies include steak and ale or chicken and mushroom, while there are also hearty favourites such as steaks, honey and mustard chicken, fish and seafood dishes and much more.

Handy for visiting the coast, it makes the perfect place to enjoy a fine meal or drink while exploring the many sights and attractions of East Yorkshire. Patrington is an ancient village with a beautiful Gothic church is dedicated to St Patrick, from whom the town is said to derive its name, and from the churchyard there are delightful views of the Humber and its fertile shores as far as Spurn point and the opposite shores of Lincolnshire.

77 The Kingstown Hotel

Hull Road, Hedon, Hull, Yorkshire HU12 8DJ
Tel: 01482 890461

Real Ales, Bar Food, Restaurant Menu, Accommodation, No Smoking Area, Disabled Facilities

78 Light Dragoon

Main Street, Etton, Beverley,
North Humberside HU17 7PQ
Tel: 01430 810282

Bar Food, Restaurant Menu, No Smoking Area, Disabled Facilities

79 Manor Court Hotel

53 Main Street, Carnaby, Bridlington,
North Humberside YO16 4UJ
Tel: 01262 606468

Real Ales, Bar Food, Restaurant Menu, Accommodation, No Smoking Area

80 The Marine

The Promenade, Withernsea,
North Humberside HU19 2DP
Tel: 01964 612434

Bar Food, Restaurant Menu, No Smoking Area

81 Mariners Arms

Eastgate South, Driffield,
North Humberside YO25 6LR
Tel: 01377 253708

Real Ales, No Smoking Area

82 Marquis Of Granby

North Churchside, Easington, Hull,
Yorkshire HU12 0TW
Tel: 01964 650108

Bar Food, Accommodation, Disabled Facilities

83 The Mermaid

Bessingby Gate, Bridlington,
North Humberside YO16 4RB
Tel: 01262 673708

No Smoking Area

84 Middleton Arms

North Grimston, Malton,
North Yorkshire YO17 8AX
Tel: 01944 768255

Real Ales, Bar Food, Restaurant Menu, No Smoking Area, Disabled Facilities

85 Molescroft Inn

75 Molescroft Road, Beverley,
North Humberside HU17 7EG
Tel: 01482 862968

Real Ales, Bar Food, Restaurant Menu, No Smoking
Area, Disabled Facilities

86 The Nags Head

1 Sproatley Road, Preston, Hull,
Yorkshire HU12 8TT
Tel: 01482 897517

Bar Food, No Smoking Area, Disabled Facilities

87 **The Nancy Inn**

Back Lane, Burton Pidsea, Hull,
Yorkshire HU12 9AN
Tel: 01964 670444

Real Ales, Bar Food, No Smoking Area

See panel opposite

88 New Inn

44 South Street, Leven, Beverley,
North Humberside HU17 5NZ
Tel: 01964 542223

Real Ales, Accommodation

89 The New Inn

Main Street, Tickton, Beverley,
North Humberside HU17 9SH
Tel: 01964 542371

Real Ales, Bar Food, No Smoking Area

90 Norseman Pub & Club

Middle Street North, Driffield,
North Humberside YO25 6SW
Tel: 01377 240033

91 The Old Falcon Inn

57 Market Place, Driffield,
North Humberside YO25 6AW
Tel: 01377 255829

92 The Original Keys

Market Place, Driffield,
North Humberside YO25 6AP
Tel: 01377 253343

Real Ales, Bar Food

93 Pack Horse Inn

Main Street, Cranswick, Driffield,
North Humberside YO25 9QY
Tel: 01377 270298

94 Pier Hotel

9 Seaside Road, Withernsea,
North Humberside HU19 2DL
Tel: 01964 612069

Accommodation

95 Pike & Heron

21 Market Place, Hornsea,
North Humberside HU18 1AN
Tel: 01964 536312

Disabled Facilities

96 Pipe & Glass

West End, South Dalton, Beverley,
North Humberside HU17 7PN
Tel: 01430 810246

Real Ales, Bar Food, Restaurant Menu,
Accommodation, No Smoking Area, Disabled Facilities

97 The Plough Inn

Northside Road, Hollym, Withernsea,
North Humberside HU19 2RS
Tel: 01964 612049

Real Ales, Bar Food, Accommodation

98 Plough Inn

Foston-on-The-Wolds, Driffield,
North Humberside YO25 8BJ
Tel: 01262 488303

Real Ales, Bar Food, Restaurant Menu,
No Smoking Area

99 Queens Head Hotel

14 St. Augustines Gate, Hedon, Hull,
Yorkshire HU12 8EX
Tel: 01482 891432

Bar Food, Restaurant Menu, Disabled Facilities

100 The Railway Inn

New Ellerby, Hull, Yorkshire HU11 5AP
Tel: 01964 563770

Real Ales, Bar Food, Restaurant Menu,
Accommodation, No Smoking Area

87 The Nancy Inn

Burton-Pidsea, Hull, East Yorkshire HU12 9AN
☎ 01964 670444

Real Ales, Bar Food, No Smoking Area

- 12 miles east of Hull off the B1362
- Marstons Cask Bitter, Banks Bitter and guest ales
- 12-2 & Mon and Weds 5-8, Thurs-Sat 5-9
- Live music at weekends
- Car park, beer garden, disabled access
- All the major cards
- No smoking areas
- Hull, Tunstall, Halsham, Withernsea

Dating back to the early 1800s, The Nancy Inn is an excellent village pub that began life as a coaching inn and has some original features still intact. Charming and welcoming, the atmosphere at this convivial pub is always warm and comfortable. It's a marvellous place to stop while exploring the East Riding and the coast to enjoy a good drink or meal.

The menu and specials board boast a range of hearty favourites and more innovative dishes, all made with the freshest local ingredients. A small sample from the evening menu includes tasty meals such as steaks, Jamaican chicken curry, lamb in a Port and redcurrant sauce, tuna steak and more.

101 The Red Lion

57 Middle Street North, Driffield,
North Humberside YO25 6SS
Tel: 01377 252289

Real Ales, Bar Food, Accommodation,
Disabled Facilities

See panel on page 148

102 Red Lion

1 Finkle Street, Market Weighton, York,
Yorkshire YO43 3JL
Tel: 01430 872452

Real Ales, Bar Food, Restaurant Menu,
No Smoking Area

103 Robin Hood Inn

1 Beverley Road, Middleton on the Wolds, Driffield,
North Humberside YO25 9UF
Tel: 01377 217319

Real Ales, Bar Food, Disabled Facilities

104 Rose & Crown Inn

York Road, Little Driffield, Driffield,
North Humberside YO25 5XA
Tel: 01377 252211

No Smoking Area

105 Rose & Crown

Market Place, Hornsea,
North Humberside HU18 1AN
Tel: 01964 535756

Real Ales, Bar Food, Disabled Facilities

106 Rose & Crown

North Street, Driffield,
North Humberside YO25 6AS
Tel: 01377 253041

Real Ales, Bar Food, Disabled Facilities

107 Rose & Crown

Chapel Lane, Middleton On The Wolds, Driffield,
North Humberside YO25 9UE
Tel: 01377 217333

Real Ales, Bar Food, Restaurant Menu,
No Smoking Area

101 The Red Lion

Middle Street, Driffield, East Yorkshire YO25 6SS
☎ 01377 252289

Real Ales, Bar Food, Accommodation, Disabled
Facilities

- 10 miles north of Beverley on the A614
- John Smiths Cask
- All day snacks
- 5 en suite rooms
- Car park, disabled access, beer garden and patio
- Midday to 1 a.m.
- The Wolds Way, Sledmere House, Burton Agnes Hall and Manor House, Bridlington

Dating back to the early 1800s, The Red Lion in Driffield is a large and welcoming inn with all-day snacks, real ale and great accommodation. Owner Alison Smith and her capable, friendly staff offer all their guests genuine hospitality.

This convivial town centre inn is located just off the High Street and has a range of drinks include real ale, lagers, wines, spirits, cider, stout and soft drinks, while the all-day food features freshly made sandwiches including hearty favourites such as bacon, sausage, tuna, cheese and ham. The interior is warm and welcoming, while the accommodation is comfortable and features every modern amenity. The inn makes a good base from which to explore the region.

108 The Royal Oak

59 Victoria Road, Driffield, North Humberside
YO25 6TY
Tel: 01377 252038

109 Shakespere Inn

Baxtergate, Hedon, Hull, Yorkshire HU12 8JN
Tel: 01482 898371

Real Ales, Bar Food, Disabled Facilities

110 Ship Inn

Scarborough Road, Langtoft, Driffield,
North Humberside YO25 3TH
Tel: 01377 267243

Real Ales, Bar Food, Restaurant Menu,
Accommodation, No Smoking Area

111 The Ship Inn

York Road, Shiptonthorpe, Yorkshire YO43 3PG
Tel: 01430 872006

Real Ales, Bar Food, Restaurant Menu,
Accommodation, No Smoking Area, Disabled Facilities

See panel opposite

112 Ship Inn

Main Street, Keyingham, Hull, Yorkshire HU12 9RD
Tel: 01964 603132

Real Ales, Bar Food, Restaurant Menu,
No Smoking Area, Disabled Facilities

113 The Ship Inn

Cliff Road, Sewerby, Bridlington,
North Humberside YO15 1EW
Tel: 01262 672374

Real Ales, Bar Food, No Smoking Area

114 Skippers Tavern

Grampian Way, Bransholme, Hull,
Yorkshire HU7 5BJ
Tel: 01482 824616

115 Spread Eagle Inn

Exchange Street, Driffield,
North Humberside YO25 6LJ
Tel: 01377 253073

Real Ales

111 The Ship Inn

30 York Road, Shiptonthorpe,
East Yorkshire YO43 3PG
☎ 01430 872006

Real Ales, Bar Food, Restaurant Menu, Accommodation, No Smoking Area, Disabled Facilities

☛ On the A1079 close to the junction with the A614

🍺 John Smiths

🍴 12-2.30 & 5-8

🛏 6 en suite rooms

🎵 Open-mike night Thurs

🅿 Parking, patio, disabled access

💳 All major cards

🚫 No smoking in restaurant

🕐 Mon-Fri 12-2.30 & 5-2 a.m., Sat 12-2 a.m., Sun 12-11

🏛 Beverley, York, Pocklington, Malton, the coast

The Ship Inn is a handsome 19th-century inn with great food, drink and accommodation. Real ale lovers will feel right at home, while the menu boasts several excellent and hearty dishes including stuffed plaice, filled giant Yorkshire puddings and all-day breakfast. The bedrooms are handsome and comfortable, and include one adapted for guests with disabilities.

116 The Star

King Street, Sancton, York, Yorkshire YO43 4QP
Tel: 01430 827269

Real Ales, Bar Food, Restaurant Menu,
No Smoking Area

117 Star Inn

21 Exchange Street, Driffield,
North Humberside YO25 6LJ
Tel: 01377 241883

Real Ales

118 Star Inn

North Dalton, Driffield,
North Humberside YO25 9UX
Tel: 01377 217688

Real Ales, Bar Food, Restaurant Menu

119 The Star Inn

Main Street, North Frodingham, Driffield,
North Humberside YO25 8JX
Tel: 01262 488365

Real Ales, Bar Food, Restaurant Menu,
No Smoking Area, Disabled Facilities

120 The Star Inn

5 North Street, Nafferton, Driffield,
North Humberside YO25 4JW
Tel: 01377 254396

Real Ales, Restaurant Menu, Accommodation,
No Smoking Area

121 The Station Buffet

Middle Street South, Driffield,
North Humberside YO25 6QE
Tel: 01377 254421

Real Ales, Bar Food, Restaurant Menu,
No Smoking Area, Disabled Facilities

122 Station Hotel

Souttergate, Hedon, Hull, Yorkshire HU12 8JR
Tel: 01482 897544

123 The Sun

Church Lane, Skirlaugh, Hull, Yorkshire HU11 5EU
Tel: 01964 562338

124 The Swan & Cygnet

Main Street, Swanland, North Ferriby,
North Humberside HU14 3QP
Tel: 01482 634571

Real Ales, Bar Food, No Smoking Area

125 Three Tuns Inn

West Lutton, Malton, North Yorkshire YO17 8TA
Tel: 01944 738200

Real Ales

126 The Tiger Inn

The Green, North Newbald, York,
Yorkshire YO43 4SA
Tel: 01430 827759

Real Ales, Bar Food, Restaurant Menu,
No Smoking Area

127 Tiger Inn

Main Street, Beeford, Driffield,
North Humberside YO25 8AS
Tel: 01262 488733

Real Ales, Bar Food, Restaurant Menu,
No Smoking Area, Disabled Facilities

128 The Tiger Inn

Market Place, Driffield,
North Humberside YO25 6AP
Tel: 01377 257490

Real Ales, Disabled Facilities

129 Tow Bar Inn

Hornsea Road, Skipsea, Driffield,
North Humberside YO25 8SY
Tel: 01262 469191

Bar Food, Restaurant Menu, No Smoking Area,
Disabled Facilities

130 The Victoria

39 Market Place, Hornsea,
North Humberside HU18 1AN
Tel: 01964 533133

Real Ales, Restaurant Menu

See panel below

131 Wards Hotel

Main Road, Gilberdyke, Brough,
North Humberside HU15 2SL
Tel: 01430 440356

Real Ales

132 Watts Arms

Main Street, Ottringham, Hull, Yorkshire HU12 0AG
Tel: 01964 622034

Real Ales, Bar Food, No Smoking Area,
Disabled Facilities

---

130 The Victoria

Marketplace, Hornsea, East Yorkshire HU18 1AN
☎ 01964 533133

Real Ales, Restaurant Menu

- 13 miles northeast of Hull on the B1242
- Black Sheep, Tetleys Cask, guest ale
- 12-9 (to 10 p.m. Saturday)
- Acoustic night every other Tuesday, food theme nights
- Car park, beer garden, small function room, disabled access
- All the major cards
- Member of the *Daily Telegraph* Fine Dining Club
- No smoking in restaurant or at the bar
- 11.30-11
- Seaside, Hornsea Folk Museum, Hornsea Mere RSPB reserve

Unmissable as you enter Hornsea, The Victoria Bars & Restaurant is a convivial and welcoming place to enjoy a great selection of food and drink. For over 200 years there has been an inn on this site, and owner Brian

Thompson – a former professional golfer – continues to uphold the proud tradition of great service and hospitality for all his guests.

With two bars, beer garden and sunny patio, there are plenty of places to enjoy the hand-pulled beers and other libations available, while the bar snacks, extensive menu and specials board offer a range of delicious and hearty dishes such as roasts, seafood, Indian specialities and more. Brian also presides over the Black Horse Inn at Atwick, another fine place to stop for a great drink or meal while exploring the region.

138 The Wolds Inn

Driffield Road, Huggate, East Yorkshire YO42 1YH
☎ 01377 288217

Real Ales, Bar Food, Restaurant Menu, Accommodation, No Smoking Area

- Off the A166 west of Driffield
- Tetleys and Timothy Taylor Landlord
- Tues-Sun 12-2 & 6.30-9, closed Fri lunch (A la Carte menu, bar meals & Sunday Roast served)
- 3 en suite rooms
- Parking, beer gardens, small function room
- All major cards
- 3 Diamonds AA
- No smoking in restaurant & bedrooms
- Tues-Thurs, Sat 12-2 & 6.30-11, Fri 6.30-11, Sun 12-2 & 6.30-10.30 (6-10.30 June-Sept)
- York, Stamford Bridge, Driffield, Market Weighton, Pocklington, great walking

The Wolds Inn is a traditional country inn dating back to the 1500s. Hidden away amid superb countryside, it is well worth seeking out for the quality of its real ales, excellent food and comfortable accommodation. With a full range of drinks from real ales to wines, spirits and soft drinks, there's something to quench every thirst. The accent is firmly on excellent food here, with two full-time chefs creating varied and seasonal à la carte menus and daily specials that are hearty and delicious. The accommodation comprises three attractive and welcoming guest bedrooms, and throughout the inn there are numerous traditional features combined with every modern comfort.

---

133 The Wellington Inn

19 The Green, Lund, Driffield,
North Humberside YO25 9TE
Tel: 01377 217294

Real Ales, Bar Food, Restaurant Menu,
No Smoking Area

134 Wentworth House Hotel

Seaside Road, Aldbrough, Hull, Yorkshire HU11 4RX
Tel: 01964 527246

Accommodation, No Smoking Area, Disabled Facilities

135 White Hart Inn

Westgate, North Cave, Brough,
North Humberside HU15 2NJ
Tel: 01430 422432

136 The White Horse

South Church Side, Easington, Yorkshire HU12 0TR
Tel: 01964 650310

Bar Food

137 White Horse Inn

Main Road, Gilberdyke, Brough,
North Humberside HU15 2UP
Tel: 01430 440269

Disabled Facilities

138 The Wolds Inn

Driffield Road, Huggate, York, Yorkshire YO42 1YH
Tel: 01377 288217

Real Ales, Bar Food, Restaurant Menu,
Accommodation, No Smoking Area

See panel above

139 Wrygarth Inn

Station Road, Great Hatfield, Yorkshire HU11 4UY
Tel: 01964 536994

Real Ales, Bar Food, Restaurant Menu,
No Smoking Area, Disabled Facilities

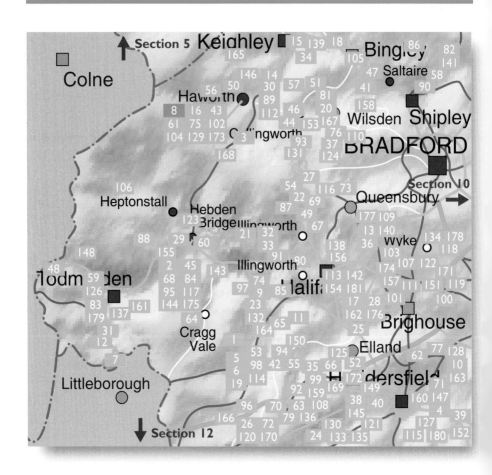

Section 5

Keighley
165
15 139 18
34

Colne

Bingley
105
86
141
82

Haworth
56 50
146 14
30 57 51
89
47 Saltaire
41
58
90

8 16 43
61 75 102
104 129 173
168
112 46
44 153 167
93
131
81
20
76
37
124
158
Wilsden Shipley
110
BRADFORD

ngworth

Heptonstall
106

Hebden
Bridge Illingworth
123
27
54 116 73
22 69
87 49
21 32 67

Queensbury
Section 10
177 109
13 140
36

88 29 60
148
155
33
91
138
156
wyke
103
134 178
118

Todmorden
48
59
126
83
179
137
31
12
7
161
2 45
68 84
95 117
144 175
64
143
74
97 85
23
132 65
164
Illingworth
80
113 142
154 181
17 28
162 176
25
Halifax
174 107 122
157
171
111 151 119
101
100

Cragg
Vale

Littleborough

1
5 53 94
6 98 42 55 35 66
19 114
92 159
96 70 63 108
166
26 72 79 136
120 170
150
125
99
169
38 40
145
130
24 133 135
121
127
Elland
52
62 77 128
71 10
163
Brighouse

Huddersfield
160 147
4 39
115 180 152

Section 12

SECTION 9

Bradford

Bradford is a city with much to offer the visitor. In terms of numbers, the most popular attraction is undoubtedly the **National Museum of Photography, Film and Television**, which houses IMAX, one of the largest cinema screens in the world.

Hainworth

The **Worth Way** is an interesting five-mile walk from the heart of Keighley to the eastern edge of the Worth Valley at Oxenhope. En route, the Worth Way passes close to the village of Hainworth, which stands high on the hillside and commands some grand views of Harden Moor.

Halifax

Halifax boasts one of Yorkshire's most impressive examples of municipal architecture, the glorious 18th-century **Piece Hall**. The **Town Hall** is another notable building, designed by Sir Charles Barry, architect of the Houses of Parliament, and

there's an attractive Borough Market, constructed in cast iron and glass with an ornate central clock. Halifax also boasts the largest parish church in England. The **Calderdale Industrial Museum** houses still-working looms and mill machinery and hand textile demonstrations. From the Great Wheel to the Spinning Jenny, from mining to moquette, from steam engines (in live steam) to toffee, the museum provides a riveting insight into Halifax's industrial heritage. Situated next to Halifax railway station, **Eureka!** is Britain's first and only interactive museum designed especially for children between three and 12 years old. **Shibden Hall and Park**, about a mile out of town, is somewhere very special that should not be missed, set in 90 acres of parkland.

Piece Hall, Halifax

Haworth

Once a bleak moorland town in a dramatic setting that fired the romantic imaginations of the Brontë sisters, Haworth has been transformed into a lively, attractive place, with wonderful tea houses, street theatre, and antique and craft shops. It is worth exploring the ginnels and back roads off the steeply rising high street, to get a feeling of what the place was like in the days of the Brontës. At the **Brontë Parsonage Museum** the Brontë Society has restored the interior to resemble as closely as possible the house in which the sisters lived with their father and brother. The **Brontë Way** is a 40-mile linear footpath with a series of four guided walks. The most exhilarating and popular excursion is that to **Top Withins**, inspiration for the 'Wuthering Heights' of the novel. The route also takes into account a great variety of scenery, from wild moorlands to pastoral countryside. Haworth is headquarters of the **Keighley & Worth Valley Railway**, a thriving volunteer-run railway which serves six stations (most of them gas-lit) in the course of its 4¾-mile length.

Hebden Bridge

This mill town is characterised by the stepped formation of its houses which were stacked one on top of the other up the steep sides of the Calder valley. **Hebden Bridge Mill** has, for almost 700 years now, been powered by the fast-flowing waters of the River Hebden. For over four centuries this was a manorial corn mill before it was converted into a textile mill that was finally abandoned in the 1950s. Now lovingly restored, the mill is home to various stylish shops, restaurants and craft workshops. The **Rochdale Canal**, which slices through the town, was completed in 1798.

Heptonstall

The village, one of the main tourist centres in Calderdale, overlooks Hebden Bridge and **Hardcastle Crags**. This beautiful wooded valley is protected and cared for by the National Trust and, from the crags, there are several interesting walks along the purpose built footpaths.

Main Street, Haworth

Huddersfield

With its steep, often cobbled streets, millstone grit cottages and larger Victorian dwellings, Huddersfield has a very distinctive character all its own. The **Tolson Memorial Museum** has displays that range from the tools of the earliest settlers

Saltaire Mill

in the area to modern day collections contributed by local people. **Huddersfield Art Gallery** holds the Kirklees Collection of British Art covering the last 150 years. The town is also home to the **Huddersfield Broad Canal** and **Huddersfield Narrow Canal**, linking the town with Ashton-under-Lyne. Its centrepiece, the Standedge Tunnel, took 17 years to complete and is the longest, highest and deepest canal tunnel in the country.

Keighley

The centre of Keighley is dominated by impressive Victorian civic buildings. Outside the town centre is **Cliffe Castle** which, despite its deceptive name, is – in fact – a grand late-19th-century mansion complete with a tower, battlements and parkland. To the south of Keighley runs the line of the **Keighley and Worth Valley Railway** to Haworth and Oxenhope. This restored steam railway line passes through some

attractive small villages and some notable stations complete with vintage advertising signs, gas lighting and coal fires in the waiting rooms.

Saltaire

Saltaire is the model village created by Titus Salt for the workers at his mill. The Victoria Boat House was built in 1871 and has been beautifully restored, with an open fire, pianola and wind-up gramophone, all recreating a traditional parlour atmosphere where you can enjoy cream teas and attend special Victorian evenings in the dress of that time. The former Salt's Mill has been converted into the **1853 David Hockney Gallery** which displays the world's largest collection of paintings by the internationally acclaimed artist who was born in Bradford in 1937.

Scapegoat Hill

About a mile south of the oddly-named Scapegoat Hill the **Colne Valley Museum** is housed in three 19th-century weavers' cottages near the parish church. Visitors can see a loom chamber with working hand looms and a Spinning Jenny; a weavers' living room of 1850 and a gas-lit clogger's shop of 1910.

Shipley

Although Shipley town is mainly industrial, **Shipley Glen** is a very popular area for tourists. Within the grounds is a narrow gauge, cable hauled tramway, built in 1895, that carries passengers a quarter of a mile up the side of a steep hill, passing en route through Walker Wood, famous for its bluebells.

Todmorden

The magnificent **Town Hall** was designed by John Gibson and opened in 1875. One of the finest municipal buildings of its size in the country, the grand old building stands half in Yorkshire and half in Lancashire. So the ornate carving in the pediment represents the farming and iron trades of Yorkshire in the right panel; the cotton trade of Lancashire in the left.

1 The Aima Inn

Four Lane Ends, Sowerby Bridge,
West Yorkshire HX6 4NS
Tel: 01422 823334

Real Ales, Restaurant Menu, Accommodation,
No Smoking Area, Disabled Facilities

2 The Albert

Albert Street, Hebden Bridge,
West Yorkshire HX7 8AH
Tel: 01422 842417

Real Ales

3 The Bay Horse

Upper Town, Oxenhope, Keighley,
West Yorkshire BD22 9LN
Tel: 01535 642209

Real Ales, Bar Food, Restaurant Menu

4 The Beaumont Arms

Church Lane, Kirkheaton, Huddersfield,
Yorkshire HD5 0BH
Tel: 01484 517777

Real Ales, Bar Food, Restaurant Menu,
No Smoking Area

5 The Beehive Inn

Hob Lane, Ripponden, Sowerby Bridge,
West Yorkshire HX6 4LU
Tel: 01422 824670

Real Ales, Bar Food, Restaurant Menu,
No Smoking Area

6 Besom

Oldham Road, Sowerby Bridge,
West Yorkshire HX6 4EB
Tel: 01422 823018

7 Bird-In-The-Hand

Rochdale Road, Todmorden, Lancashire OL14 6UH
Tel: 01706 378145

Real Ales, Bar Food, Restaurant Menu

8 The Black Bull

Main Street, Haworth, Keighley,
West Yorkshire BD22 8DP
Tel: 01535 642249

Real Ales, Bar Food, Restaurant Menu,
Accommodation, No Smoking Area, Disabled Facilities

See panel on page 158

9 The Black Lion

Burnley Road, Luddendenfoot, Halifax,
West Yorkshire HX2 6AR
Tel: 01422 886964

Real Ales, Bar Food, Accommodation,
No Smoking Area

10 Blacksmiths Arms

106 Heaton Moor Road, Huddersfield,
Yorkshire HD5 0PH
Tel: 01484 422529

Real Ales, Bar Food, Restaurant Menu,
No Smoking Area

11 The Blue Ball Inn

Norland, Sowerby Bridge,
West Yorkshire HX6 3RQ
Tel: 01422 831490

Real Ales, Restaurant Menu, No Smoking Area

12 The Boarder Rose Inn

772 Rochdale Road, Todmorden,
Lancashire OL14 7UA
Tel: 01706 812142

Real Ales, Bar Food, Restaurant Menu,
No Smoking Area, Disabled Facilities

13 The Bottomley's Arms

Wade House Road, Halifax,
West Yorkshire HX3 7NU
Tel: 01274 678649

Real Ales, Bar Food, Restaurant Menu

14 The Bracken Arms

Bracken Bank Grove, Keighley,
West Yorkshire BD22 7BE
Tel: 01535 605366

8 The Black Bull

119 Main Street, Haworth,
West Yorkshire BD22 8DP
☎ 01535 642249
🌐 www.blackbullhaworth.co.uk

Real Ales, Bar Food, Restaurant Menu, Accommodation, No Smoking Area, Disabled Facilities

- 8½ miles northwest of Bradford off the A6033
- Deuchars IPA and 2 guest ales
- 12-6.30
- 3 en suite rooms
- Tuesday quiz night
- Parking, patio terrace, disabled access
- All major cards
- 11.30-11
- Brontë Parsonage Museum, Top Withins, Keighley and Worth Valley Railway, Saltaire

A small sample from the menu and specials board includes steak and ale pie made with prime Aberdeen Angus beef, wholetail Whitby scampi, roast of the day and local lamb. There are also all-days snacks such as tasty sandwiches and baguettes, roast beef, ploughman's, platters, and more.

This excellent inn will soon also offer brand new accommodation in the shape of three comfortable and attractive guest bedrooms, furnished and decorated with taste and style and providing guests with every modern amenity while maintaining a traditional feel in keeping with the rest of the inn. The Black Bull is ideally situated to make a perfect base from which to explore Haworth, the Moors and the many sights and attractions of the region.

Here in the lively and attractive village of Haworth with its wonderful antique and craft shops and, of course, sights and attractions associated with the Brontë sisters, The Black Bull is a superb 17th-century stonebuilt pub located at the very top of Haworth's famous Main Street. Owners Melanie Chantack and James Williams, together with their friendly, conscientious staff, offer all their guests a warm welcome and the best in food, drink and hospitality. Real ales are on tap to quench your thirst, together with a good selection of wines, soft drinks, spirits, lagers, cider and stout.

The food is a big draw here, as the inn's chefs create a range of tempting dishes at lunch and dinner, including hearty favourites and more creative dishes.

15 The Bridge Inn

Bradford Road, Keighley, West Yorkshire BD21 4EB
Tel: 01535 602300

Real Ales, Bar Food, Restaurant Menu,
No Smoking Area, Disabled Facilities

16 Bronte Hotel

Lees Lane, Haworth, Keighley,
West Yorkshire BD22 8RA
Tel: 01535 644112

Real Ales, Bar Food, Restaurant Menu,
Accommodation, No Smoking Area, Disabled Facilities

17 The Brown Horse Inn

Denholme Gate Road, Hipperholme, Halifax,
West Yorkshire HX3 8HX
Tel: 01422 202112

Real Ales, Bar Food, Restaurant Menu,
No Smoking Area, Disabled Facilities

18 Busfield Arms

Main Road, East Morton, Keighley,
West Yorkshire BD20 5SP
Tel: 01274 550931

Real Ales, Bar Food, Restaurant Menu

19 The Butchers Arms

Rochdale Road, Ripponden, Sowerby Bridge,
West Yorkshire HX6 4JU
Tel: 01422 823100

Real Ales, Bar Food, Restaurant Menu

20 C Bell

114 Main Street, Wilsden, Bradford,
West Yorkshire BD15 0AB
Tel: 01535 272551

Real Ales, Bar Food, Disabled Facilities

21 Catlith Well Inn

Lower Saltonstall, Halifax, West Yorkshire HX2 7TS
Tel: 01422 244841

Real Ales, Bar Food, Restaurant Menu,
No Smoking Area

22 The Cause Way Foot Inn

13 Causeway Foot, Ogden, Halifax,
West Yorkshire HX2 8XX
Tel: 01422 240052

Real Ales, Bar Food, Restaurant Menu,
No Smoking Area

23 The Church Stile Inn

Sowerby New Road, Sowerby, Sowerby Bridge,
West Yorkshire HX6 1JZ
Tel: 01422 831871

24 The Coach & Horses

1054 Manchester Road, Linthwaite, Huddersfield,
Yorkshire HD7 5QQ
Tel: 01484 842113

Real Ales, Disabled Facilities

25 The Colliers Arms

66 Park Road, Elland, West Yorkshire HX5 9HZ
Tel: 01422 372007

Real Ales, Bar Food, No Smoking Area,
Disabled Facilities

26 Commercial Inn

Swallow Lane, Golcar, Huddersfield,
Yorkshire HD7 4NB
Tel: 01484 652483

Real Ales

27 Copper Kettle

Brighouse Road, Denholme, Bradford,
West Yorkshire BD13 4HE
Tel: 01274 832482

Disabled Facilities

28 Country House Inn

Halifax Road, Hipperholme, Halifax,
West Yorkshire HX3 8HQ
Tel: 01422 202232

No Smoking Area

29 Cross Inn

46 Towngate, Heptonstall, Hebden Bridge,
West Yorkshire HX7 7NB
Tel: 01422 843833

Real Ales, Bar Food, No Smoking Area

30 Cross Roads Inn

Cross Roads, Keighley, West Yorkshire BD22 9BG
Tel: 01535 643047

Real Ales, Bar Food, Restaurant Menu,
No Smoking Area, Disabled Facilities

31 Crosskeys

649 Rochdale Road, Todmorden,
Lancashire OL14 6SX
Tel: 01706 815185

Real Ales, Bar Food, Restaurant Menu,
Accommodation, No Smoking Area

32 The Crossroads Inn

Wainstalls, Halifax, West Yorkshire HX2 7TB
Tel: 01422 245316

Real Ales, Bar Food, Restaurant Menu,
Accommodation, No Smoking Area

33 Delvers

Wainstalls Road, Halifax, West Yorkshire HX2 7TE
Tel: 01422 244863

Real Ales, Bar Food, Restaurant Menu, No Smoking Area

34 The Druids Arms

Thwaites Brow Road, Keighley,
West Yorkshire BD21 4SQ
Tel: 01535 607963

Real Ales

35 Duke Of York

Stainland Road, Stainland, Halifax,
West Yorkshire HX4 9HF
Tel: 01422 370217

Real Ales, Bar Food, No Smoking Area

36 The Duke Of York

West Street, Halifax, West Yorkshire HX3 7LN
Tel: 01422 202056

Real Ales, Bar Food, Restaurant Menu,
Accommodation, No Smoking Area, Disabled Facilities

37 The Duke Of York Inn

Old Allen Road, Thornton, Bradford,
West Yorkshire BD13 3RT
Tel: 01274 832462

Real Ales, Bar Food, Restaurant Menu,
No Smoking Area, Disabled Facilities

38 Dusty Miller Inn

2 Gilead Road, Huddersfield, Yorkshire HD3 4XH
Tel: 01484 651763

Real Ales, No Smoking Area

39 The Fenay Bridge Inn

Penistone Road, Fenay Bridge, Huddersfield,
Yorkshire HD8 0AS
Tel: 01484 609870

Bar Food, Restaurant Menu, No Smoking Area,
Disabled Facilities

40 The Fieldhead

219 Quarmby Road, Huddersfield,
Yorkshire HD3 4FB
Tel: 01484 654581

Real Ales

41 The Fishermans

Wagon Lane, Bingley, West Yorkshire BD16 1TS
Tel: 01274 561697

Real Ales, Bar Food, Restaurant Menu,
No Smoking Area, Disabled Facilities

42 Fleece Inn

Ripponden Bank, Barkisland, Halifax,
West Yorkshire HX4 0DJ
Tel: 01422 822598

Real Ales, Bar Food, Restaurant Menu,
Accommodation, No Smoking Area

43 The Fleece Inn

Daisy Street, Haworth, Keighley,
West Yorkshire BD22 8AD
Tel: 01535 642172

Real Ales, Bar Food, Restaurant Menu,
Accommodation, No Smoking Area, Disabled Facilities

44 The Fleece Inn

Cullingworth Gate, Cullingworth, Bradford,
West Yorkshire BD13 5DH
Tel: 01535 272439

Real Ales, Bar Food, Restaurant Menu,
No Smoking Area, Disabled Facilities

45 The Fox & Goose Inn

9 Heptonstall Road, Hebden Bridge,
West Yorkshire HX7 6AZ
Tel: 01422 842649

Real Ales, No Smoking Area

46 George Hotel

Station Road, Cullingworth, Bradford,
West Yorkshire BD13 5HN
Tel: 01535 272203

Bar Food, No Smoking Area, Disabled Facilities

47 The Glen

Gilstead Lane, Bingley, West Yorkshire BD16 3LN
Tel: 01274 563589

Bar Food, No Smoking Area

48 The Glen View Inn

853 Burnley Road, Todmorden,
Lancashire OL14 7EW
Tel: 01706 812796

Real Ales, Bar Food, No Smoking Area,
Disabled Facilities

49 The Golden Fleece Inn

1 Bradshaw Lane, Halifax, West Yorkshire HX2 9UZ
Tel: 01422 244350

50 The Golden Fleece Inn

126-128 Lane Ends, Oakworth, Keighley,
West Yorkshire BD22 7PR
Tel: 01535 642574

Real Ales

51 The Golden Fleece Inn

38 Long Lane, Harden, Bingley,
West Yorkshire BD16 1HP
Tel: 01535 273970

Real Ales, Bar Food, No Smoking Area

52 The Golden Fleece Inn

Lindley Road, Blackley, Elland,
West Yorkshire HX5 0TE
Tel: 01422 372704

Real Ales, Bar Food, No Smoking Area

53 The Golden Lion Hotel

Halifax Road, Ripponden, Sowerby Bridge,
West Yorkshire HX6 4BQ
Tel: 01422 822887

Real Ales, Accommodation

54 The Goose Inn Restaurant

24 Causeway Foot, Halifax,
West Yorkshire HX2 8YB
Tel: 01422 244542

Real Ales, Bar Food, Restaurant Menu,
No Smoking Area

55 The Griffin Inn

Stainland Road, Barkisland, Halifax,
West Yorkshire HX4 0AQ
Tel: 01422 823873

Real Ales, Restaurant Menu, No Smoking Area

56 The Grouse Inn

Harehills, Oldfield, Keighley,
West Yorkshire BD22 0RX
Tel: 01535 643073

Real Ales, Bar Food, Restaurant Menu,
Disabled Facilities

57 The Guide Inn

Keighley Road, Hainworth, Keighley,
West Yorkshire BD21 5QP
Tel: 01535 272138

Real Ales

58 The Halfway House Inn

45 Otley Road, Charlestown, Shipley,
West Yorkshire BD17 7PY
Tel: 01274 584610

Bar Food, Restaurant Menu, No Smoking Area

59 Hare & Hounds

Burnley Road, Todmorden, Lancashire OL14 8EA
Tel: 01706 818820

Real Ales, Bar Food, Restaurant Menu,
No Smoking Area, Disabled Facilities

60 The Hare & Hounds Inn
Wadsworth, Hebden Bridge,
West Yorkshire HX7 8TN
Tel: 01422 842671

Real Ales, Bar Food, Restaurant Menu,
Accommodation

61 Haworth Old Hall
Sun Street, Haworth, Keighley,
West Yorkshire BD22 8BP
Tel: 01535 642709

Real Ales, Bar Food, Restaurant Menu,
Accommodation, No Smoking Area, Disabled Facilities

62 The High Park
Bradley Road, Huddersfield, Yorkshire HD2 1PX
Tel: 01484 534226

Real Ales, Bar Food, Restaurant Menu,
No Smoking Area, Disabled Facilities

63 Highlander
New Hey Road, Huddersfield, Yorkshire HD3 3FJ
Tel: 01422 370711

Real Ales, Bar Food, Restaurant Menu

64 Hinchliffe Arms Free House
Cragg Vale, Hebden Bridge,
West Yorkshire HX7 5TA
Tel: 01422 883256

Real Ales, Bar Food, Restaurant Menu,
Accommodation, No Smoking Area, Disabled Facilities

65 The Hobbit Country Inn
Hob Lane, Ripponden, Sowerby Bridge,
West Yorkshire HX6 4LU
Tel: 01422 832202

Real Ales, Bar Food, Restaurant Menu,
Accommodation, No Smoking Area, Disabled Facilities

66 The Hollowmell Inn
249 Stainland Road, Holywell Green, Halifax,
West Yorkshire HX4 9AJ
Tel: 01422 374358

67 Holdsworth House Hotel
Holdsworth Road, Holmfield, Halifax,
West Yorkshire HX2 9TG
Tel: 01422 240024

Bar Food, Restaurant Menu, Accommodation,
No Smoking Area, Disabled Facilities

68 The Hole In The Wall
Hangingroyd Lane, Hebden Bridge,
West Yorkshire HX7 7DD
Tel: 01422 844059

Real Ales

69 Innings
16 Bradshaw Lane, Halifax,
West Yorkshire HX2 9XB
Tel: 01422 243735

Bar Food, Restaurant Menu, No Smoking Area

70 Jack O'Mitre
New Hey Road, Scammonden, Huddersfield,
Yorkshire HD3 3FJ
Tel: 01484 842604

Bar Food, Restaurant Menu, No Smoking Area

71 Junction Inn
4 Town Road, Huddersfield, Yorkshire HD5 0HW
Tel: 01484 544770

72 Junction Inn
1 Knowl Road, Golcar, Huddersfield,
Yorkshire HD7 4AN
Tel: 01484 652184

No Smoking Area, Disabled Facilities

73 The Junction Inn
Lane Side, Queensbury, Bradford,
West Yorkshire BD13 1NE
Tel: 01274 880278

Real Ales, Bar Food, Restaurant Menu,
No Smoking Area, Disabled Facilities

74 Kershaw House Inn
Luddenden Lane, Luddendenfoot, Halifax,
West Yorkshire HX2 6NW
Tel: 01422 882222

Real Ales, Bar Food, Restaurant Menu

75 Kings Arms

2 Church Street, Haworth, Keighley,
West Yorkshire BD22 8DR
Tel: 01535 647302

Real Ales, Bar Food, Restaurant Menu,
Accommodation, No Smoking Area

76 The Ling Bob

Ling Bob, Wilsden, Bradford,
West Yorkshire BD15 0JU
Tel: 01535 272201

Real Ales, Bar Food, No Smoking Area

77 Little John

Keldregate, Huddersfield, Yorkshire HD2 1TA
Tel: 01484 452424

Disabled Facilities

78 Lord Nelson Inn

High Street, Luddenden, Halifax,
West Yorkshire HX2 6PX
Tel: 01422 882176

Real Ales, Accommodation, No Smoking Area

79 Lower Royal George Inn

New Hey Road, Scammonden, Huddersfield,
Yorkshire HD3 3FW
Tel: 01484 842455

Real Ales, Bar Food, Restaurant Menu,
Accommodation, No Smoking Area, Disabled Facilities

80 Macmillans

Long Lane, Wheatley, Halifax,
West Yorkshire HX3 5AD
Tel: 01422 353950

Real Ales

81 The Malt Shovel Inn

Harden Beck, Harden, Bingley,
West Yorkshire BD16 1JQ
Tel: 01535 272357

Real Ales, Bar Food, No Smoking Area

82 Marriott Hollings Hall Hotel

Hollins Hill, Baildon, Shipley,
West Yorkshire BD17 7QW
Tel: 01274 530053

Real Ales, Bar Food, Restaurant Menu,
Accommodation, No Smoking Area

83 The Masons Arms

Bacup Road, Todmorden, Lancashire OL14 7PN
Tel: 01706 812180

Real Ales

84 Mayles Hotel

6-10 New Road, Hebden Bridge,
West Yorkshire HX7 8AD
Tel: 01422 845272

Real Ales, Restaurant Menu, Accommodation,
No Smoking Area, Disabled Facilities

85 The Maypole Inn

32-34 Warley Town, Halifax,
West Yorkshire HX2 7RZ
Tel: 01422 831106

Real Ales, Bar Food, Restaurant Menu,
No Smoking Area

86 Moor Valley Park Motel

Mill Lane, Hawksworth, Leeds, Yorkshire LS20 8PQ
Tel: 01943 876083

Accommodation, No Smoking Area, Disabled Facilities

87 Moorlands Inn

Keighley Road, Ogden, Halifax,
West Yorkshire HX2 8XD
Tel: 01422 248943

Real Ales, Bar Food, Restaurant Menu,
Accommodation, No Smoking Area

88 New Delight Inn

Jack Bridge, Blackshaw Head, Hebden Bridge,
Yorkshire HX7 7HT
Tel: 01422 846178

Real Ales, Bar Food, Restaurant Menu,
No Smoking Area

89 The New Inn
Bocking, Cross Roads, Keighley,
West Yorkshire BD22 9AP
Tel: 01535 643191

Disabled Facilities

90 The New Inn
Otley Road, Charlestown, Shipley,
West Yorkshire BD17 7JN
Tel: 01274 586530

Real Ales, Bar Food

91 The New Inn
33 Heath Hill Road, Halifax, West Yorkshire HX2 0UT
Tel: 01422 244801

Real Ales, Bar Food, No Smoking Area

92 The New Inn
Forest Hill Road, Holywell Green, Halifax,
West Yorkshire HX4 9LB
Tel: 01422 310937

Real Ales, Bar Food, Restaurant Menu, No Smoking Area

93 The New Inn
Keighley Road, Denholme, Bradford,
West Yorkshire BD13 4JT
Tel: 01274 833871

Real Ales, Disabled Facilities

94 The New Rock
Barkisland, Halifax, West Yorkshire HX4 0DE
Tel: 01422 823578

Bar Food, No Smoking Area, Disabled Facilities

95 The Nutclough House Hotel
Nutclough Mill, Hebden Bridge,
West Yorkshire HX7 8EZ
Tel: 01422 844361

Real Ales, Bar Food, Restaurant Menu

96 The Old Boar
Oldham Road, Rishworth, Sowerby Bridge,
West Yorkshire HX6 4QT
Tel: 01422 822291

Real Ales, Restaurant Menu, Accommodation,
No Smoking Area, Disabled Facilities

97 Old Brandy Wine
Station Road, Luddendenfoot, Halifax,
West Yorkshire HX2 6AD
Tel: 01422 886173

Real Ales, Bar Food, Restaurant Menu,
No Smoking Area

98 The Old Bridge Inn
Priest Lane, Ripponden, Sowerby Bridge,
West Yorkshire HX6 4DF
Tel: 01422 822595

Real Ales, Bar Food, Restaurant Menu,
No Smoking Area, Disabled Facilities

99 Old Golf House Hotel
New Hey Road, Outlane, Huddersfield,
Yorkshire HD3 3YP
Tel: 01422 379311

Bar Food, Restaurant Menu, Accommodation,
No Smoking Area

100 Old Packhorse Inn
High Moor Lane, Cleckheaton,
West Yorkshire BD19 6LW
Tel: 01274 873452

Real Ales, No Smoking Area, Disabled Facilities

101 The Old Pond Inn
Spout House Lane, Brighouse,
West Yorkshire HD6 2PL
Tel: 01484 712396

Real Ales, Disabled Facilities

102 Old Sun Hotel
79 West Lane, Haworth, Keighley,
West Yorkshire BD22 8EL
Tel: 01535 642780

Real Ales, Bar Food, Restaurant Menu,
Accommodation

103 The Old White Bear
Village Street, Norwood Green, Halifax,
West Yorkshire HX3 8QG
Tel: 01274 676645

Real Ales, Bar Food, Restaurant Menu, No Smoking Area

104 Old White Lion Hotel
West Lane, Haworth, Keighley,
West Yorkshire BD22 8DU
Tel: 01535 642313

Real Ales, Bar Food, Restaurant Menu,
Accommodation, No Smoking Area

105 The Oskwood Hall Hotel
Lady Lane, Bingley, West Yorkshire BD16 4AW
Tel: 01274 564123

Real Ales, Bar Food, Restaurant Menu,
Accommodation, No Smoking Area, Disabled Facilities

106 The Pack Horse Inn
Widdop, Hebden Bridge, West Yorkshire HX7 7AT
Tel: 01422 842803

Real Ales, Bar Food, Restaurant Menu,
Accommodation

107 The Pear Tree
Station Road, Norwood Green, Halifax,
West Yorkshire HX3 8QD
Tel: 01274 676036

Real Ales, Bar Food, Restaurant Menu, No Smoking Area

108 Pennine Manor Hotel
Nettleton Hill Road, Scapegoat Hill, Golcar,
Huddersfield HD7 4NH
Tel: 01484 642368

Bar Food, Restaurant Menu, Accommodation,
No Smoking Area, Disabled Facilities

109 Prince Of Orange Inn
Carr House Road, Halifax, West Yorkshire HX3 7RJ
Tel: 01274 679112

110 Prune Park Bar
Prune Park Lane, Allerton, Bradford,
West Yorkshire BD15 9BJ
Tel: 01274 483516

Real Ales, Bar Food, Restaurant Menu,
No Smoking Area, Disabled Facilities

111 Punch Bowl Hotel
635 Bradford Road, Brighouse,
West Yorkshire HD6 4DY
Tel: 01484 713718

112 The Quarry House Inn
Bingley Road, Lees Moor Road, Keighley,
West Yorkshire BD21 5QE
Tel: 01535 642239

Real Ales, Bar Food, Restaurant Menu

113 The Queen Victoria Inn
10 Victoria Place, Northowram, Halifax,
West Yorkshire HX3 7HY
Tel: 01422 202952

Real Ales

114 The Queens
Ripponden, Sowerby Bridge,
West Yorkshire HX6 4BQ
Tel: 01422 825634

115 The Radcliffe Arms
59 Westgate, Almondbury, Huddersfield,
Yorkshire HD5 8XF
Tel: 01484 300663

Real Ales

116 The Raggaids Country Inn
Brighouse & Denholme Road, Queensbury,
Bradford, West Yorkshire BD13 1NA
Tel: 01274 884421

Real Ales, Bar Food, Restaurant Menu,
No Smoking Area, Disabled Facilities

117 The Railway Hotel
12 New Road, Hebden Bridge,
West Yorkshire HX7 8AD
Tel: 01422 844088

Real Ales, No Smoking Area, Disabled Facilities

118 The Richardsons Arms
Bradford Road, Oakenshaw, Bradford, West
Yorkshire BD12 7EN
Tel: 01274 675722

Real Ales, Bar Food, No Smoking Area,
Disabled Facilities

119 Ring Of Bells
127 Westgate, Cleckheaton,
West Yorkshire BD19 5DR
Tel: 01274 873861

120 The Rising Sun
Leymoor Road, Golcar, Huddersfield,
Yorkshire HD7 4QF
Tel: 01484 659290

Bar Food, Restaurant Menu

121 Rising Sun Inn
27 Crosland Hill Road, Huddersfield,
Yorkshire HD4 5NZ
Tel: 01484 653636

Real Ales

122 The Rising Sun Inn
Scholes Lane, Scholes, Cleckheaton,
West Yorkshire BD19 6NR
Tel: 01274 874397

Real Ales, Bar Food, Restaurant Menu,
No Smoking Area, Disabled Facilities

123 Robin Hood Inn
Keighley Road, Pecket Well, Hebden Bridge,
West Yorkshire HX7 8QR
Tel: 01422 842593

Real Ales, Bar Food, Restaurant Menu,
Accommodation, No Smoking Area

124 Rock & Heifer Inn
Rock Lane, Thornton, Bradford,
West Yorkshire BD13 3RH
Tel: 01274 833490

Disabled Facilities

125 The Rock Inn Hotel
22 Broad Carr, Holywell Green, Halifax,
West Yorkshire HX4 9BS
Tel: 01422 379721

Bar Food, Restaurant Menu, Accommodation

126 Roebuck Inn
Burnley Road, Todmorden, Lancashire OL14 8PY
Tel: 01706 816179

Bar Food, Restaurant Menu, No Smoking Area,
Disabled Facilities

127 The Rose & Crown
43 Northgate, Almondbury, Huddersfield,
Yorkshire HD5 8RX
Tel: 01484 549090

Disabled Facilities

128 The Royal & Ancient
19 Dalton Bank Road, Huddersfield,
Yorkshire HD5 0RE
Tel: 01484 425461

Real Ales, Bar Food, Restaurant Menu, No Smoking Area

129 The Royal Oak
2 Mill Hey, Haworth, Keighley,
West Yorkshire BD22 8NQ
Tel: 01535 643257

Real Ales

130 The Royal Oak Inn
826 Manchester Road, Linthwaite, Huddersfield,
Yorkshire HD7 5QS
Tel: 01484 842469

Real Ales, Disabled Facilities

131 Royal Public House
Main Road, Denholme, Bradford,
West Yorkshire BD13 4DD
Tel: 01274 831622

Real Ales, No Smoking Area, Disabled Facilities

132 The Rushcart
Sowerby Green, Sowerby, Sowerby Bridge,
West Yorkshire HX6 1JJ
Tel: 01422 831956

Real Ales, Bar Food, No Smoking Area,
Disabled Facilities

133 The Sair Inn
139 Lane Top, Linthwaite, Huddersfield,
Yorkshire HD7 5SG
Tel: 01484 842370

Real Ales, No Smoking Area

134 The Salthorn
760 Cleckheaton Road, Oakenshaw, Bradford,
West Yorkshire BD12 7AE
Tel: 01274 691844

Real Ales, Disabled Facilities

135 Sands House Inn

Blackmoorfoot Road, Crosland Hill, Huddersfield,
Yorkshire HD4 7AF
Tel: 01484 654478

Real Ales, Bar Food, Restaurant Menu, No Smoking Area

136 Scapehouseinn

74 High Street, Golcar, Huddersfield,
Yorkshire HD7 4NJ
Tel: 01484 654144

Real Ales, Bar Food, Restaurant Menu,
No Smoking Area, Disabled Facilities

137 Shepherds Rest Inn

Lumbutts Road, Todmorden, Lancashire OL14 6JJ
Tel: 01706 813437

Real Ales, Bar Food, Restaurant Menu,
No Smoking Area, Disabled Facilities

138 Shibden Mill Inn

1 Shibden Mill Fold, Shibden, Halifax,
West Yorkshire HX3 7UL
Tel: 01422 365840

Real Ales, Bar Food, Restaurant Menu,
Accommodation, No Smoking Area, Disabled Facilities

139 Shoulder Of Mutton

Thwaites, Keighley, West Yorkshire BD21 4NG
Tel: 01535 608684

Real Ales

140 The Shoulder Of Mutton

Carr House Lane, Halifax, West Yorkshire HX3 7RB
Tel: 01274 679179

Real Ales, Bar Food, No Smoking Area

141 The Shoulder Of Mutton

30 Otley Road, Charlestown, Shipley,
West Yorkshire BD17 7QA
Tel: 01274 584071

Real Ales, Bar Food, No Smoking Area,
Disabled Facilities

142 Shoulder Of Mutton

Mutton Fold, Northowram, Halifax,
West Yorkshire HX3 7EA
Tel: 01422 206229

Real Ales, Bar Food, Restaurant Menu, No Smoking Area

143 Shoulder Of Mutton Inn

New Road, Mytholmroyd, Hebden Bridge,
West Yorkshire HX7 5DZ
Tel: 01422 883165

Real Ales, Bar Food, No Smoking Area

144 Shoulder Of Mutton Inn

Bridge Gate, Hebden Bridge,
West Yorkshire HX7 8EX
Tel: 01422 842585

Real Ales, Restaurant Menu

145 The Slip Inn

156a Longwood Gate, Longwood, Huddersfield,
Yorkshire HD3 4XF
Tel: 01484 654423

Real Ales, Disabled Facilities

146 The Snooty Fox

Colne Road, Oakworth, Keighley,
West Yorkshire BD22 7PB
Tel: 01535 642689

Real Ales

147 Spangled Bull Inn

10 Bankfield Lane, Huddersfield,
Yorkshire HD5 0JG
Tel: 01484 480204

Real Ales

148 Sportsmans Arms

Kebs Road, Todmorden, Lancashire OL14 8SB
Tel: 01706 813449

Real Ales, No Smoking Area, Disabled Facilities

149 Spotted Cow

New Hey Road, Huddersfield, Yorkshire HD3 4GP
Tel: 01484 651325

Bar Food

150 The Spring Rock Inn

Norland Road, Greetland, Halifax,
West Yorkshire HX4 8PT
Tel: 01422 377722

Real Ales, Bar Food, No Smoking Area

151 Stafford Arms

Scholes Lane, Scholes, Cleckheaton,
West Yorkshire BD19 6LS
Tel: 01274 873475

Real Ales, Bar Food, No Smoking Area,
Disabled Facilities

152 The Star

1 Penistone Road, Fenay Bridge, Huddersfield,
Yorkshire HD8 0AS
Tel: 01484 603448

Bar Food, Restaurant Menu, No Smoking Area

153 The Station Hotel

122 Harecroft, Wilsden, Bradford,
West Yorkshire BD15 0BP
Tel: 01535 272430

Real Ales

154 The Stocks Arms

22 Square, Northowram, Halifax,
West Yorkshire HX3 7HW
Tel: 01422 201099

155 Stubbing Wharf

King Street, Bridge, Hebden Bridge,
West Yorkshire HX7 6LU
Tel: 01422 844107

Real Ales, Bar Food, Restaurant Menu,
No Smoking Area, Disabled Facilities

156 Stump Cross Inn

Godley Lane, Halifax, West Yorkshire HX3 6XG
Tel: 01422 321066

Bar Food, Restaurant Menu, No Smoking Area

157 The Sun Inn

152-154 Wakefield Road, Lightcliffe, Halifax,
West Yorkshire HX3 8TH
Tel: 01422 202230

Real Ales, Bar Food, Restaurant Menu, No Smoking Area

158 Sun Inn

Bradford Old Road, Cottingly, Bingley,
West Yorkshire BD16 1SA
Tel: 01274 550981

Real Ales, Bar Food, Restaurant Menu,
No Smoking Area, Disabled Facilities

159 The Swan Inn

748 New Hey Road, Huddersfield, Yorkshire HD3 3YJ
Tel: 01422 379007

Real Ales, Bar Food, No Smoking Area

160 The Tandem

39 Wakefield Road, Tandem, Huddersfield,
Yorkshire HD5 0AN
Tel: 01484 304574

Real Ales

161 Top Brink Inn

Brink Top, Todmorden, Lancashire OL14 6JB
Tel: 01706 812696

Real Ales, Bar Food, Restaurant Menu,
No Smoking Area, Disabled Facilities

162 The Travellers Inn

Tanhouse Hill, Halifax, West Yorkshire HX3 8HN
Tel: 01422 202494

Real Ales, No Smoking Area, Disabled Facilities

163 Travellers Rest

252 Hopton Lane, Mirfield,
West Yorkshire WF14 8EJ
Tel: 01924 493898

Real Ales, Bar Food, No Smoking Area

164 Triangle Inn

Rochdale Road, Triangle, Sowerby Bridge,
West Yorkshire HX6 3NE
Tel: 01422 831512

Real Ales, No Smoking Area, Disabled Facilities

165 The Turkey Inn

Goose Eye, Oakworth, Keighley,
West Yorkshire BD22 0PD
Tel: 01535 681339

Real Ales, Bar Food, Restaurant Menu,
No Smoking Area

166 Turnpike Inn

Rishworth, Sowerby Bridge,
West Yorkshire HX6 4RH
Tel: 01422 822789

Real Ales, Bar Food, Restaurant Menu,
Accommodation, No Smoking Area, Disabled Facilities

167 The Villager
Peel Street, Wilsden, Bradford,
West Yorkshire BD15 0JE
Tel: 01535 275700

Real Ales

168 The Waggon & Horses Inn
Dyke Nook, Oxenhope, Keighley,
West Yorkshire BD22 9QE
Tel: 01535 643302

Real Ales, Bar Food, Accommodation, No Smoking Area

169 The Wagon & Horses
805 New Hey Road, Huddersfield, Yorkshire HD3 3YP
Tel: 01422 374764

Real Ales, Bar Food, Restaurant Menu,
No Smoking Area, Disabled Facilities

170 The Walkers Arms
Parkwood Road, Golcar, Huddersfield,
Yorkshire HD7 4QW
Tel: 01484 654300

Real Ales, Bar Food

171 Walkers Arms
Scholes Lane, Scholes, Cleckheaton,
West Yorkshire BD19 6NR
Tel: 01274 872346

Real Ales, Disabled Facilities

172 Wappy Spring Inn
Lindley Moor Road, Huddersfield, Yorkshire HD3 3TD
Tel: 01422 372324

Real Ales, Bar Food, Restaurant Menu, No Smoking Area

173 Weavers Restaurant & Bar
15 West Lane, Haworth, Keighley,
West Yorkshire BD22 8DU
Tel: 01535 643822

Bar Food, Restaurant Menu, Accommodation,
No Smoking Area

174 The White Horse Inn
Leeds Road, Halifax, West Yorkshire HX3 8SX
Tel: 01422 202343

Real Ales, Bar Food, Restaurant Menu, No Smoking Area

175 White Lion Hotel
Bridge Gate, Hebden Bridge,
West Yorkshire HX7 8EX
Tel: 01422 842197

Real Ales, Bar Food, Restaurant Menu,
Accommodation, No Smoking Area, Disabled Facilities

176 The Whitehall
Leeds Road, Halifax, West Yorkshire HX3 8NA
Tel: 01422 202088

Real Ales

177 Windmill Inn
17 Stanage Lane, Halifax, West Yorkshire HX3 7PR
Tel: 01274 679027

Bar Food, No Smoking Area

178 The Woodlands
Mill Carr Hill Road, Oakenshaw, Bradford,
West Yorkshire BD12 7EZ
Tel: 01274 676742

Real Ales, Bar Food, Restaurant Menu,
No Smoking Area

179 The Woodpecker Inn
Rochdale Road, Todmorden, Lancashire OL14 7NU
Tel: 01706 816088

Real Ales

180 The Woolpack
19 Westgate, Almondbury, Huddersfield,
Yorkshire HD5 8XF
Tel: 01484 435702

Real Ales, Restaurant Menu

181 The Yew Tree Inn
20 Northowram Green, Halifax,
West Yorkshire HX3 7JE
Tel: 01422 202316

Real Ales, Disabled Facilities

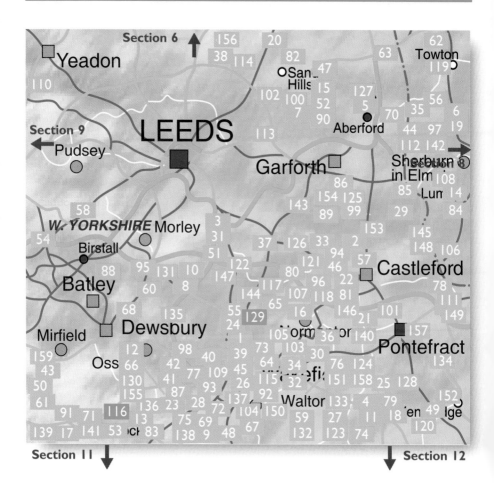

Section 6

Yeadon

156
20
82
63
62
Towton
119
38 114
47
102 100
San
Hills
15
127
52
5
90
70 35 56
7
6
97 19

Section 9
Pudsey

LEEDS
113
Aberford
44
112 142

Garforth
Sherburn
in Elm
108
85 Lum 14
86
154 125
143
89 99
29
84

W. YORKSHIRE Morley
58
54
3
31
51
37 126 33
2
153
145
148 106

Birstall
88
95 131 10
147
122
80
94
46 57
121
96 22
Castleford
88
60
8
144
117
107 118 81
78
111

68
135
55
129
65
16
146 21
101
149
Dewsbury
24
105 orm tor 140
157

Mirfield
12
98
40
39
73 103 30
76 124
Pontefract
134

159
43
50
Oss 66
130
42
41 77 109 45
26
64 34
115 32
151 158 25 128

61
155
87
93
137
92
Waltor
133 4 79
152

91 71 116
136 23 28 72
104 150
59
27
11
18 en 49 lge
120

139 17 141 53 cH 83
138 9 48 67
132 123 74

Section 11

Section 12

11	Pub or Inn Reference Number	- Detailed Information
12	Pub or Inn Reference Number	- Summary Entry
● ■	Place of interest mentioned in the chapter introduction	

SECTION 10

Aberford

To the southeast of this village lies an elegant Edwardian mansion **Lotherton Estate and Gardens**, providing a fascinating insight into life in the days before the First World War. The collections include superb 19th- and 20th-century decorative art as well as costume and Oriental art. Other attractions include the Edwardian formal gardens, a walled garden with some quirky spiral topiary, a bird garden with more than 200 species of rare and endangered birds, a 12th-century Chapel of Ease, deer park and café.

Birstall

This town is home to **Oakwell Hall**, an Elizabethan manor house that dates from 1583 and is one of England's most charming historic houses. Now set out as a 17th-century home, the panelled rooms contain a fine collection of oak furniture, reproduction soft furnishings and items of domestic life. The gardens contain period plants, including culinary and medicinal herbs.

Leeds

In recent years, the city of Leeds has seen something of a renaissance. The **Leeds City Art Gallery** showcases an exceptional collection of Victorian and French Post-Impressionist paintings along with major works by Courbet, Lowry, Sickert, Stanley Spencer and Bridget Riley. Linked to the gallery is the **Henry Moore Institute**, the first centre in Europe devoted to the display and study of sculpture of all periods. There's also a Craft & Design shop selling cards, jewellery and pottery, and an art library. The **Thackray Medical Museum**, one of the largest museums of its kind in Europe, possesses more than 25,000 extraordinary objects in its collection. Opened by Queen Elizabeth II in 1998, the **Royal Armouries** trace the development of arms and armour from the 5th century BC to modern times. A few miles north of Leeds city centre is one of the UK's most popular garden tourist attractions and home to the largest collection of tropical plants outside Kew Gardens – **Tropical World**. A couple of miles southwest of the city is **Temple Newsam House**, often referred to as the 'Hampton Court of the North'.

Civic Hall, Leeds

Normanton

A former mining town, Normanton has a spacious park, a moat round a hill where the Romans built a camp, and a large, mostly 15th-century church with a fine 500-year-old font. The stained glass windows here are something of an oddity since none of them originally belonged to the church. They were part of a collection amassed by a 19th-century resident of the town who was himself a glass painter and bequeathed the unrelated pieces to the church. The most striking is a 15th-century *Pietà* in the east window which has been identified as Flemish in origin.

Pontefract

The great shattered towers of **Pontefract Castle** stand on a crag to the east of the town. The town's most famous products, of course, are Pontefract Cakes. Liquorice root has been grown here since monastic times and there's even a small planting of liquorice in the local park. The town celebrates this unique heritage with the five-day **Pontefract Liquorice Fayre** in mid-August.

Wakefield

One of the oldest towns in Yorkshire, Wakefield stands on a hill guarding an important crossing of the River Calder. **Wakefield Cathedral** was begun in Norman times, rebuilt in 1329 and refashioned in 1470 when its magnificent 247-foot high spire – the highest in Yorkshire – was added. Just south of the city centre stands **Sandal Castle**, a 12th-century motte-and-bailey fortress that was

later replaced by a stone structure. It overlooks the site of the Battle of Wakefield in 1460.

A visit to the **National Coal Mining Museum for England** at Caphouse Colliery in Overton, a few miles southwest of Wakefield, includes a guided tour 450 feet underground. Over to the southeast, **Nostell Priory** is one of the most popular tourist venues in this area, and is not a priory as such but in fact a large Palladian building erected on the site of an old Augustinian priory, where Robert Adam, between 1766 and 1776, produced an incomparable sequence of interiors. The Priory also boasts the most comprehensive collection in the world of Chippendale's work.

Wintersett

Found on the historic estate of Walton Hall is the **Heronry and Waterton Countryside Discovery Centre**, which provides information and exhibitions about the surrounding country park.

Woolley

Newmillerdam Country Park and Boathouse was, in the 19th century, part of the Chevet Estate and a playground for the local Pilkington family. The boathouse, built in the 1820s, has been restored as a visitors' centre (open Sundays and Bank Holiday Mondays), while the rest of the 240-acre park offers ample opportunity for walking and viewing wildlife at close quarters. Just to the northwest lies Woolley Edge, from where there are wonderful views out across Emley Moor.

1 Aagrah Restaurant & Hotel

108 Barnsley Road, Wakefield,
West Yorkshire WF1 5NX
Tel: 01924 258725

Restaurant Menu, Accommodation, No Smoking Area,
Disabled Facilities

2 The Anchor Inn

Victoria Street, Allerton Bywater, Castleford,
West Yorkshire WF10 2DF
Tel: 01977 603119

3 Angel Inn

55 Wakefield Road, Rothwell, Leeds,
Yorkshire LS26 0SF
Tel: 01132 822202

Bar Food, Restaurant Menu, No Smoking Area,
Disabled Facilities

4 Angel Inn

Wakefield Road, Ackworth, Pontefract,
West Yorkshire WF7 7AB
Tel: 01977 611276

Real Ales, Bar Food, Restaurant Menu,
No Smoking Area, Disabled Facilities

5 The Arabian Horse Inn

Main Street North, Aberford, Leeds,
Yorkshire LS25 3AA
Tel: 01132 813312

Real Ales, Bar Food, Restaurant Menu,
Disabled Facilities

6 The Ash Tree

London Road, Barkston Ash, Tadcaster,
North Yorkshire LS24 9PP
Tel: 01937 557247

Real Ales, Bar Food, Restaurant Menu,
No Smoking Area, Disabled Facilities

7 Barley Corn Inn

68 Main Street, Scholes, Leeds, Yorkshire LS15 4DH
Tel: 01132 646956

Real Ales, Bar Food, No Smoking Area

8 Bay Horse

Bradford Road, East Ardsley, Wakefield,
West Yorkshire WF3 2HQ
Tel: 01924 825926

Bar Food, Restaurant Menu, No Smoking Area,
Disabled Facilities

9 Bay Horse

30 Stoney Lane, Chapelthorpe, Wakefield,
West Yorkshire WF4 3JN
Tel: 01924 256673

Disabled Facilities

10 Bedford Arms

54 Main Street, East Ardsley, Wakefield,
West Yorkshire WF3 2AT
Tel: 01924 823127

No Smoking Area

11 Beverley Arms

Doncaster Road, Ackworth, Pontefract,
West Yorkshire WF7 7BX
Tel: 01977 615945

Real Ales, Bar Food, Restaurant Menu,
No Smoking Area, Disabled Facilities

12 Bingley Arms

Bridge Road, Horbury, Wakefield,
West Yorkshire WF4 5NL
Tel: 01924 281331

Real Ales, Bar Food, Disabled Facilities

13 The Black Bull

21 Bar Lane, Midgley, Wakefield,
West Yorkshire WF4 4JJ
Tel: 01924 830260

Real Ales, Bar Food, Restaurant Menu,
No Smoking Area

14 Black Bull Inn

Low Street, South Milford, Leeds,
Yorkshire LS25 5AS
Tel: 01977 682591

Real Ales

15 The Black Swan
7 The Cross, Barwick in Elmet, Leeds,
Yorkshire LS15 4JP
Tel: 01132 813065

Real Ales, Bar Food, Restaurant Menu,
No Smoking Area

16 Black Swan Hotel
Castleford Road, Normanton,
West Yorkshire WF6 2DP
Tel: 01924 893294

Real Ales, No Smoking Area

17 Blacksmiths Arms
64 Wakefield Road, Grange Moor, Wakefield,
West Yorkshire WF4 4DS
Tel: 01924 848531

Real Ales, Bar Food, Restaurant Menu,
No Smoking Area, Disabled Facilities

18 The Boot & Shoe
Wakefield Road, Ackworth, Pontefract,
West Yorkshire WF7 7DF
Tel: 01977 610218

Real Ales, Disabled Facilities

19 Boot & Shoe Inn
Main Street, Barkston Ash, Tadcaster,
North Yorkshire LS24 9PR
Tel: 01937 557374

Real Ales, No Smoking Area

20 The Bracken Fox
Wetherby Road, Scarcroft, Leeds, Yorkshire LS14 3AT
Tel: 01132 896101

Real Ales, Restaurant Menu

21 The Bradley Arms
Cutsyke Road, Featherstone, Pontefract,
West Yorkshire WF7 6BD
Tel: 01977 792284

Real Ales

22 The Bridge Inn
Altofts Lane, Castleford, West Yorkshire WF10 5PZ
Tel: 01977 550498

Real Ales, Bar Food, Restaurant Menu,
Accommodation, No Smoking Area

23 The British Oak
Denby Dale Road, Calder Grove, Wakefield,
West Yorkshire WF4 3DL
Tel: 01924 275286

Real Ales, Bar Food, Restaurant Menu,
No Smoking Area, Disabled Facilities

24 British Oak Hotel
55 Aberford Road, Wakefield,
West Yorkshire WF1 4AW
Tel: 01924 374381

Bar Food, Restaurant Menu, No Smoking Area,
Disabled Facilities

25 Brown Cow
Pontefract Road, Ackworth, Pontefract,
West Yorkshire WF7 7EL
Tel: 01977 704735

Real Ales, Bar Food, Disabled Facilities

26 Castle Inn
343 Barnsley Road, Wakefield,
West Yorkshire WF2 6AS
Tel: 01924 229031

Real Ales, Bar Food, No Smoking Area,
Disabled Facilities

27 The Catchpenny
Lane Ends Close, Fitzwilliam, Pontefract,
West Yorkshire WF9 5NJ
Tel: 01977 611984

Real Ales, Bar Food, Restaurant Menu,
No Smoking Area

28 Cedar Court Hotel
Denby Dale Road, Calder Grove, Wakefield,
West Yorkshire WF4 3QZ
Tel: 01924 276310

Bar Food, Restaurant Menu, Accommodation,
No Smoking Area, Disabled Facilities

29 Chequers Inn
Claypit Lane, Ledsham, Leeds, Yorkshire LS25 5LP
Tel: 01977 683135

Real Ales, Bar Food, Restaurant Menu,
No Smoking Area

30 Clifton Properties

1 Whinney Lane, Streethouse, Pontefract,
West Yorkshire WF7 6BY
Tel: 01977 780403

Real Ales

31 Coach & Horses

71 Wakefield Road, Rothwell, Leeds,
Yorkshire LS26 0SF
Tel: 01132 821021

Real Ales, Bar Food, No Smoking Area,
Disabled Facilities

32 The Cock & Crown

570 Doncaster Road, Crofton, Wakefield,
West Yorkshire WF4 1PP
Tel: 01924 862344

Bar Food, Restaurant Menu, No Smoking Area,
Disabled Facilities

33 Commercial

12 Main Street, Methley, Leeds, Yorkshire LS26 9JE
Tel: 01977 553556

Real Ales, Bar Food, No Smoking Area,
Disabled Facilities

34 The Crofton Arms

Doncaster Road, Crofton, Wakefield,
West Yorkshire WF4 1RP
Tel: 01924 862391

Bar Food, Restaurant Menu, No Smoking Area,
Disabled Facilities

35 Crooked Billet Inn

Wakefield Road, Saxton, Tadcaster,
North Yorkshire LS24 9QN
Tel: 01937 557389

Real Ales, Bar Food, No Smoking Area,
Disabled Facilities

36 Cross Keys Hotel

New Road, Old Snydale, Pontefract,
West Yorkshire WF7 6HB
Tel: 01924 892238

Real Ales, Bar Food, No Smoking Area,
Disabled Facilities

37 Devere Oulton Hotel

Rothwell Lane, Oulton, Leeds, Yorkshire LS26 8HN
Tel: 01132 821000

Bar Food, Restaurant Menu, Accommodation,
No Smoking Area, Disabled Facilities

38 The Dexter

Wigton Lane, Leeds, Yorkshire LS17 8RZ
Tel: 01132 034991

Real Ales, Bar Food, Restaurant Menu,
No Smoking Area, Disabled Facilities

39 Duke Of York

93 Agbrigg Road, Wakefield, West Yorkshire WF1 5AP
Tel: 01924 255332

40 The Duke Wellington

220 Horbury Road, Wakefield,
West Yorkshire WF2 8RE
Tel: 01924 372640

Disabled Facilities

41 The Fleece Inn

High Street, Horbury, Wakefield,
West Yorkshire WF4 5LG
Tel: 01924 274293

Real Ales

42 The Fleece Inn

Spa Street, Ossett, West Yorkshire WF5 0HP
Tel: 01924 273685

Real Ales, Bar Food, Restaurant Menu,
No Smoking Area, Disabled Facilities

43 The Flower Pot

65 Calder Road, Mirfield,
West Yorkshire WF14 8NN
Tel: 01924 496939

Bar Food, Restaurant Menu, No Smoking Area

44 Foresters Arms

35 Kirkgate, Sherburn in Elmet, Leeds,
Yorkshire LS25 6BH
Tel: 01977 682629

45 Foresters Arms

187 Barnsley Road, Wakefield,
West Yorkshire WF1 5NU
Tel: 01924 250245

46 The Fourways Hotel

Methley Road, Castleford West Yorkshire WF10 1PW
Tel: 01977 554376

Real Ales, Bar Food, Restaurant Menu,
No Smoking Area, Disabled Facilities

47 The Fox & Grapes

York Road, Leeds, Yorkshire LS15 4NJ
Tel: 01133 935009

Real Ales, Bar Food, Restaurant Menu,
No Smoking Area, Disabled Facilities

48 The Fox & Hounds

672 Barnsley Road, Newmillerdam, Wakefield,
West Yorkshire WF2 6QQ
Tel: 01924 255474

Bar Food, Restaurant Menu, No Smoking Area

49 The Fox & Hounds

Pontefract Road, Thorpe Audlin, Pontefract,
West Yorkshire WF8 3EL
Tel: 01977 620082

Real Ales, Bar Food, Restaurant Menu,
No Smoking Area, Disabled Facilities

50 Freemasons Arms

Hopton Hall Lane, Mirfield,
West Yorkshire WF14 8EA
Tel: 01924 492093

Real Ales

51 Gardener'S Arms

383 Leeds Road, Lofthouse, Wakefield,
West Yorkshire WF3 3QE
Tel: 01924 872607

Real Ales, Bar Food, Restaurant Menu,
No Smoking Area, Disabled Facilities

52 Gascoigne Arms

2 Main Street, Barwick in Elmet, Leeds,
Yorkshire LS15 4JQ
Tel: 01132 812265

Bar Food, No Smoking Area

53 George & The Dragon

257 Barnsley Road, Flockton, Wakefield,
West Yorkshire WF4 4AL
Tel: 01924 840975

Real Ales, Bar Food, Restaurant Menu,
No Smoking Area, Disabled Facilities

54 The Golden Fleece

23 Whitehall Road East, Birkenshaw, Bradford,
West Yorkshire BD11 2EQ
Tel: 01274 651743

Real Ales

55 The Graziers Inn

116 Aberford Road, Stanley, Wakefield,
West Yorkshire WF3 4NN
Tel: 01924 200283

Bar Food

56 The Greyhound Inn

Main Street, Saxton, Tadcaster,
North Yorkshire LS24 9PY
Tel: 01937 557202

Real Ales, Bar Food, Restaurant Menu,
No Smoking Area, Disabled Facilities

57 Griffin Inn

Lock Lane, Castleford, West Yorkshire WF10 2LB
Tel: 01977 557551

Real Ales, Restaurant Menu

58 Guesthouse Tavern

Whitehall Road, Drighlington, Bradford,
West Yorkshire BD11 1NE
Tel: 01132 852561

Bar Food

59 Hammer & Anvil

91 Station Road, Ryhill, Wakefield,
West Yorkshire WF4 2BZ
Tel: 01226 722475

60 Hare & Hounds

Batley Road, Tingley, Wakefield,
West Yorkshire WF3 1DU
Tel: 01132 526030

Real Ales, Disabled Facilities

61 Hare & Hounds Inn

Liley Lane, Mirfield, West Yorkshire WF14 8EE
Tel: 01924 481021

Real Ales, Bar Food, No Smoking Area,
Disabled Facilities

62 The Hare & Hounds Inn

Manor Road, Stutton, Tadcaster,
North Yorkshire LS24 9BR
Tel: 01937 833164

Real Ales, Bar Food, Restaurant Menu,
No Smoking Area

63 Hazlewood Castle

Paradise Lane, Hazlewood, Tadcaster,
North Yorkshire LS24 9NJ
Tel: 01937 535353

Bar Food, Restaurant Menu, Accommodation,
No Smoking Area, Disabled Facilities

64 Horse & Groom Inn

Horse Race End, Heath, Wakefield,
West Yorkshire WF1 5SG
Tel: 01924 371110

Bar Food, Restaurant Menu, No Smoking Area,
Disabled Facilities

65 Horse & Jockey

47 Church Road, Normanton,
West Yorkshire WF6 2NU
Tel: 01924 892994

Real Ales, Bar Food, Restaurant Menu,
No Smoking Area

66 Horse & Jockey Inn

Bridge Road, Horbury, Wakefield,
West Yorkshire WF4 5PP
Tel: 01924 275141

Real Ales, Bar Food, No Smoking Area,
Disabled Facilities

67 Hotel St Pierre

733 Barnsley Road, Newmillerdam, Wakefield,
West Yorkshire WF2 6QG
Tel: 01924 255596

Bar Food, Restaurant Menu, Accommodation,
No Smoking Area, Disabled Facilities

68 Huntsman Inn

Chidswell Lane, Dewsbury,
West Yorkshire WF12 7SE
Tel: 01924 275700

Real Ales, Bar Food, No Smoking Area

69 The Jolly Miller

Hendal Lane, Wakefield, West Yorkshire WF2 7PB
Tel: 01924 254499

Real Ales, Bar Food, Disabled Facilities

70 Joseph's Well Tavern

Copley Lane, Aberford, Leeds, Yorkshire LS25 3ED
Tel: 01132 031861

Bar Food, No Smoking Area, Disabled Facilities

71 Kaye Arms

Wakefield Road, Grange Moor, Wakefield,
West Yorkshire WF4 4BG
Tel: 01924 848385

Real Ales, Bar Food, Restaurant Menu,
No Smoking Area

72 The Kettlethorpe

Deffer Road, Wakefield, West Yorkshire WF2 7HB
Tel: 01924 255997

Disabled Facilities

73 The Kings Arms

Heath, Wakefield, West Yorkshire WF1 5SL
Tel: 01924 377527

Real Ales, Bar Food, Restaurant Menu,
No Smoking Area, Disabled Facilities

74 Kinsley Hotel

Wakefield Road, Kinsley, Pontefract,
West Yorkshire WF9 5EH
Tel: 01977 617379

Real Ales

75 Lord Nelson Inn

163 High Street, Crigglestone, Wakefield,
West Yorkshire WF4 3EF
Tel: 01924 255680

Real Ales

76 Lord Of The Manor

Santingley Lane, New Crofton, Wakefield,
West Yorkshire WF4 1LG
Tel: 01924 864597

Real Ales, Disabled Facilities

77 Lupset

328 Horbury Road, Wakefield,
West Yorkshire WF2 8JF
Tel: 01924 373382

Bar Food, Restaurant Menu, No Smoking Area,
Disabled Facilities

78 Magnet Inn

Fishergate, Ferrybridge, Knottingley,
West Yorkshire WF11 8NB
Tel: 01977 674136

Real Ales, Accommodation

79 Mason Arms

Bell Lane, Ackworth, Pontefract,
West Yorkshire WF7 7JD
Tel: 01977 610488

Real Ales, Accommodation, No Smoking Area

80 The Mexborough Arms

Watergate, Methley, Leeds, Yorkshire LS26 9DQ
Tel: 01977 515319

Disabled Facilities

81 Mexborough Arms

Wood Lane, Whitwood, Castleford,
West Yorkshire WF10 5PJ
Tel: 01977 553162

Real Ales

82 The Mexborough Arms

Main Street, Thorner, Leeds, Yorkshire LS14 3DX
Tel: 01132 892316

Real Ales, Bar Food, No Smoking Area,
Disabled Facilities

83 Midgley Lodge Motel

Bar Lane, Midgley, Wakefield, West Yorkshire WF4 4JJ
Tel: 01924 830069

Real Ales, Accommodation, No Smoking Area,
Disabled Facilities

84 Milford Hall

Lumby Lane, South Milford, Leeds, Yorkshire LS25 5DA
Tel: 01977 685933

Real Ales, Bar Food, Restaurant Menu,
No Smoking Area, Disabled Facilities

85 Milford Lodge

Great North Road, Peckfield, Garforth,
Leeds LS25 5LQ
Tel: 01977 681800

Bar Food, Restaurant Menu, Accommodation,
No Smoking Area, Disabled Facilities

86 The Moorgate

Leeds Road, Kippax, Leeds, Yorkshire LS25 7EP
Tel: 01132 862884

Real Ales

87 Navigation Inn

Broad Cut Road, Calder Grove, Wakefield,
West Yorkshire WF4 3DS
Tel: 01924 274361

Real Ales, Bar Food, Restaurant Menu,
No Smoking Area, Disabled Facilities

88 Needless Inn

Scotchman Lane, Morley, Leeds, Yorkshire LS27 0NZ
Tel: 01924 472986

Real Ales, Bar Food, Restaurant Menu,
No Smoking Area

89 The New Inn

Berry Lane, Great Preston, Woodiesford,
Leeds LS26 8AX
Tel: 01132 871703

No Smoking Area

90 New Inn

Main Street, Barwick In Elmet, Leeds,
Yorkshire LS15 4JF
Tel: 01132 812289

Real Ales, Bar Food

91 The New Inn

2 Briestfield Road, Grange Moor, Wakefield,
West Yorkshire WF4 4DX
Tel: 01924 848523

Real Ales, Bar Food, Restaurant Menu

92 New Inn

144 Shay Lane, Walton, Wakefield,
West Yorkshire WF2 6LA
Tel: 01924 255447

Real Ales, Bar Food, Restaurant Menu, No Smoking
Area, Disabled Facilities

93 The New Inn

419 Denby Dale Road East, Durkar, Wakefield,
West Yorkshire WF4 3AX
Tel: 01924 255897

Real Ales, No Smoking Area

94 New Queen

Lower Mickletown, Methley, Leeds,
Yorkshire LS26 9AN
Tel: 01977 515382

Real Ales, Bar Food, Restaurant Menu,
Accommodation, No Smoking Area

95 The New Scarborough

Dewsbury Road, Tingley, Wakefield,
West Yorkshire WF3 1LH
Tel: 01132 534762

Real Ales, Bar Food, Disabled Facilities

96 The New Wheatsheaf

Altofts Lane, Castleford, West Yorkshire WF10 5PZ
Tel: 01977 553052

Bar Food, Restaurant Menu, No Smoking Area

97 Oddfellows Arms

40 Low Street, Sherburn in Elmet, Leeds,
Yorkshire LS25 6BA
Tel: 01977 682368

Bar Food, Accommodation, No Smoking Area,
Disabled Facilities

98 The Old Malt Shovel

270 Wakefield Road, Ossett,
West Yorkshire WF5 9AB
Tel: 01924 201561

99 Old Tree Inn

53 High Street, Kippax, Leeds, Yorkshire LS25 7AH
Tel: 01132 875790

Real Ales, Disabled Facilities

100 Orlando's At The Buffer

Rakehill Road, Scholes, Leeds, Yorkshire LS15 4AL
Tel: 01132 732455

Bar Food, Restaurant Menu, No Smoking Area,
Disabled Facilities

101 Parkside Hotel

Park Road, Pontefract, West Yorkshire WF8 4QD
Tel: 01977 709911

Real Ales, Bar Food, Restaurant Menu,
Accommodation, No Smoking Area, Disabled Facilities

102 Pendas Arms

Naburn Approach, Leeds, Yorkshire LS14 2DF
Tel: 01132 651648

Real Ales, Bar Food

103 Pineapple Inn

Wakefield Road, Warmfield, Wakefield,
West Yorkshire WF1 5TR
Tel: 01924 899998

Real Ales, Bar Food, Restaurant Menu,
No Smoking Area

104 The Pledwick Well Inn

434 Barnsley Road, Wakefield,
West Yorkshire WF2 6QE
Tel: 01924 255088

Real Ales, Bar Food, No Smoking Area

105 The Plough

45 Warmfield Lane, Warmfield, Wakefield,
West Yorkshire WF1 5TL
Tel: 01924 892007

Real Ales, Bar Food, Restaurant Menu,
Accommodation, No Smoking Area, Disabled Facilities

106 Plough Inn

Main Street, Burton Salmon, Leeds,
Yorkshire LS25 5JS
Tel: 01977 672422

Real Ales, Disabled Facilities

107 The Poplar Inn

Church Road, Normanton, West Yorkshire WF6 2QR
Tel: 01924 893416

Real Ales

108 Queen Of T'Owd Thatch
101 High Street, South Milford, Leeds,
Yorkshire LS25 5AQ
Tel: 01977 682367

Real Ales, Bar Food, No Smoking Area,
Disabled Facilities

109 Queens Arms
159 Denby Dale Road, Wakefield,
West Yorkshire WF2 8ED
Tel: 01924 202141

Bar Food, No Smoking Area, Disabled Facilities

110 The Queens Hotel
Apperley Lane, Bradford, West Yorkshire BD10 0NS
Tel: 01132 507829

Real Ales, Bar Food, Restaurant Menu,
No Smoking Area, Disabled Facilities

111 Railway Hotel
88 Pontefract Road, Knottingley,
West Yorkshire WF11 8RN
Tel: 01977 672707

Disabled Facilities

112 The Red Bear Hotel
4 Low Street, Sherburn in Elmet, Leeds,
Yorkshire LS25 6BG
Tel: 01977 683634

No Smoking Area

113 The Red Lion
Cross Gates Lane, Leeds, Yorkshire LS15 7PF
Tel: 01133 909779

Bar Food, Restaurant Menu, No Smoking Area,
Disabled Facilities

114 The Red Lion
60 Main Street, Shadwell, Leeds, Yorkshire LS17 8HH
Tel: 01132 737463

Real Ales, Bar Food, Restaurant Menu,
No Smoking Area

115 Redbeck Motel
Doncaster Road, Crofton, Wakefield,
West Yorkshire WF4 1RR
Tel: 01924 862730

Restaurant Menu, Accommodation, Disabled Facilities

116 The Reindeer Inn & Restaurant
Family run Free House
204 Old Road, Overton, Wakefield,
West Yorkshire WF4 4RL
☎ 01924 848374

Real Ales, Bar Food, Disabled Facilities

🚩	Off the A642 7 miles southwest of Wakefield
🍺	John Smiths Cask & Boddingtons Smooth
🍴	Tues 12-2.30; Weds-Sat 12-2.30 & 7-9.30; Sun 12-7; Traditional Sunday Lunch all day
🎵	Weds night quiz
⛱	Parking, disabled access, beer garden, patio
💳	All major cards
🕐	Mon 3-12; Tues-Sun 12-12
🏛	National Coal Mining Museum, Wakefield Cathedral, Harewood House, Yorkshire Sculpture Park Bretton

Good food is assured at The Reindeer Inn, which enjoys a well-earned reputation for its home-cooked, honest Yorkshire fare.

This stonebuilt 16th-century former coaching inn is well worth seeking out, having an attractive décor, comfortable seating and a warm and welcoming ambience.

116 The Reindeer Inn & Restaurant
Old Road, Overton, Wakefield,
West Yorkshire WF4 4RL
Tel: 01924 848374

Real Ales, Bar Food, Disabled Facilities

See panel above

117 The Rising Sun
Bottom Boat Road, Stanley, Wakefield,
West Yorkshire WF3 4AU
Tel: 01924 822297

Real Ales

118 Rising Sun Hotel
Whitwood Common Lane, Castleford,
West Yorkshire WF10 5PT
Tel: 01977 554766

Real Ales, Bar Food, Restaurant Menu, No Smoking Area

119 Rockingham Arms

Main Street, Towton, Tadcaster,
North Yorkshire LS24 9PB
Tel: 01937 832811

Bar Food, Restaurant Menu, No Smoking Area

120 Rogerthorpe Manor Hotel

Thorpe Lane, Badsworth, Pontefract,
West Yorkshire WF9 1AB
Tel: 01977 643839

Real Ales, Bar Food, Restaurant Menu,
Accommodation, No Smoking Area, Disabled Facilities

121 The Rose & Crown

24 Church Side, Methley, Leeds, Yorkshire LS26 9EE
Tel: 01977 668235

Real Ales, Bar Food, Restaurant Menu,
No Smoking Area, Disabled Facilities

122 Rose & Crown Hotel

253 Leeds Road, Lofthouse, Wakefield,
West Yorkshire WF3 3LW
Tel: 01924 870485

Real Ales, Bar Food, Restaurant Menu,
No Smoking Area

123 The Rovers Return

Wakefield Road, Fitzwilliam, Pontefract,
West Yorkshire WF9 5AJ
Tel: 01977 610203

Real Ales

124 Royal Oak

High Street, Crofton, Wakefield,
West Yorkshire WF4 1NF
Tel: 01924 863433

125 The Royal Oak

Cross Hills, Kippax, Leeds, Yorkshire LS25 7JP
Tel: 01132 862423

Real Ales, Bar Food, Restaurant Menu

126 The Royal Oak Inn

102 Leeds Road, Methley, Leeds, Yorkshire LS26 9EP
Tel: 01977 515576

Disabled Facilities

127 Royal Oak Inn

Main Street North, Aberford, Leeds,
Yorkshire LS25 3AH
Tel: 01132 813248

Real Ales, Bar Food, Restaurant Menu,
No Smoking Area

128 Rustic Arms

7 Long Lane, Ackworth, Pontefract,
West Yorkshire WF7 7EZ
Tel: 01977 794136

Real Ales, Bar Food, Restaurant Menu,
No Smoking Area, Disabled Facilities

129 **The Ship Inn**

186 Ferry Lane, Stanley, Wakefield,
West Yorkshire WF3 4LY
Tel: 01924 372420

Real Ales, Bar Food, Restaurant Menu,
No Smoking Area, Disabled Facilities

See panel on page 182

130 Ship Inn

201 Bridge Road, Horbury, Wakefield,
West Yorkshire WF4 5PR
Tel: 01924 272795

Bar Food, No Smoking Area

131 The Smithy

Westerton Road, Tingley, Wakefield,
West Yorkshire WF3 1PZ
Tel: 01132 532071

Real Ales

132 Sportsman Inn

124 Station Road, Ryhill, Wakefield,
West Yorkshire WF4 2BZ
Tel: 01226 722797

Real Ales, Bar Food, Restaurant Menu,
No Smoking Area, Disabled Facilities

133 The Spread Eagle

Doncaster Road, Wragby, Wakefield,
West Yorkshire WF4 1QX
Tel: 01977 616369

Real Ales, Bar Food, Restaurant Menu

129 The Ship Inn

Ferry Lane, Stanley, West Yorkshire WF3 4LY
☎ 01924 373420

Real Ales, Bar Food, Restaurant Menu, No Smoking
Area, Disabled Facilities

☛ Just off the A642, 2 miles northeast of
Wakefield

🍺 Courage Directors, Ruddles Best, Theakstons,
John Smiths Cask

🍴 Tues-Sat 12-2 & 5.30-8.30; Sun 12-3

� Parking, disabled access, beer garden, children's
play area

🚫 No smoking in restaurant and one lounge

🕐 11.30-11

🏛 Wakefield Cathedral, Sandal Castle, Nostell
Priory, National Coal Mining Museum

Adjacent to the Aire and Calder Navigation
Canal, with the marina just a few yards
away, The Ship Inn is a picturesque place dating
back to 1807 and justly popular with boaters,
walkers and everyone interested in excellent
food, drink and hospitality. Cosy and
comfortable, there's also a large and attractive
beer garden.

134 The Spread Eagle

Estcourt Road, Darrington, Pontefract,
West Yorkshire WF8 3AP
Tel: 01977 699698

Real Ales, Bar Food, Restaurant Menu,
No Smoking Area

135 The Star Inn

Batley Road, Kirkhamgate, Wakefield,
West Yorkshire WF2 0RZ
Tel: 01924 374431

Bar Food, Restaurant Menu, No Smoking Area,
Disabled Facilities

136 The Star Inn

211 Netherton Lane, Netherton, Wakefield,
West Yorkshire WF4 4HJ
Tel: 01924 274496

Real Ales

137 Star Inn

42 Standbridge Lane, Wakefield,
West Yorkshire WF2 7DY
Tel: 01924 255254

Real Ales, Bar Food, Restaurant Menu,
No Smoking Area

138 The Station

Cliff Road, Crigglestone, Wakefield,
West Yorkshire WF4 3EQ
Tel: 01924 259544

Real Ales, Bar Food, Restaurant Menu

139 Sun Inn

137 Highgate Lane, Lepton, Huddersfield,
Yorkshire HD8 0HJ
Tel: 01484 607506

Real Ales

140 Sun Inn

11 Ackton Lane, Featherstone, Pontefract,
West Yorkshire WF7 6AP
Tel: 01977 702055

Real Ales, Bar Food, Restaurant Menu,
No Smoking Area

141 The Sun Inn

62 Barnsley Road, Flockton, Wakefield,
West Yorkshire WF4 4DW
Tel: 01924 848437

Real Ales, Bar Food, Restaurant Menu,
No Smoking Area, Disabled Facilities

142 Swan At Sherburn

Low Street, Sherburn In Elmet, Leeds,
Yorkshire LS25 6BG
Tel: 01977 682235

Real Ales

143 Swillington Hotel

40 Wakefield Road, Swillington, Leeds,
Yorkshire LS26 8DJ
Tel: 01132 862410

No Smoking Area

144 Thatched House

434 Aberford Road, Stanley, Wakefield,
West Yorkshire WF3 4AA
Tel: 01924 823361

Real Ales, Bar Food, Restaurant Menu

145 Three Horse Shoes

Gauk Street, Fairburn, Knottingley,
West Yorkshire WF11 9JS
Tel: 01977 672543

Real Ales, Bar Food, Restaurant Menu,
Disabled Facilities

146 The Trading Post

Pioneer Way, Castleford, West Yorkshire WF10 5QG
Tel: 01977 519587

Real Ales, Bar Food, Restaurant Menu,
No Smoking Area

147 Waggon & Horses

156 Leeds Road, Lofthouse, Wakefield,
West Yorkshire WF3 3LR
Tel: 01924 824128

148 Waggon & Horses

Great North Road, Fairburn, Knottingley,
West Yorkshire WF11 9JY
Tel: 01977 675459

Real Ales, Bar Food, No Smoking Area

149 The Wallbottle

50 Hazel Road, Knottingley,
West Yorkshire WF11 0QG
Tel: 01977 673117

No Smoking Area, Disabled Facilities

150 Waterton Park Hotel

The Balk, Walton, Wakefield,
West Yorkshire WF2 6PW
Tel: 01924 257911

Bar Food, Restaurant Menu, Accommodation,
No Smoking Area, Disabled Facilities

151 Weavers Green

Slack Lane, Crofton, Wakefield,
West Yorkshire WF4 1HE
Tel: 01924 860243

152 Wentbridge House Hotel

Wentbridge, Pontefract, West Yorkshire WF8 3JJ
Tel: 01977 620444

Real Ales, Bar Food, Restaurant Menu,
Accommodation, No Smoking Area

153 The White Horse

30 Main Street, Allerton Bywater, Castleford,
West Yorkshire WF10 2DL
Tel: 01977 553069

Real Ales, Bar Food, Restaurant Menu,
No Smoking Area

154 The White Swan

15 Cross Hills, Kippax, Leeds, Yorkshire LS25 7JP
Tel: 01132 862052

Real Ales

155 White Swan Hotel

93 New Road, Middlestown, Wakefield,
West Yorkshire WF4 4NS
Tel: 01924 262015

Real Ales, Bar Food

156 Wike Ridge Inn

Wike Ridge Lane, Wike, Leeds, Yorkshire LS17 9JW
Tel: 01132 886000

Bar Food, Restaurant Menu, No Smoking Area

157 The Willow Park Hotel

Baghill Lane, Pontefract, West Yorkshire WF8 2HB
Tel: 01977 796537

Real Ales

158 The Windmill Inn

733 Doncaster Road, Crofton, Wakefield,
West Yorkshire WF4 1PX
Tel: 01924 860971

Real Ales, Accommodation, No Smoking Area

159 The Yorkshire Volunteer

36 Calder Road, Mirfield, West Yorkshire WF14 8PJ
Tel: 01924 496862

Real Ales

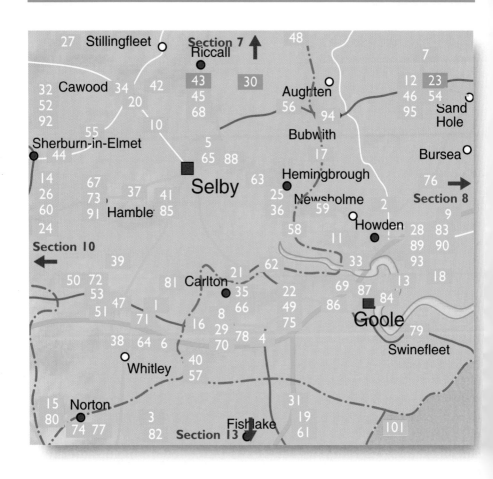

27 Stillingfleet
Riccall
Section 7
48
7
32 Cawood 34 42
43 30
Aughten
12 23
46 54
52 20
45
56
95 Sand
92
68
94
Hole
55
10
Bubwith
Sherburn-in-Elmet
5
17
Bursea
44
65 88
76
14 67
Selby 63
Hemingbrough
Section 8
26 73 37 41
25
Newsholme
9
60 91 Hamble 85
36
59 2
24
58
Howden
28 83
Section 10
11
89 90
39
33
93
50 72 53
21 62
13 18
81 Carlton
69 87 84
51 47 1
35
22
86
71
8 66
49 75
Goole 79
38 64 6
16
29 78 4
70
Swinefleet
Whitley
40
57
15 Norton
31
80
3
19
101
74 77
82 Section 13
Fishlake 61

Section 10
Section 13
Goole

11 Pub or Inn Reference Number - Detailed Information
12 Pub or Inn Reference Number - Summary Entry
● ■ Place of interest mentioned in the chapter introduction

SECTION 11

Carlton

A mile or so south of Camblesforth, off the A1041, is **Carlton Towers**, a stately home that should on no account be missed. This extraordinary building, 'something between the Houses of Parliament and St Pancras Station', was created in the 1870s by two young English eccentrics, Henry, 9th Lord Beaumont, and Edward Welby Pugin, son of the eminent Victorian architect, AG Pugin.

Fishlake

Set along the banks of the River Don, which is known here as the Dutch River, Fishlake is effectively an island since it is surrounded by rivers and canals and can only be entered by crossing a bridge. It's a charming village with a striking medieval church famous for its elaborately carved Norman doorway, an ancient windmill and a welcoming traditional inn.

Goole

Britain's most inland port, some 50 miles from the sea, Goole lies at the hub of a waterways network that includes the River Ouse, the River Don (known here as the Dutch River), the River Aire and the Aire & Calder Navigation. The **Waterways Museum**, located on the dockside, tells the story of Goole's development as a canal terminus and also as a port connecting to the North Sea. The museum displays model ships and many photographs dating from 1905 to the present day, and visitors can explore an original Humber Keel, *Sobriety*,

and watch crafts people at work. There are also occasional short boat trips available.

Hemingbrough

Anyone interested in remarkable churches should seek out **St Mary's Church** at Hemingbrough. Built in a pale rose-coloured brick, it has an extraordinarily lofty and elegant spire soaring 190 feet high and, inside, what is believed to be Britain's oldest misericord, dating back to around AD 1200.

Howden

Despite the fact that its chancel collapsed in 1696 and has not been used for worship ever since, **Howden Minster** is still one of the largest parish churches in East Yorkshire and also one of its most impressive, cathedral-like in size. From the top of its soaring tower, 135 feet high, there are wonderful views of the surrounding countryside – but it's not for the faint-hearted. The ruined chapter house, lavishly decorated with a wealth of carved mouldings, has been described as one of the most exquisite small buildings in England. Howden town is a pleasing jumble of narrow, flagged and setted streets with a picturesque stone and brick Market Hall in the marketplace. The celebrated aircraft designer Barnes Wallis knew Howden well: he lived here while working on the R100 airship which was built at Hedon airfield nearby. It made its maiden flight in 1929 and successfully crossed the Atlantic. At the nearby Breighton Aerodrome is the **Real Aeroplane Museum**, which illustrates the history of flight through the work of Yorkshire aviation pioneers.

Norton

This sizeable village is located close to the borders with North and West Yorkshire and was once busy with farming, mining and quarrying. Nowadays it's a peaceful place, with an ancient parish church whose splendid 14th-century west tower is considered by many to be the finest in Yorkshire.

Riccall

Riccall is popular with walkers: from the village you can either go southwards alongside the River Ouse to Selby, or strike northwards towards Bishopthorpe on the outskirts of York following the track of the dismantled York to Selby railway. This latter path is part of the 150-mile-long Trans Pennine Trail linking Liverpool and Hull.

Skipwith Common Nature Reserve is 500 acres of lowland heath and one of the last such areas remaining in the north of England. Of national importance, its principal interest is the variety of insect and birdlife, but the reserve also contains a number of ancient burial sites.

Selby

Selby Abbey was built with a lovely cream-coloured stone, and is a sublime sight. Devotees of railway history will also want to pay their respects to Selby's old railway station. Built at the incredibly early date of 1834, it is the oldest surviving station in Britain. From Selby the railway track runs straight as a ruler for 18 miles to Hull – the longest such stretch in Britain.

Sherburn-in-Elmet

This attractive village was once the capital of the Celtic Kingdom of Elmete. Well worth visiting is **All Saints' Church** which stands on a hill to the west and dates from about 1120. Its great glory is the nave with its mighty Norman pillars and arcades. A curiosity here is a 15th-century Janus cross which was discovered in the churchyard during the 1770s. The vicar and churchwarden of the time both claimed it as their own. Unable to resolve their dispute, they had the cross sawn in half: the two beautifully carved segments are displayed on opposite sides of the south aisle.

1 Anchor Inn
Main Street, Hensall, Goole,
North Humberside DN14 0QZ
Tel: 01977 663026

Real Ales, Bar Food, Restaurant Menu,
No Smoking Area

2 Barnes Wallis
Station Road, North Howden, Goole,
North Humberside DN14 7LF
Tel: 01430 430639

Real Ales, Bar Food, Restaurant Menu,
No Smoking Area, Disabled Facilities

3 The Baxter Arms
Fenwick Lane, Fenwick, Doncaster,
 South Yorkshire DN6 0EZ
Tel: 01302 702671

Bar Food, No Smoking Area

4 The Bay Horse
Snaith Road, East Cowick, Goole,
North Humberside DN14 9DA
Tel: 01405 869467

Accommodation, Disabled Facilities

5 Bay Horse Inn
York Road, Barlby, Selby, North Yorkshire YO8 5JH
Tel: 01757 703878

Real Ales

6 Bay Horse Inn
Great Heck, Goole, North Humberside DN14 0BE
Tel: 01977 661125

Real Ales, Bar Food, Restaurant Menu,
No Smoking Area, Disabled Facilities

7 The Black Horse
South End, Seaton Ross, York, Yorkshire YO42 4LZ
Tel: 01759 318481

Real Ales, Bar Food, Restaurant Menu

8 Black Lion Inn
Selby Road, Snaith, Goole,
North Humberside DN14 9HT
Tel: 01405 861144

Real Ales

9 The Black Swan
High Street, Eastrington, Goole,
North Humberside DN14 7PR
Tel: 01430 410339

Real Ales

10 The Black Swan
Church Hill, Wistow, Selby, North Yorkshire YO8 3UU
Tel: 01757 268305

Real Ales

11 The Black Swan
Asselby, Goole, North Humberside DN14 7HE
Tel: 01757 630409

Real Ales, Bar Food, Restaurant Menu,
No Smoking Area, Disabled Facilities

12 Blacksmiths Arms
79 High Street, Holme-on-spalding-Moor, York,
Yorkshire YO43 4AA
Tel: 01430 860668

Real Ales

13 The Blacksmiths Arms
High Street, Hook, Goole,
North Humberside DN14 5NY
Tel: 01405 763482

Real Ales, Bar Food, Restaurant Menu,
Accommodation, No Smoking Area, Disabled Facilities

14 The Blue Bell Inn
86 Main Street, Monk Fryston, Leeds,
Yorkshire LS25 5DU
Tel: 01977 683236

Real Ales

15 Blue Bell Inn
Great North Road, Wentbridge, Pontefract,
West Yorkshire WF8 3JF
Tel: 01977 620697

Real Ales, Bar Food, Restaurant Menu

16 The Boot & Shoe Inn
Main Street, Gowdall, Goole,
North Humberside DN14 0AL
Tel: 01405 862787

No Smoking Area

17 The Breighton Ferry

Breighton, Selby, North Yorkshire YO8 6DH
Tel: 01757 288407

Real Ales, Bar Food, No Smoking Area,
Disabled Facilities

18 Bricklayers Arms

Front Street, Laxton, Goole, North Humberside
DN14 7TS
Tel: 01430 430111

Real Ales, Bar Food, Restaurant Menu,
Accommodation, Disabled Facilities

19 The Buffalo

Marshland Road, Moorends, Doncaster,
South Yorkshire DN8 4SY
Tel: 01405 816355

No Smoking Area, Disabled Facilities

20 Castle Inn

7 Wistowgate, Cawood, Selby,
North Yorkshire YO8 3SH
Tel: 01757 268324

Real Ales, Bar Food, Restaurant Menu,
No Smoking Area, Disabled Facilities

21 The Comus Inn

Selby Road, Camblesforth, Selby,
North Yorkshire YO8 8HR
Tel: 01757 618234

Real Ales, Bar Food, Disabled Facilities

22 Creykes Arms Hotel

50 High Street, Rawcliffe, Goole,
North Humberside DN14 8QW
Tel: 01405 839707

No Smoking Area, Disabled Facilities

23 The Cross Keys

80 Moor End, Holme-on-spalding-Moor, York,
Yorkshire YO43 4DR
Tel: 01430 860342

Real Ales, Bar Food, Restaurant Menu

See panel below

24 Cross Keys Inn

The Square, Hillam, Leeds, Yorkshire LS25 5HE
Tel: 01977 683840

Real Ales, Bar Food, Restaurant Menu,
No Smoking Area, Disabled Facilities

---

23 The Cross Keys

80 Moor End, Holme on Spalding Moor, East
Yorkshire YO43 4DR
☎ 01430 860342

Real Ales, Bar Food, Restaurant Menu

- On the A614 towards Goole
- John Smiths Cask
- 12-6 then seasonal opening
- Quiz every other Thursday night, live music Saturday nights
- Parking, patio, conservatory restaurant
- All major cards
- 12-00.30
- Howden Minster, Wressle Castle, Blacktoft Sands RSPB Reserve, Londesborough Park, the Wolds Way

The Cross Keys is a spacious and charming pub with good food and drink and a welcoming ambience. This pleasant village pub with a view of Capability Brown landscaping is well worth seeking out. The food here is very good, much of it home-made, with hearty and tasty favourites such as steak and ale pie. Owned and personally run by Hayley and Gary Walker, who offer all their guests genuine hospitality and a high standard of service, it makes an excellent place to stop off for a relaxing drink or meal while exploring the sights and attractions of this part of Yorkshire.

25 The Crown Inn
Main Street, Hemingbrough, Selby,
North Yorkshire YO8 6QE
Tel: 01757 638434

Real Ales, Bar Food

26 Crown Inn
75 Main Street, Monk Fryston, Leeds,
Yorkshire LS25 5DU
Tel: 01977 682468

Real Ales, Bar Food, Restaurant Menu,
No Smoking Area, Disabled Facilities

27 The Crown Inn
Bolton Percy, York, Yorkshire YO23 7AG
Tel: 01904 744255

Real Ales, Bar Food, Restaurant Menu,
No Smoking Area, Disabled Facilities

28 David Donoghue
1-2 Corn Market Hill, Howden, Goole,
North Humberside DN14 7BU
Tel: 01430 430447

Real Ales, Accommodation, No Smoking Area,
Disabled Facilities

29 The Downs Arms
15 Market Place, Snaith, Goole,
North Humberside DN14 9HE
Tel: 01405 860544

Real Ales, Bar Food, No Smoking Area,
Disabled Facilities

30 The Drovers Arms
Skipwith, Selby, North Yorkshire YO8 5SF
Tel: 01757 288433

Real Ales, Bar Food, Restaurant Menu,
No Smoking Area, Disabled Facilities

See panel on page 190

31 The Dutchman
Goole Road, Moorends, Doncaster,
South Yorkshire DN8 4JY
Tel: 01405 812668

Disabled Facilities

32 Fenton Flyer
Main Street, Church Fenton, Tadcaster,
North Yorkshire LS24 9RF
Tel: 01937 557009

Real Ales, Bar Food, Restaurant Menu,
No Smoking Area

33 Ferry Boat Inn
Boothferry Road, Howden, Goole,
North Humberside DN14 7ED
Tel: 01430 430300

Bar Food, Restaurant Menu, No Smoking Area,
Disabled Facilities

34 Ferry Inn
2 King Street, Cawood, Selby,
North Yorkshire YO8 3TL
Tel: 01757 268515

Real Ales, Bar Food, Restaurant Menu,
Accommodation, No Smoking Area, Disabled Facilities

35 The Foresters Arms
High Street, Carlton, Goole,
North Humberside DN14 9LY
Tel: 01405 860315

Accommodation

36 Fox & Pheasant
Main Street, Hemingbrough, Selby,
North Yorkshire YO8 6QE
Tel: 01757 638327

Real Ales, Disabled Facilities

37 Fox Inn
Leeds Road, Thorpe Willoughby, Selby,
North Yorkshire YO8 9LX
Tel: 01757 704273

Real Ales, Bar Food, Restaurant Menu,
No Smoking Area

38 The George & Dragon
Doncaster Road, Whitley, Goole,
North Humberside DN14 0HY
Tel: 01977 661319

Real Ales, Bar Food, Disabled Facilities

30 The Drovers Arms

Skipwith, Selby, North Yorkshire YO8 5SF
☎ 01757 288433

Real Ales, Bar Food, Restaurant Menu, No Smoking Area, Disabled Facilities

- Off the A163 east of Selby
- Spitfire, Black Sheep
- 12-2.30 & 6-9
- Quiz night Friday, annual Burns night, barbecue in summer
- Parking, disabled access, beer gardens
- All major cards
- No smoking in restaurant
- 11.30-11
- Skipwith Common Nature Reserve, Selby Abbey, Yorkshire Air Museum (Elvington), Tadcaster

Dating back to the 19th century, The Drovers Arms is an impressive brickbuilt inn in the heart of the charming and stylish village of Skipwith near Selby. Spacious and attractive, the inn's decor is traditional without sacrificing comfort, pristine and welcoming. There is a varied selection of real ales, a good wine list and a choice of lagers, spirits and soft drinks, together with cider and stout on tap.

All the food is home-cooked, with an impressive range of dishes from the menu and specials board that include steak and ale pie, venison sausages, crispy fried duck, stuffed

peppers and other hearty favourites, all expertly prepared and presented. The owners are Daniel and Catherine, who have been here since late 2004 and bring a great deal of enthusiasm and zeal, offering all their guests a warm welcome. They and their friendly, efficient staff offer all their guests a high standard of service and quality.

The ambience is always relaxed, and the pub makes a good place to stop and enjoy a quiet drink or meal while exploring this part of Yorkshire, which boasts such sights and attractions as York, Selby, Tadcaster and the Vale of York. Part of the Trans Pennine Trail linking the west coast at Liverpool with Hull on the east coast runs nearby. The Yorkshire Wildlife Trust maintain the Skipwith Common Nature Reserve, some 500 acres of lowland heath that is one of the last such areas remaining in the north of England. Regarded as nationally important, the principal interest here is the variety of birdlife. The reserve also contains a number of ancient burial sites.

43 The Greyhound

Riccall, North Yorkshire YO19 6TE
☎ 01757 249101

Real Ales, Restaurant Menu, No Smoking Area,
Disabled Facilities

- ☛ 4 miles north of Selby off the A19
- ♙ Taylors Landlord, John Smiths Cask, Black Sheep, guest ales
- ⍸ Sunday carvery 12-2
- ♫ Live music monthly on a Saturday night, Sunday quiz night
- ⚒ Parking, beer gardens, disabled access, small function room
- ✎ All major cards
- ⊘ No smoking at the bar or food areas
- ⏲ Mon-Thurs 12-3 & 5.30-11, Fri & Sat 12-11, Sun 12-10.30
- 🏛 River Ouse walking, Trans Pennine Trail, Skipwith Common Nature Reserve, Selby

The Greyhound is a pristine and welcoming pub in the heart of the ancient village of Riccall. This convivial village pub dates back to the 1800s and offers quality ales together with a good range of lagers, cider, stout, wines, spirits and soft drinks. Relaxed and warm, the ambience is always a draw here, making the inn popular with locals and visitors alike – many of whom are in the region to enjoy the excellent walking and many sights and attractions of Selby, York and the surrounding area. The Sunday carvery is justly popular with several roasts and all the trimmings. Owners Bob, Christine and Anne and their efficient, friendly staff offer all their guests a warm welcome.

39 The George & Dragon

Main Street, West Haddlesey, Selby,
North Yorkshire YO8 8QA
Tel: 01757 228198

Real Ales, Bar Food, Restaurant Menu,
No Smoking Area

40 George & Dragon Inn

Main Street, Pollington, Goole,
North Humberside DN14 0DN
Tel: 01405 862668

Real Ales, Bar Food, No Smoking Area,
Disabled Facilities

41 The Grey Horse

Doncaster Road, Brayton, Selby,
North Yorkshire YO8 9HD
Tel: 01757 702719

42 The Grey Horse

Main Street, Kelfield, York, Yorkshire YO19 6RG
Tel: 01757 248339

Bar Food, Restaurant Menu

43 The Greyhound

82 Main Street, Riccall, York, Yorkshire YO19 6TE
Tel: 01757 249101

Real Ales, Restaurant Menu, No Smoking Area,
Disabled Facilities

See panel above

44 Half Moon Inn

Bishopdyke Road, Sherburn In Elmet, Leeds,
Yorkshire LS25 6JG
Tel: 01977 689797

Bar Food, Restaurant Menu, No Smoking Area,
Disabled Facilities

45 Hare & Hounds

8 Silver Street, Riccall, York, Yorkshire YO19 6PA
Tel: 01757 248255

Real Ales, Bar Food

46 Hare & Hounds Inn

57 High Street, Holme-on-spalding-Moor, York,
Yorkshire YO43 4EN
Tel: 01430 860445

Real Ales, Accommodation

47 Horse & Jockey Hotel
Weeland Road, Eggborough, Goole,
North Humberside DN14 0RX
Tel: 01977 661295

Bar Food, Restaurant Menu, Accommodation,
No Smoking Area, Disabled Facilities

48 Jefferson Arms
Main Street, Thorganby, York, Yorkshire YO19 6DB
Tel: 01904 448316

Real Ales, Bar Food, Restaurant Menu,
No Smoking Area, Disabled Facilities

49 Jemmy Hirst At The Rose & Crown
26 Riverside, Rawcliffe, Goole,
North Humberside DN14 8RN
Tel: 01405 831038

Real Ales

50 The Jenny Wren
Main Street, Beal, Goole,
North Humberside DN14 0SS
Tel: 01977 673487

Real Ales, Bar Food, Restaurant Menu,
No Smoking Area, Disabled Facilities

51 Jolly Miller
Kellington Lane, Eggborough, Goole,
North Humberside DN14 0LB
Tel: 01977 661348

Real Ales, Bar Food, Restaurant Menu

52 Junction Inn
Station Road, Church Fenton, Tadcaster,
North Yorkshire LS24 9RA
Tel: 01937 557257

Real Ales, Bar Food, Disabled Facilities

53 Kellington Manor
Whales Lane, Kellington, Goole,
North Humberside DN14 0SB
Tel: 01977 661000

Real Ales, Bar Food, Restaurant Menu,
Accommodation, No Smoking Area, Disabled Facilities

54 The Kingfisher
Stocks Hill, Holme-on-Spalding-Moor,
Holme-on-Spaidinq-Moor, York YO43 4AF
Tel: 01430 861415

Real Ales, Bar Food, Restaurant Menu

55 Kingfisher
Biggin, Leeds, Yorkshire LS25 6HJ
Tel: 01977 682344

Real Ales, Bar Food, Restaurant Menu,
No Smoking Area

56 Kings Arms
Main Street, North Duffield, Selby,
North Yorkshire YO8 5RG
Tel: 01757 288492

Real Ales, Restaurant Menu

57 Kings Head
Main Street, Pollington, Goole,
North Humberside DN14 0DN
Tel: 01405 861507

Real Ales, Bar Food

58 The Kings Head
High Street, Barmby-on-The-Marsh, Goole,
North Humberside DN14 7HT
Tel: 01757 630705

Real Ales, Bar Food, Restaurant Menu,
No Smoking Area, Disabled Facilities

59 Loftsome Bridge Coaching House
Wressle, Selby, North Yorkshire YO8 6EN
Tel: 01757 630070

Bar Food, Restaurant Menu, Accommodation,
No Smoking Area, Disabled Facilities

60 Monk Fryston Hall Hotel
Main Street, Monk Fryston, Leeds,
Yorkshire LS25 5DU
Tel: 01977 682369

Bar Food, Restaurant Menu, Accommodation,
No Smoking Area, Disabled Facilities

61 Moorends Hotel

156 Marshland Road, Moorends, Doncaster,
South Yorkshire DN8 4SU
Tel: 01405 812170

Bar Food, Accommodation, Disabled Facilities

62 The New Huntsman Inn

105 Main Road, Drax, Selby,
North Yorkshire YO8 8NT
Tel: 01757 617431

Real Ales, Bar Food

63 The New Inn

York Road, Cliffe, Selby, North Yorkshire YO8 6NU
Tel: 01757 630837

Real Ales, Bar Food

64 New Inn

Main Street, Great Heck, Goole,
North Humberside DN14 0BQ
Tel: 01977 661414

Real Ales, Bar Food, Restaurant Menu,
No Smoking Area

65 New Inn

Howden Road, Barlby, Selby,
North Yorkshire YO8 5JE
Tel: 01757 702349

Real Ales, Bar Food, Restaurant Menu,
No Smoking Area, Disabled Facilities

66 The Oddfellow Arms

High Street, Carlton, Goole,
North Humberside DN14 9LY
Tel: 01405 860254

No Smoking Area

67 The Owl Hotel

Main Road, Hambleton, Selby,
North Yorkshire YO8 9JH
Tel: 01757 228374

Bar Food, Restaurant Menu, Accommodation,
No Smoking Area, Disabled Facilities

68 Park View Hotel & Restaurant

20 Main Street, Riccall, York, Yorkshire YO19 6PX
Tel: 01757 248458

Bar Food, Restaurant Menu, Accommodation,
No Smoking Area, Disabled Facilities

69 The Percy Arms

89 High Street, Airmyn, Goole,
North Humberside DN14 8LD
Tel: 01405 764408

Real Ales, Bar Food, Restaurant Menu,
No Smoking Area, Disabled Facilities

70 The Plough Inn

Shearburn Terrace, Snaith, Goole,
North Humberside DN14 9JJ
Tel: 01405 860751

Real Ales

71 Railway Tavern

Station Road, Hensall, Goole,
North Humberside DN14 0QJ
Tel: 01977 661478

Real Ales, Bar Food

72 The Red Lion

1 Ings Lane, Kellington, Goole,
North Humberside DN14 0NT
Tel: 01977 661008

73 Red Lion

Main Road, Hambleton, Selby,
North Yorkshire YO8 9JL
Tel: 01757 228297

Real Ales

74 Royal Hotel

West End Road, Norton, Doncaster,
South Yorkshire DN6 9DH
Tel: 01302 700749

Real Ales, No Smoking Area, Disabled Facilities

75 The Royal Oak

West End, Rawcliffe, Goole,
North Humberside DN14 8RW
Tel: 01405 839899

76 Royal Oak Inn

Holme Road, Spaldington, Goole,
North Humberside DN14 7NA
Tel: 01430 430563

Real Ales, Bar Food, Restaurant Menu,
No Smoking Area, Disabled Facilities

77 The School Boy

High Street, Norton, Doncaster,
South Yorkshire DN6 9EL
Tel: 01302 700264

Bar Food, Restaurant Menu, No Smoking Area,
Disabled Facilities

78 The Ship

73 High Street, West Cowick, Goole,
North Humberside DN14 9EB
Tel: 01405 869555

Real Ales

79 The Ship Inn75

High Street, Swinefleet, Goole,
North Humberside DN14 8AQ
Tel: 01405 704436

Real Ales

80 The Shoulder Of Mutton

Main Street, Kirk Smeaton, Pontefract,
West Yorkshire WF8 3JY
Tel: 01977 620348

Real Ales

81 The Sloop Inn

Main Street, Temple Hirst, Selby,
North Yorkshire YO8 8QN
Tel: 01757 270267

Real Ales, Bar Food, Restaurant Menu,
No Smoking Area

82 The Star Inn

Moss Road, Moss, Doncaster,
South Yorkshire DN6 0HQ
Tel: 01302 700497

Real Ales, Bar Food, Accommodation,
No Smoking Area, Disabled Facilities

83 The Station

4 Bridgegate, Howden, Goole,
North Humberside DN14 7AB
Tel: 01430 431301

Real Ales, Bar Food, Restaurant Menu,
No Smoking Area, Disabled Facilities

84 The Steam Packet

Cheviot Avenue, Goole,
North Humberside DN14 6HT
Tel: 01405 762981

Real Ales, No Smoking Area, Disabled Facilities

85 Swan Inn

Doncaster Road, Brayton, Selby,
North Yorkshire YO8 9EG
Tel: 01757 703870

Real Ales, Bar Food, Restaurant Menu,
No Smoking Area, Disabled Facilities

86 Travel Inn

Rawcliffe Road, Airmyn, Goole,
North Humberside DN14 8JS
Tel: 08701 977177

Bar Food, Restaurant Menu, Accommodation,
No Smoking Area, Disabled Facilities

87 The Vikings

Western Road, Goole,
North Humberside DN14 6RG
Tel: 01405 721821

Real Ales, Bar Food, Restaurant Menu,
No Smoking Area, Disabled Facilities

88 Wadkin Arms

Cliffe Road, Osgodby, Selby,
North Yorkshire YO8 5HU
Tel: 01757 702391

Real Ales

89 Wellington Hotel

31 Bridgegate, Howden, Goole,
North Humberside DN14 7JG
Tel: 01430 430258

Real Ales, Bar Food, Restaurant Menu,
Accommodation, No Smoking Area, Disabled Facilities

90 Wheatsheaf

83 Hailgate, Howden, Goole,
North Humberside DN14 7SX
Tel: 01430 432334

Real Ales, Bar Food, Restaurant Menu,
No Smoking Area, Disabled Facilities

91 Wheatsheaf Inn

87 Main Road, Hambleton, Selby,
North Yorkshire YO8 9JD
Tel: 01757 228294

No Smoking Area

92 The White Horse

Main Street, Church Fenton, Tadcaster,
North Yorkshire LS24 9RF
Tel: 01937 557143

Real Ales, Bar Food, Restaurant Menu,
No Smoking Area, Disabled Facilities

93 White Horse Inn

10 Market Place, Howden, Goole,
North Humberside DN14 7BJ
Tel: 01430 430326

Real Ales, Bar Food, No Smoking Area,
Disabled Facilities

94 White Swan

9 Main Street, Bubwith, Selby,
North Yorkshire YO8 6LT
Tel: 01757 288209

Real Ales

95 Ye Olde Red Lion

25 Old Road, Holme-on-spalding-Moor, York,
Yorkshire YO43 4AD
Tel: 01430 860220

Real Ales, Bar Food, Restaurant Menu

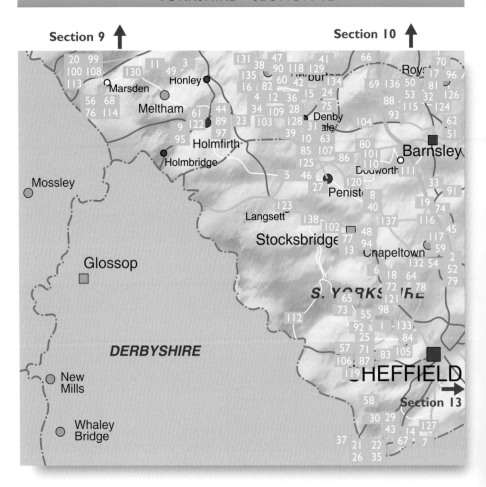

Section 9 ↑   Section 10 ↑

20 99
100 108
113
        130   11 49 3
    Marsden   Honley
                         131 38 47
                         135 90 118 129 41   66   Roy 70
                         16 82 60 42 134   69 136 50 17 96
56 68   4 12 36 15 24   53 32 81 126
76 114   Meltham   34 109 28 75   88 115 124
              61 44   103 128 31 Denby   93   62
           9 122 89 23   39 ale   104   51
              95 97   10 63
         Holmfirth   85 107 80   Barnsley
       Holmbridge   125 86 101 110 Dodworth 111
                                    5 46 120   33 91
Mossley   27   Penist 8   19 74
                              123   40   116
                     Langsett 138 102 48 137   45
                  Stocksbridge 77 94   117
                                13 Chapeltown 59 2
Glossop   6 18 64 132 54 52
                                  72 78 79
                     S. YORKSIRE 65 121
                              73 55 98
                           112 92 1 -133
                              25   84
                  DERBYSHIRE   57 71 83 105
                              106 87
New   119 SHEFFIELD →
Mills   58   Section 13
                              30 29
Whaley   43 14 127
Bridge   37 21 22 67 7
                              26 35

■ 11 Pub or Inn Reference Number - Detailed Information

■ 12 Pub or Inn Reference Number - Summary Entry

● ■ Place of interest mentioned in the chapter introduction

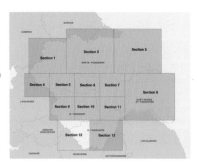

SECTION 12

Barnsley

The town's most impressive museum is actually located a few miles to the west, in the village of Cawthorne. **Cannon Hall** is a magnificent 18th-century country house set in formal gardens and historic parkland. It offers unique collections of pottery, furniture, glassware and paintings, along with the 'Charge Gallery' which documents the story of the 13th/18th Royal Hussars. Southeast, situated in attractive South Yorkshire countryside just off the M1 (J36), the **Elsecar Heritage Centre** is an imaginative science and history centre which is fun and educational for all the family.

Clayton West

A popular attraction at Clayton West is the **Kirklees Light Railway**, a 15-inch gauge steam railway which runs along the old Lancashire & Yorkshire Clayton West branch line. The **Yorkshire Sculpture Park** is one of the leading attractions of the area and is found about three miles northeast of Clayton West, conveniently close to Junction 38 of the M1. Alongside the programme of indoor and outdoor exhibitions, more permanent features include the YSP collection of works in many different styles (from 19th-century bronzes by Rodin to contemporary sculptures), and a display of monumental bronzes by Henry Moore sited within the adjacent 100-acre Bretton Country Park.

Denby Dale

Denby Dale is, of course, famous for its production of gigantic meat pies. The first of these Desperate Dan-sized dishes was baked in 1788 to celebrate George III's return to sanity; later ones marked the victory of Waterloo and Queen Victoria's Jubilee. The most recent pie was made in 2000 as part of the town's Millennium celebrations. It weighed a hearty 12 tonnes.

Holmbridge

This charming village stands at the head of a steep-sided valley and enjoys picture-postcard views of the Pennines and the Holme valley. There are cottages here dating from the 1700s and the area is known for its unusual style of architecture, four-decker cottages dug into the hillside. The lower cottage is approached from the front, the upper cottage is reached by a steep flight of stone steps leading round the back.

Holmfirth

BBC-TV's longest running situation comedy, *Last of the Summer Wine*, has made the little Pennine town of Holmfirth familiar to viewers around the world. Holmfirth has a lovely Georgian church, built in 1777-8 in neo-classical style to the designs of Joseph Jagger. The gable faces the street and the tower is constructed at the eastern end against a steep hillside.

Honley

The centre of this delightful little Pennine village has been designated as a Site of Historic Interest. There are charming terraces of weavers' cottages and lots of interesting alleyways, and the old village stocks still stand in the churchyard of St Mary's. The Coach and Horses Inn has strong connections with the Luddite movement of the early 1800s.

Penistone

Perched 700 feet above sea level, Penistone forms a gateway to the Peak District National Park which extends for some 30 miles to the south of the town. Penistone's oldest building is the 15th-century tower of its parish church which overlooks a graveyard in which ancestors of the poet William Wordsworth are buried. Later centuries added an elegant Dissenters' Chapel (in the 1600s) and a graceful Cloth Hall in the 1700s.

Sheffield

Among the city's many museums is the **Kelham Island Museum** which tells the story of Sheffield in a living museum. Visitors can see the mighty River Don Engine in steam – the most powerful working steam engine in Europe; reconstructed workshops; the 'Little Mesters' working cutler; and craftspeople demonstrating traditional 'Made in Sheffield' skills. The **Millenium Galleries** have helped to establish the city as a cultural

force in the north of England. Sheffield's most picturesque museum is undoubtedly the **Bishop's House Museum** which dates from around 1500 and is the earliest timber-framed house still standing in the city. Many original features survive and the bedchamber and great parlour are furnished in the style of the home of a prosperous 17th-century yeoman. There are also displays on Sheffield in Tudor and Stuart times, and changing exhibitions on local history themes.

Silkstone

The travel writer Arthur Mee dubbed Silkstone's parish church 'The Minster of the Moors' and it is indeed a striking building. Parts of the church date back to Norman times but most of it was built during the golden age of English ecclesiastical architecture, the 15th century. Outside, there are graceful flying buttresses and wonderfully weird gargoyles. Inside, the ancient oak roofs sprout floral bosses on moulded beams, and old box-pews and lovely medieval screens all add to the charm.

Sheffield Cathedral

1 Admiral Rodney

592 Loxley Road, Loxley, Sheffield, Yorkshire S6 6RU
Tel: 01142 856521

Real Ales, Bar Food, Restaurant Menu,
No Smoking Area, Disabled Facilities

2 The Ball Inn

Hesley Lane, Thorpe Hesley, Rotherham,
South Yorkshire S61 2PT
Tel: 01142 467681

3 Beaumont Arms

Meltham Road, Netherton, Huddersfield,
Yorkshire HD4 7EL
Tel: 01484 661984

Real Ales, Bar Food

4 The Black Bull

1 Marsh Lane, Shepley, Huddersfield,
Yorkshire HD8 8AE
Tel: 01484 603640

Disabled Facilities

5 The Blacksmiths Arms

Manchester Road, Millhouse Green, Sheffield,
Yorkshire S36 9NQ
Tel: 01226 762211

Restaurant Menu

6 Blue Ball Inn

281 Main Road, Wharncliffe Side, Sheffield,
Yorkshire S35 0DQ
Tel: 01142 862429

Real Ales, Bar Food, No Smoking Area,
Disabled Facilities

7 Bradway Hotel

Bradway Road, Sheffield, Yorkshire S17 4QW
Tel: 01142 368131

Real Ales, No Smoking Area, Disabled Facilities

8 The Bridge Inn

Cote Lane, Thurgoland, Sheffield, Yorkshire S35 7AE
Tel: 01142 882016

Real Ales, Bar Food, No Smoking Area

9 Bridge Tavern

Woodhead Road, Holmbridge, Holmfirth,
Yorkshire HD9 2NQ
Tel: 01484 683794

Real Ales, Bar Food, Restaurant Menu

10 The Britannia Inn

85 Sheffield Road, Penistone, Sheffield,
Yorkshire S36 6HH
Tel: 01226 762278

11 The Bulls Head

31 Blackmoorfoot, Linthwaite, Huddersfield,
Yorkshire HD7 5TR
Tel: 01484 842715

Real Ales, Bar Food, Restaurant Menu,
No Smoking Area, Disabled Facilities

12 The Cask & Spindle

Abbey Road, Shepley, Huddersfield,
Yorkshire HD8 8EL
Tel: 01484 607238

Real Ales, Bar Food, Restaurant Menu,
No Smoking Area, Disabled Facilities

13 The Castle Inn

Bolsterstone, Sheffield, Yorkshire S36 3ZB
Tel: 01142 888097

Real Ales, Bar Food, Restaurant Menu,
No Smoking Area

14 Castle Inn

Twentywell Road, Bradway, Sheffield,
Yorkshire S17 4PT
Tel: 01142 353028

Real Ales, Bar Food, Restaurant Menu,
No Smoking Area

15 The Chartist

74 Commercial Road, Skelmanthorpe, Huddersfield,
Yorkshire HD8 9DS
Tel: 01484 863766

16 Clothiers Arms

Station Road, Stocksmoor, Huddersfield,
Yorkshire HD4 6XN
Tel: 01484 602752

Real Ales, Restaurant Menu, No Smoking Area

17 Cobbys

High Street, Royston, Barnsley,
South Yorkshire S71 4RF
Tel: 01226 722038

Real Ales, Disabled Facilities

18 The Cock Inn

5 Bridge Hill, Oughtibridge, Sheffield,
Yorkshire S35 0FL
Tel: 01142 862373

19 The Cock Inn

Pilley Hill, Birdwell, Barnsley, South Yorkshire S70 5UD
Tel: 01226 742155

Real Ales, Bar Food, Restaurant Menu, No Smoking
Area

20 Commercial Hotel

Carr Lane, Slaithwaite, Huddersfield,
Yorkshire HD7 5AN
Tel: 01484 842920

21 The Cricket Inn

Penny Lane, Totley, Sheffield, Yorkshire S17 3AZ
Tel: 01142 365256

Real Ales, Bar Food, Restaurant Menu,
No Smoking Area, Disabled Facilities

22 Cross Scythes

Baslow Road, Sheffield, Yorkshire S17 4AE
Tel: 01142 360204

Real Ales, Bar Food, Restaurant Menu,
Accommodation, No Smoking Area, Disabled Facilities

23 The Crossroads Inn

Penistone Road, New Mill, Holmfirth,
Yorkshire HD9 7JL
Tel: 01484 683567

Real Ales, Bar Food, Restaurant Menu,
No Smoking Area

24 The Crown

183 Wakefield Road, Scissett, Huddersfield,
Yorkshire HD8 9JL
Tel: 01484 862358

Real Ales, Bar Food, Restaurant Menu,
No Smoking Area, Disabled Facilities

25 Crown & Glove

96 Upper Gate Road, Stannington, Sheffield,
Yorkshire S6 6BY
Tel: 01142 345522

Real Ales, Bar Food

26 Crown Inn

Hillfoot Road, Totley, Sheffield, Yorkshire S17 3AX
Tel: 01142 360789

Real Ales, Bar Food, No Smoking Area,
Disabled Facilities

27 Cubley Hall

Mortimer Road, Cubley, Penistone,
Sheffield S36 9DF
Tel: 01226 766086

Real Ales, Bar Food, Restaurant Menu,
Accommodation, No Smoking Area, Disabled Facilities

28 The Dalesman

408 Wakefield Road, Denby Dale, Huddersfield,
Yorkshire HD8 8RP
Tel: 01484 863508

Real Ales, Disabled Facilities

29 The Devonshire Arms

11 High Street, Dore, Sheffield, Yorkshire S17 3GU
Tel: 01142 351716

Real Ales, Bar Food, No Smoking Area,
Disabled Facilities

30 Dore Moor Inn

Hathersage Road, Dore, Sheffield,
Yorkshire S17 3AB
Tel: 01142 355121

Bar Food, Restaurant Menu, No Smoking Area,
Disabled Facilities

31 Dunkirk Inn

231 Barnsley Road, Denby Dale, Huddersfield,
Yorkshire HD8 8TX
Tel: 01484 862646

Real Ales, Bar Food, Restaurant Menu,
No Smoking Area

32 Eastfield Arms

Bar Lane, Mapplewell, Barnsley,
South Yorkshire S75 6DQ
Tel: 01226 382265

Restaurant Menu, No Smoking Area,
Disabled Facilities

33 The Edmund Arms

25 Worsbrough Village, Worsbrough, Barnsley,
South Yorkshire S70 5LW
Tel: 01226 206865

Real Ales, Bar Food, Restaurant Menu,
No Smoking Area

34 Farmers Boy Inn

44 Marsh Lane, Shepley, Huddersfield,
Yorkshire HD8 8AP
Tel: 01484 605941

Real Ales, Restaurant Menu, No Smoking Area,
Disabled Facilities

35 Fleur De Lys

Totley Hall Lane, Sheffield, Yorkshire S17 4AA
Tel: 01142 360707

Real Ales, Bar Food, Restaurant Menu,
No Smoking Area, Disabled Facilities

36 Foresters Inn

2 Shelley Woodhouse Lane, Lower Cumberworth,
Huddersfield, Yorkshire HD8 8PH
Tel: 01484 862493

Real Ales, Bar Food, Restaurant Menu,
No Smoking Area

37 The Fox House

Hathersage Road, Sheffield, Yorkshire S11 7TY
Tel: 01433 630374

Restaurant Menu, Accommodation, No Smoking Area,
Disabled Facilities

38 The Foxglove

Penistone Road, Kirkburton, Huddersfield,
Yorkshire HD8 0PQ
Tel: 01484 602101

Real Ales, Bar Food, Restaurant Menu,
Accommodation, No Smoking Area, Disabled Facilities

39 The George Inn

Denby Lane, Upper Denby, Huddersfield,
Yorkshire HD8 8UE
Tel: 01484 861347

No Smoking Area

40 Green Dragon

Halifax Road, Thurgoland, Sheffield,
Yorkshire S35 7AJ
Tel: 01142 882297

Restaurant Menu, No Smoking Area

41 Green Dragon Inn

30 Church Street, Emley, Huddersfield,
Yorkshire HD8 9RW
Tel: 01924 848275

Real Ales, Bar Food, Restaurant Menu,
No Smoking Area

42 The Grove Inn

1 Station Road, Skelmanthorpe, Huddersfield,
Yorkshire HD8 9AU
Tel: 01484 863082

Accommodation, Disabled Facilities

43 The Hare & Hounds

1-7 Church Lane, Dore, Sheffield, Yorkshire S17 3GR
Tel: 01142 355061

Real Ales, Bar Food, Restaurant Menu,
No Smoking Area, Disabled Facilities

44 Hervey's Wine Bar

Norridge Bottom, Holmfirth, Yorkshire HD9 7BB
Tel: 01484 686925

Real Ales, Bar Food, Disabled Facilities

45 Horse Shoe Inn

Harley Road, Harley, Rotherham,
South Yorkshire S62 7UD
Tel: 01226 742204

Real Ales, No Smoking Area

46 The Huntsman

136 Manchester Road, Thurlstone, Sheffield,
Yorkshire S36 9QW
Tel: 01226 764892

Real Ales, Bar Food, No Smoking Area

47 The Junction Inn

32 Paddock Road, Kirkburton, Huddersfield,
Yorkshire HD8 0TW
Tel: 01484 602038

Real Ales, Bar Food, Restaurant Menu,
No Smoking Area

48 The King & Miller

4-6 Manchester Road, Deepcar, Sheffield,
Yorkshire S36 2RD
Tel: 01142 884462

No Smoking Area, Disabled Facilities

49 Kings Arms

23-25 Midway, South Crosland, Huddersfield,
Yorkshire HD4 7DA
Tel: 01484 661669

Real Ales, Restaurant Menu, No Smoking Area,
Disabled Facilities

50 Kings Head Inn

Darton Lane, Mapplewell, Barnsley,
South Yorkshire S75 6AP
Tel: 01226 382386

Real Ales, Disabled Facilities

51 Lundwood Hotel

Pontefract Road, Barnsley, South Yorkshire S71 5JH
Tel: 01226 296276

Real Ales, No Smoking Area

52 The Masons Arms

Thorpe Street, Thorpe Hesley, Rotherham,
South Yorkshire S61 2RP
Tel: 01142 468079

Real Ales, Bar Food

53 Mason'S Arms

166 New Road, Staincross, Barnsley, Yorkshire S75 6PP
Tel: 01226 382904

No Smoking Area

54 The Miners Arms

125 Warren Lane, Chapeltown, Sheffield,
Yorkshire S35 2YD
Tel: 01142 570092

Real Ales, Bar Food, Restaurant Menu, No Smoking
Area, Disabled Facilities

55 The Nags Head

Stacey Bank, Loxley, Sheffield, Yorkshire S6 6SJ
Tel: 01142 851202

Real Ales, Bar Food, Restaurant Menu,
No Smoking Area

56 New Inn

Manchester Road, Marsden, Huddersfield,
Yorkshire HD7 6EZ
Tel: 01484 844384

Real Ales, Bar Food, Accommodation,
No Smoking Area, Disabled Facilities

57 The New Norfolk

Manchester Road, Hollow Meadows, Sheffield,
Yorkshire S6 5SJ
Tel: 01142 309253

Real Ales, Bar Food, No Smoking Area

58 Norfolk Arms

2 Ringinglow Village, Sheffield, Yorkshire S11 7TS
Tel: 01142 302197

Real Ales, Bar Food, Restaurant Menu,
Accommodation, No Smoking Area, Disabled Facilities

59 Norfolk Arms

29 White Lane, Chapeltown, Sheffield,
Yorkshire S35 2YG
Tel: 01142 402016

Real Ales, Bar Food, Restaurant Menu,
Accommodation, No Smoking Area, Disabled Facilities

60 The Oddfellows

95 Huddersfield Road, Shelley, Huddersfield,
Yorkshire HD8 8HF
Tel: 01484 602463

Real Ales

61 Old Bridge Hotel

Market Walk, Holmfirth, Huddersfield,
Yorkshire HD9 7DA
Tel: 01484 681212

Real Ales, Bar Food, Restaurant Menu,
Accommodation, No Smoking Area

62 The Old Bridge Inn
Burton Road, Barnsley, South Yorkshire S71 5RP
Tel: 01226 716580
No Smoking Area, Disabled Facilities

63 Old Crown
6 Market Street, Penistone, Sheffield,
Yorkshire S36 6BZ
Tel: 01226 762422
Bar Food, Restaurant Menu, Accommodation,
No Smoking Area

64 The Old Harrow
165 Main Street, Grenoside, Sheffield,
Yorkshire S35 8PP
Tel: 01142 468801
Real Ales, Bar Food

65 Old Horns Inn
High Bradfield, Bradfield, Sheffield, Yorkshire S6 6LG
Tel: 01142 851207
Real Ales, Bar Food, Restaurant Menu,
No Smoking Area

66 Old Manor House
19 Sycamore Lane, Bretton, Wakefield,
West Yorkshire WF4 4JR
Tel: 01924 830324
Accommodation, No Smoking Area, Disabled Facilities

67 Old Mother Red Cap
87 Everard Avenue, Sheffield, Yorkshire S17 4LY
Tel: 01142 360179
Real Ales, Bar Food, No Smoking Area

68 The Old New Inn
4 Carrs Road, Marsden, Huddersfield,
Yorkshire HD7 6JE
Tel: 01484 844459
Real Ales, Bar Food

69 The Old Post Office
600 Huddersfield Road, Haigh, Barnsley,
South Yorkshire S75 4DE
Tel: 01226 387619
Real Ales, Bar Food, No Smoking Area

70 Oliver Twist
Bleakley Lane, Notton, Wakefield,
West Yorkshire WF4 2NU
Tel: 01226 722562
Bar Food, Restaurant Menu, No Smoking Area

71 Peacockinn
714 Stannington Road, Stannington, Sheffield,
Yorkshire S6 6AJ
Tel: 01142 852463
Real Ales, Bar Food, No Smoking Area,
Disabled Facilities

72 The Pheasant
59 Station Lane, Oughtibridge, Sheffield,
Yorkshire S35 0HS
Tel: 01142 862483
Real Ales, Bar Food, Restaurant Menu,
No Smoking Area, Disabled Facilities

73 Plough Inn
New Road, Bradfield, Sheffield, Yorkshire S6 6HW
Tel: 01142 851280
Real Ales, Bar Food, No Smoking Area

74 The Prince Of Wales
Sheffield Road, Hoyland Common, Barnsley,
South Yorkshire S74 0DQ
Tel: 01226 742417

75 Queens Head
191 Wakefield Road, Scissett, Huddersfield,
Yorkshire HD8 9JL
Tel: 01484 862296
Real Ales, Bar Food, Restaurant Menu,
Disabled Facilities

76 The Railway Inn
34 Station Road, Marsden, Huddersfield,
Yorkshire HD7 6DH
Tel: 01484 841541
Real Ales, Bar Food, Restaurant Menu,
No Smoking Area

77 ## The Red Grouse

Spink Hall Lane, Stocksbridge, Sheffield,
Yorkshire S36 1FL
Tel: 01142 882286

Real AlesReal Ales

78 ## The Red Lion

93-95 Penistone Road, Grenoside, Sheffield,
Yorkshire S35 8QH
Tel: 01142 460084

Bar Food, Restaurant Menu, No Smoking Area,
Disabled Facilities

79 ## The Red Lion Inn

Brook Hill, Thorpe Hesley, Rotherham,
South Yorkshire S61 2PY
Tel: 01142 570946

Bar Food, Restaurant Menu, Accommodation,
Disabled Facilities

80 ## Red Lion Inn

69 High Street, Silkstone, Barnsley,
South Yorkshire S75 4JR
Tel: 01226 790455

Real Ales

81 ## Ring O'Bells Inn

Royston Lane, Royston, Barnsley,
South Yorkshire S71 4NJ
Tel: 01226 727681

82 ## The Rising Sun

162 Penistone Road, Shelley, Huddersfield,
Yorkshire HD8 8JB
Tel: 01484 602435

Real Ales

83 ## Rivelin Hotel

Tofts Lane, Stannington, Sheffield, Yorkshire S6 5SL
Tel: 01142 333247

Real Ales, Bar Food, No Smoking Area

84 ## Robin Hood

Greaves Lane, Stannington, Sheffield, Yorkshire S6 6BG
Tel: 01142 344565

Real Ales, Bar Food, Restaurant Menu,
Accommodation, No Smoking Area, Disabled Facilities

85 ## The Rose & Crown

Shrewsbury Road, Penistone, Sheffield,
Yorkshire S36 6DY
Tel: 01226 763609

Real Ales

86 ## The Rose & Crown

Barnsley Road, Hoylandswaine, Sheffield,
Yorkshire S36 7JA
Tel: 01226 762227

Real Ales, Restaurant Menu, No Smoking Area

87 ## Rose & Crown

Bankfield Lane, Stannington, Sheffield,
Yorkshire S6 6BR
Tel: 01142 345096

Bar Food, Restaurant Menu, No Smoking Area

88 ## Rose & Crown Hotel

Barnsley Road, Darton, Barnsley,
South Yorkshire S75 5NQ
Tel: 01226 382352

Bar Food, Restaurant Menu, No Smoking Area

89 ## Rose & Crown Inn

Victoria Square, Holmfirth, Yorkshire HD9 2DN
Tel: 01484 683960

Real Ales, Bar Food, Restaurant Menu

90 ## The Royal

64 North Road, Kirkburton, Huddersfield,
Yorkshire HD8 0RW
Tel: 01484 602521

Bar Food, Disabled Facilities

91 ## Royal Albert

Wentworth Road, Blacker Hill, Barnsley,
South Yorkshire S74 0RL
Tel: 01226 742193

Real Ales, No Smoking Area

92 ## Royal Hotel

Main Road, Dungworth, Bradfield, Sheffield S6 6HF
Tel: 01142 851213

Real Ales, Bar Food, Restaurant Menu,
Accommodation, No Smoking Area

93 The Royal Hotel

Barnsley Road, Barugh Green, Barnsley,
South Yorkshire S75 1LS
Tel: 01226 382363

Real Ales, Bar Food, Restaurant Menu,
No Smoking Area, Disabled Facilities

94 The Royal Oak

31 Manchester Road, Deepcar, Sheffield,
Yorkshire S36 2QX
Tel: 01142 882208

Real Ales, No Smoking Area

95 Shepherds Rest

116 Woodhead Road, Holmbridge, Holmfirth,
Yorkshire HD9 2NL
Tel: 01484 682329

Real Ales

96 Ship Inn

Midland Road, Royston, Barnsley,
South Yorkshire S71 4AY
Tel: 01226 725681

Disabled Facilities

97 Shoulder Of Mutton

2 Dunford Road, Holmfirth, Yorkshire HD9 2DP
Tel: 01484 684414

No Smoking Area

98 Shoulder Of Mutton

19 Top Road, Worrall, Sheffield, Yorkshire S35 0AQ
Tel: 01142 862101

Real Ales, Bar Food, No Smoking Area,
Disabled Facilities

99 Shoulder Of Mutton Inn

9 Church Street, Slaithwaite, Huddersfield,
Yorkshire HD7 5AS
Tel: 01484 844661

Real Ales

100 Silent Woman Inn

Nabbs Lane, Slaithwaite, Huddersfield,
Yorkshire HD7 5AU
Tel: 01484 842819

Disabled Facilities

101 Silkstone Lodge

Cone Lane, Silkstone, Barnsley, Yorkshire S75 4LY
Tel: 01226 790456

Real Ales, Restaurant Menu, Accommodation,
No Smoking Area, Disabled Facilities

102 The Silver Fox

839 Unsliven Road, Stocksbridge, Sheffield,
Yorkshire S36 1FT
Tel: 01142 883926

Real Ales, Bar Food, Restaurant Menu,
No Smoking Area

103 Soverign Inn

172-174 Penistone Road, Shepley, Huddersfield,
Yorkshire HD8 8BE
Tel: 01484 601901

Restaurant Menu, No Smoking Area,
Disabled Facilities

104 Spencer Arms

Church Street, Cawthorne, Barnsley,
South Yorkshire S75 4HL
Tel: 01226 791398

Real Ales, Bar Food, Restaurant Menu,
No Smoking Area

105 The Sportsman

2 Oldfield Road, Stannington, Sheffield,
Yorkshire S6 6DT
Tel: 01142 336400

No Smoking Area, Disabled Facilities

106 Sportsman Inn

569 Redmires Road, Sheffield, Yorkshire S10 4LJ
Tel: 01142 301935

Real Ales, Bar Food, No Smoking Area,
Disabled Facilities

107 Spread Eagle

Market Street, Penistone, Sheffield, Yorkshire S36 6BZ
Tel: 01226 762025

108 The Star Hotel

1438-1440 Manchester Road, Slaithwaite,
Huddersfield, Yorkshire HD7 5JX
Tel: 01484 843043

Real Ales

109 Star Inn
64 Barnsley Road, Upper Cumberworth,
Huddersfield, Yorkshire HD8 8NS
Tel: 01484 606315
Real Ales

110 Station Inn
1 Knabs Lane, Silkstone Common, Barnsley,
South Yorkshire S75 4RB
Tel: 01226 790248
Real Ales

111 Strafford Arms Hotel
Park Drive, Stainborough, Barnsley,
South Yorkshire S75 3EW
Tel: 01226 287488
Real Ales, Bar Food, Restaurant Menu,
No Smoking Area

112 The Strines Inn
Strines, Bradfield, Sheffield, Yorkshire S6 6JE
Tel: 01142 851247
Real Ales, Bar Food, Accommodation,
No Smoking Area, Disabled Facilities

113 The Swan
Carr Lane, Slaithwaite, Huddersfield,
Yorkshire HD7 5BQ
Tel: 01484 843225
Real Ales, Bar Food

114 The Swan Hotel
5 Station Road, Marsden, Huddersfield,
Yorkshire HD7 6BS
Tel: 01484 844308
Real Ales, Bar Food, Restaurant Menu,
No Smoking Area

115 Talbot Inn Bar
Towngate, Mapplewell, Barnsley,
South Yorkshire S75 6AS
Tel: 01226 385629
Real Ales, Bar Food, Restaurant Menu

116 Tankersley Manor
Church Lane, Tankersley, Barnsley, Yorkshire S75 3DQ
Tel: 01226 744700
Real Ales, Bar Food, Restaurant Menu,
Accommodation, No Smoking Area, Disabled Facilities

117 Thorncliffe Arms
135 Warren Lane, Chapeltown, Sheffield,
Yorkshire S35 2YD
Tel: 01142 458942
Real Ales, Restaurant Menu, Accommodation,
No Smoking Area, Disabled Facilities

118 Three Acres Inn
Roydhouse, Shelley, Huddersfield, Yorkshire HD8 8LR
Tel: 01484 602606
Real Ales, Bar Food, Restaurant Menu,
Accommodation, No Smoking Area, Disabled Facilities

119 Three Merry Lads
610 Redmires Road, Sheffield, Yorkshire S10 4LJ
Tel: 01142 302824
Real Ales, Bar Food, Restaurant Menu,
No Smoking Area

120 Travellers Inn
Four Lane Ends, Oxspring, Sheffield, Yorkshire S36 8YJ
Tel: 01226 762518
Bar Food, Restaurant Menu, No Smoking Area,
Disabled Facilities

121 Travellers Rest
93 Langsett Road South, Oughtibridge, Sheffield,
Yorkshire S35 0GY
Tel: 01142 862221
Real Ales

122 Victoria Inn
Woodhead Road, Holmfirth, Yorkshire HD9 2PR
Tel: 01484 683673
Real Ales, Bar Food, Restaurant Menu,
No Smoking Area

123 Waggon & Horses
Langsett, Stocksbridge, Sheffield, Yorkshire S36 4GY
Tel: 01226 763147
Real Ales, Bar Food, Restaurant Menu,
Accommodation, No Smoking Area

124 Wellington

Laithes Lane, Athersley, Barnsley,
South Yorkshire S71 3AP
Tel: 01226 284246

Real Ales

125 Wentworth Arms Hotel

Sheffield Road, Penistone, Sheffield,
Yorkshire S36 6HG
Tel: 01226 762494

Real Ales

126 Wharncliffe Arms

Fish Dam Lane, Barnsley, South Yorkshire S71 3HF
Tel: 01226 722483

Real Ales, Bar Food, Restaurant Menu,
No Smoking Area, Disabled Facilities

127 White Hart

27 Greenhill Main Road, Sheffield, Yorkshire S8 7RA
Tel: 01142 377343

Real Ales, Bar Food, No Smoking Area,
Disabled Facilities

128 White Hart

380 Wakefield Road, Denby Dale, Huddersfield,
Yorkshire HD8 8RT
Tel: 01484 862357

Real Ales, No Smoking Area

129 The White Horse

Chapel Lane, Emley, Huddersfield, Yorkshire HD8 9SP
Tel: 01924 840937

Restaurant Menu, No Smoking Area,
Disabled Facilities

130 White House

Slaithwaite, Huddersfield, Yorkshire HD7 5TY
Tel: 01484 842245

Real Ales, Bar Food, Restaurant Menu,
Accommodation, No Smoking Area, Disabled Facilities

131 White Swan Inn

123 Penistone Road, Kirkburton, Huddersfield,
Yorkshire HD8 0RB
Tel: 01484 602132

Real Ales, Bar Food, Restaurant Menu

132 Whitley Hall Hotel

Elliott Lane, Grenoside, Sheffield,
Yorkshire S35 8NR
Tel: 01142 454444

Bar Food, Restaurant Menu, Accommodation,
No Smoking Area, Disabled Facilities

133 The Wisewood Inn

Loxley Road, Loxley, Sheffield, Yorkshire S6 6RR
Tel: 01142 349937

Real Ales, No Smoking Area, Disabled Facilities

134 Woodman Inn

Wakefield Road, Clayton West, Huddersfield,
Yorkshire HD8 9QB
Tel: 01484 863298

Real Ales

135 Woodman Inn & Restaurant

Thunderbridge, Kirkburton, Huddersfield,
Yorkshire HD8 0PU
Tel: 01484 605778

Real Ales, Bar Food, Restaurant Menu,
Accommodation, No Smoking Area

136 The Woolley

Woolley Colliery Road, Darton, Barnsley,
South Yorkshire S75 5JE
Tel: 01226 382847

Bar Food, Restaurant Menu, No Smoking Area,
Disabled Facilities

137 Wortley Hall

Wortley Village, Wortley, Sheffield,
Yorkshire S35 7DB
Tel: 01142 882100

Bar Food, Restaurant Menu, Accommodation,
No Smoking Area, Disabled Facilities

138 Ye Olde Mustard Pot

Midhopestones, Sheffield, Yorkshire S36 4GW
Tel: 01226 761155

Real Ales, Bar Food, Restaurant Menu,
Accommodation, No Smoking Area, Disabled Facilities

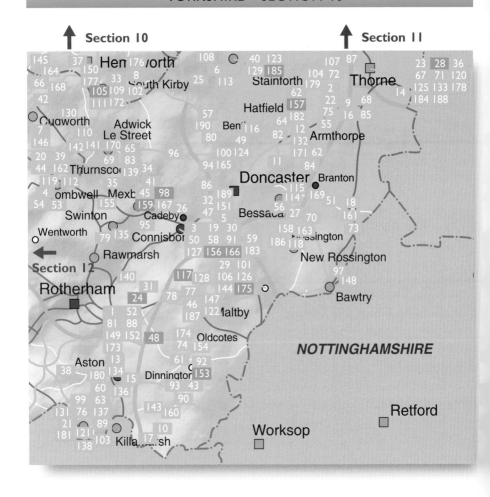

Section 10

Section 11

145 37 Hen orth 176 108 40 123 107 87 23 28 36
164 150 6 129 185 104 72 67 71 120
66 168 177 33 8 25 113 Stainforth 179 2 Thorne 125 133 178
42 105 109 102 62 14 184 188
111 172 Hatfield 157 22 9 68
130 57 182 75 16 85
Quaworth Adwick 190 Ben 116 64 82 12 132
7 110 Le Street 80 49 171 62 Armthorpe
146 142 141 170 65 100 124 84
20 39 69 83 96 94 165 11
44 162 Thunsco 139 34 86 Doncaster Branton
119 112 35 41 189 115
4 ombwell Mexb 45 98 32 151 114 169 51 18
54 53 155 159 167 26 47 56 27 70 161
Swinton Cadeby 95 5 Bessaca 158 163 73
Wentworth 79 135 Connisbo 3 19 30 186 118
50 58 91 59 sington
Rawmarsh 127 156 166 183 New Rossington
Section 12 29 101 97
140 117 128 106 126 148
Rotherham 31 78 77 144 175 Bawtry
24 46 147
1 52 187 122 altby
81 88
149 152 48 174 Oldcotes
173 74 154
Aston 13 61 92 NOTTINGHAMSHIRE
38 180 134 15 Dinnington 153
60 136 93 43
99 63 90 Retford
131 76 137 143 160
21 89 10
181 121 103 Killa sh Worksop

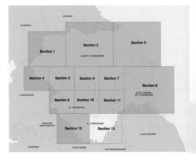

SECTION 13

Branton

Surrounded by agricultural land, Brockholes Farm has been a working farm since 1759 and one where the traditional farming skills have been passed down from one generation to the next. Today, at **Brockhole Riding and Visitor Centre**, visitors can see demonstrations of those same skills, such as those carried out by the farrier and the shepherd, as well as seeing many animals associated with traditional free-range farming. There is also a riding centre here that caters for complete beginners through to experienced riders and, along with professional instructors, has a range of horses and ponies to suit all ages and abilities.

Cadeby

Listed in the *Domesday Book* as 'Catebi', this pleasant little village is surrounded on all sides by prime agricultural land. The former village church

was designed in 1856 by Sir George Gilbert Scott, the architect of St Pancras Station in London, and resembles a medieval estate barn with its steeply pitched roofs and lofty south porch.

Conisbrough

The town is best known for the 11th-century **Conisbrough Castle** (English Heritage), the most impressive medieval building in South Yorkshire. Just to the north of Conisbrough, the charred and blackened land of two colliery sites has

Conisbrough Castle

been transformed into **Earth Centre**, an attractive complex of unusual gardens, a country park with a range of outdoor activities, a variety of specially constructed habitats for wildlife and rides such as the Water Cycle Simulator which enables visitors to travel at speed around the planet.

Doncaster

There is no one connected with the racing fraternity who has not heard of the St Leger, one of the oldest classic races, which has been held at Doncaster since 1776. Three miles or so to the northwest of Doncaster, **Brodsworth Hall** (English Heritage) is a remarkable example of a Victorian mansion that has survived with many of its original furnishings and decorations intact.

Finningley

A unique feature of this pleasant village close to the Nottinghamshire border is its five village greens, the main one having a duck pond complete with weeping willows. Finningley is a living village with a well-used Village Hall, originally a barn but which later served as the village school. Finningley has a beautiful Norman church with a rectors' list dating back to 1293 and a post office which has been in the same family for five generations. The year 2004 saw the opening of Robin Hood Aiport outside the village, which has led to increased development and investment in the area while not disturbing Finningley's traditional appeal.

North Anston

This village, separated from its neighbour

South Anston by the main road, is home to the **Tropical Butterfly House, Wildlife and Falconry Centre** where not only can visitors see the exotic butterflies, birds, snakes and crocodiles in a tropical jungle setting but also enjoy outdoor falconry displays and, at the baby farm animal area, bottle-feed lambs (depending on the season).

Renishaw

This sizeable village gives its name to **Renishaw Hall**, home of Sir Reresby and Lady Sitwell and located about a mile or so to the northwest. The beautiful formal Italian gardens and 300 acres of wooded park are open to visitors, along with a nature trail and a Sitwell family museum, an art gallery, a display of Fiori de Henriques sculptures in the Georgian stables, and a café. The Hall itself is open to group and connoisseur tours by special arrangement.

Rotherham

The town's most striking building is undoubtedly the **Church of All Saints**, one of the finest examples of perpendicular architecture in Yorkshire. **Clifton Park Museum** is a stately building whose interior has changed little since it was built in 1783. Another museum of interest is the **York and Lancaster Regimental Museum** in the Central Library. Dramatically set within the former Templeborough steelworks, **Magna** was the UK's first science adventure park, with an imaginative exploration of the power of the four natural elements – earth, air, fire and water. A little further afield, near the village of Maltby, are the dramatic ruins of **Roche Abbey** (English Heritage).only.

Stainforth

Stainforth was once an important trading centre and inland port on the River Don. It also stands on the banks of the Stainforth & Keadby Canal which still has a well-preserved dry dock and a 19th-century blacksmith's shop. This area of low, marshy ground was drained by Dutch engineers in the 1600s to produce rich, peaty farmland.

Wales

A mile or so to the west of Wales the **Rother Valley Country Park** provides excellent facilities for water sports including sailing, windsurfing, canoeing and jet skiing, as well as a cable water ski tow. Visitors can hire equipment or use their own, and training courses from beginner to instructor level are available in various water sports. About three miles northeast of Wales, at North Aston, is the **Tropical Butterfly House, Falconry and Wildlife Centre**.

1 A Methley
Main Street, Bramley, Rotherham,
South Yorkshire S66 2SF
Tel: 01709 541103

Bar Food, No Smoking Area, Disabled Facilities

2 Abbey Hotel
Station Road, Dunscroft, Doncaster,
South Yorkshire DN7 4JS
Tel: 01302 844264

3 The Aima
West Street, Conisbrough, Doncaster,
South Yorkshire DN12 3JH
Tel: 01709 864059

No Smoking Area, Disabled Facilities

4 The Albion Inn
The Green, Hemingfield, Barnsley,
South Yorkshire S73 0PT
Tel: 01226 751626

No Smoking Area

5 Alverley Inn
Springwell Lane, Doncaster,
South Yorkshire DN4 9DL
Tel: 01302 853112

Real Ales, No Smoking Area, Disabled Facilities

6 The Anne Arms
Suttonfield Road, Sutton, Doncaster,
South Yorkshire DN6 9JX
Tel: 01302 700500

Real Ales, Bar Food, Restaurant Menu,
No Smoking Area

7 Ardsley House Hotel
Doncaster Road, Barnsley, South Yorkshire S71 5EH
Tel: 01226 309955

Real Ales, Bar Food, Restaurant Menu,
Accommodation, No Smoking Area, Disabled Facilities

8 Barnsley Oak
Mill Lane, South Elmsall, Pontefract,
West Yorkshire WF9 2DT
Tel: 01977 643427

Real Ales, Bar Food, No Smoking Area, Disabled
Facilities

9 The Bay Horse
High Street, Hatfield, Doncaster,
South Yorkshire DN7 6RS
Tel: 01302 840201

Bar Food, Accommodation, No Smoking Area

10 The Beehive
16 Union Street, Harthill, Sheffield, Yorkshire S26 7YH
Tel: 01909 770205

Real Ales, Bar Food, No Smoking Area

11 The Benbow
Armthorpe Road, Doncaster,
South Yorkshire DN2 5QA
Tel: 01302 556568

Bar Food, Restaurant Menu, No Smoking Area

12 Beverley Inn
117 Thorne Road, Edenthorpe, Doncaster,
South Yorkshire DN3 2JE
Tel: 01302 882724

Real Ales, Bar Food, Restaurant Menu,
Accommodation, No Smoking Area, Disabled Facilities

13 Black Bull Hotel
29 Main Street, Aughton, Sheffield, Yorkshire S26 3XH
Tel: 01142 871020

Real Ales, Bar Food, Restaurant Menu,
Accommodation, No Smoking Area

14 The Black Bull Inn
Scunthorpe Road, Thorne, Doncaster,
South Yorkshire DN8 5SH
Tel: 01405 812744

Real Ales, Bar Food, Restaurant Menu,
No Smoking Area

15 The Blue Bell
Worksop Road, Aston, Sheffield, Yorkshire S26 2EB
Tel: 01142 878800

Real Ales, Bar Food, No Smoking Area, Disabled
Facilities

16 Blue Bell
11 Manor Road, Hatfield, Doncaster,
South Yorkshire DN7 6SA
Tel: 01302 840337

Real Ales, No Smoking Area, Disabled Facilities

17 The Bluebell

4 Woodall Lane, Harthill, Sheffield,
Yorkshire S26 7YQ
Tel: 01909 770391

Real Ales, No Smoking Area

18 Bluebell Inn

Thorne Road, Blaxton, Doncaster,
South Yorkshire DN9 3AL
Tel: 01302 770424

Real Ales, Bar Food, Restaurant Menu,
No Smoking Area, Disabled Facilities

19 The Bowman

Micklebring Grove, Conisbrough, Doncaster,
South Yorkshire DN12 2LG
Tel: 01709 865272

No Smoking Area

24 The Brush & Easel

Fleming Way, Flanderswell, Rotherham,
South Yorkshire S66 2HB
☎ 01709 549762

Real Ales, Bar Food, Restaurant Menu, No Smoking Area, Disabled Facilities

- ☛ Off the A631 2 miles east of Rotherham
- 🍺 Guest ales from local breweries
- 🍴 Mon-Fri 12-2 & 5-9; Sat 12-9; Sun 12-6
- 🎵 Quiz night Weds & Sun
- ⛴ Parking, disabled access, patio
- 💳 All major cards
- 🚫 No smoking in restaurant
- 🕐 Mon-Thurs & Sun 12-11; Fri & Sat 12-11.30
- 🏛 Ulley Country Park, Magna Science Adventure Centre, Swinton, Conisborough

The Brush & Easel is a convivial pub situated on the outskirts of Rotherham. Handsome and comfortable, real ales are provided by local breweries.

Owners Robert and Dorris Ewens are charming hosts – Robert is also an experienced chef and the food is wholesome and freshly prepared, most of it home cooked.

20 The Bridge Inn

18 Doncaster Road, Darfield, Barnsley,
South Yorkshire S73 9HH
Tel: 01226 752215

Bar Food, Restaurant Menu, No Smoking Area,
Disabled Facilities

21 The British Oak

1 Mosborough Moor, Mosborough, Sheffield,
Yorkshire S20 5AY
Tel: 01142 486442

Real Ales, Restaurant Menu, No Smoking Area

22 Broadway Hotel

Broadway, Dunscroft, Doncaster,
South Yorkshire DN7 4HB
Tel: 01302 350303

No Smoking Area

23 Brooke Arms

Wike Gate Road, Thorne, Doncaster,
South Yorkshire DN8 5PE
Tel: 01405 812029

No Smoking Area, Disabled Facilities

24 The Brush & Easel

Fleming Way, Flanderwell, Rotherham,
South Yorkshire S66 2HB
Tel: 01709 549762

Bar Food, Restaurant Menu, No Smoking Area,
Disabled Facilities

See panel adjacent

25 The Burghwallis

Scorcher Hills Lane, Burghwallis, Doncaster,
South Yorkshire DN6 9JT
Tel: 01302 723398

Real Ales, Bar Food, Restaurant Menu,
No Smoking Area, Disabled Facilities

26 Cadeby Inn

Main Street, Cadeby, Doncaster,
South Yorkshire DN5 7SW
Tel: 01709 864009

Real Ales, Bar Food, Restaurant Menu,
No Smoking Area

27 The Campanile

Bawtry Road, Doncaster, South Yorkshire DN4 7PD
Tel: 01302 370770

Bar Food, Restaurant Menu, Accommodation,
No Smoking Area, Disabled Facilities

28 **Canal Tavern**

South Parade, Thorne, Doncaster,
South Yorkshire DN8 5DZ
Tel: 01405 813688

Real Ales, Bar Food, Restaurant Menu,
No Smoking Area

See panel below

29 The Carpenters Arms

Westgate, Tickhill, Doncaster,
South Yorkshire DN11 9NE
Tel: 01302 742839

Real Ales, Bar Food, Restaurant Menu,
No Smoking Area

28 **Canal Tavern**

South Parade, Thorne, Doncaster,
South Yorkshire DN8 5DZ
☎ 01405 813688

**Real Ales, Bar Food, Restaurant Menu, No Smoking
Area**

- ☛ On the A614 10 miles northeast of
  Doncaster
- 🍺 Tetleys, John Smiths, guest ales
- 🍴 12-2.30 & 5-8, Sunday 12-3
- 🎵 Quiz night Thurs & Sun; Fri night disco
- ⛟ Parking, disabled access, patio garden
- 💳 All major cards
- 🚫 No smoking in restaurant
- 🕐 Mon-Thurs & Sun 11-11; Fri & Sat 11am-1am
- 🏛 Doncaster, Stainforth and Keadby Canal,
  Fishlake, Brockhole Riding and Visitor Centre

The Canal Tavern in Thorne is brimming
with character. This friendly pub dates back
to the 17th century and is cosy and
comfortable. Set alongside the narrow boat
canal and handy for Robin Hood Airport, this
traditional tavern has much to recommend it
including the great food and excellent choice
of real ales.

30 The Castle Inn

Minneymoor Hill, Conisbrough, Doncaster,
South Yorkshire DN12 3EN
Tel: 01709 862204

31 The Cavalier

Hollings Lane, Ravenfield, Rotherham,
South Yorkshire S65 4PU
Tel: 01709 533198

Bar Food, Restaurant Menu, Disabled Facilities

32 The Cecil

High Road, Warmsworth, Doncaster,
South Yorkshire DN4 9LU
Tel: 01302 853123

Real Ales, Bar Food, Restaurant Menu,
No Smoking Area

33 Church House

Barnsley Road, South Kirkby, Pontefract,
West Yorkshire WF9 3LA
Tel: 01977 651560

Real Ales, Bar Food, Restaurant Menu,
No Smoking Area, Disabled Facilities

34 Coach & Horses

High Street, Barnburgh, Doncaster,
South Yorkshire DN5 7EP
Tel: 01709 892306

Real Ales

35 The Collingwood

Furlong Road, Bolton-upon-Dearne, Rotherham,
South Yorkshire S63 8JA
Tel: 01709 892129

Real Ales

36 The Corner Pin

92 King Street, Thorne, Doncaster,
South Yorkshire DN8 5BA
Tel: 01405 812790

No Smoking Area

37 Cross Hill Tavern

8 Cross Hill, Hemsworth, Pontefract,
West Yorkshire WF9 4LQ
Tel: 01977 610341

38 The Cross Keys

400 Handsworth Road, Handsworth, Sheffield,
Yorkshire S13 9BZ
Tel: 01142 541050

39 Cross Keys Hotel

Church Street, Darfield, Barnsley,
South Yorkshire S73 9JX
Tel: 01226 752130

Bar Food, No Smoking Area, Disabled Facilities

40 The Crown Hotel

High Street, Askern, Doncaster,
South Yorkshire DN6 0AB
Tel: 01302 708548

Accommodation

41 The Crown Inn

Ludwell Close, Barnburgh, Doncaster,
South Yorkshire DN5 7JQ
Tel: 01709 893450

Real Ales, Bar Food, Restaurant Menu,
No Smoking Area

42 The Cudworth

Pontefract Road, Cudworth, Barnsley,
South Yorkshire S72 8AG
Tel: 01226 710385

Real Ales, Bar Food, No Smoking Area,
Disabled Facilities

43 The Cutler

Woodsetts Road, Anston, Sheffield,
Yorkshire S25 4EQ
Tel: 01909 562146

No Smoking Area, Disabled Facilities

44 The Darfield

Nanny Marr Road, Darfield, Barnsley,
South Yorkshire S73 9AW
Tel: 01226 752350

Real Ales, No Smoking Area

45 Denaby Main

Doncaster Road, Denaby Main, Doncaster,
South Yorkshire DN12 4DG
Tel: 01709 865358

Real Ales, Disabled Facilities

46 Don John Inn

High Street, Maltby, Rotherham,
South Yorkshire S66 8LH
Tel: 01709 817396

47 Doncaster Moat House

High Road, Warmsworth, Doncaster,
South Yorkshire DN4 9UX
Tel: 01302 799988

Bar Food, Restaurant Menu, Accommodation,
No Smoking Area, Disabled Facilities

48 The Double Barrel

Woodhouse Green, Thurcroft, Rotherham,
South Yorkshire S66 9AN
Tel: 01709 703571

Bar Food, Restaurant Menu, No Smoking Area

See panel on page 216

49 The Drum

Watch House Lane, Bentley, Doncaster,
South Yorkshire DN5 9NA
Tel: 01302 874488

Real Ales, Bar Food, Restaurant Menu,
No Smoking Area, Disabled Facilities

50 Eagle & Child

2 West Street, Conisbrough, Doncaster,
South Yorkshire DN12 3JH
Tel: 01709 864084

51 Eagle & Child Inn

Main Street, Auckley, Doncaster,
South Yorkshire DN9 3HS
Tel: 01302 770406

Real Ales, Bar Food, Restaurant Menu,
No Smoking Area

52 The Eiton Hotel

Main Street, Bramley, Rotherham,
South Yorkshire S66 2SE
Tel: 01709 545681

Bar Food, Restaurant Menu, Accommodation,
No Smoking Area, Disabled Facilities

48 The Double Barrel

Woodhouse Green, Thurcroft, Rotherham,
South Yorkshire S66 9AN
☎ 01709 703571

Bar Food, Restaurant Menu, No Smoking Area

☛ Just off the M18 6 miles southeast of Rotherham

🍴 Mon-Weds 12-8; Thurs-Sat 12-9; Sun 12-4

🎵 Tues night free pool; Weds night disco; Thurs night quiz; Fri & Sat night disco; Sun disco and pop quiz

⛴ Parking, disabled access, patio

💳 All major cards

🚫 No smoking in restaurant

🕐 Mon-Thurs & Sun 12-11; Fri & Sat 12-11.30

🏛 Rotherham, Doncaster, Sheffield, Finningley, Bawtry, Wales

The Double Barrel in Thurcroft, a quiet village southeast of Rotherham, is a friendly family pub and restaurant set in a residential area and handy for the many sights and attractions of the region. This welcoming inn is modern and very spacious, with a traditional interior graced with plenty of warm wood panelling and comfortable seating and handsome paintings adorning the walls. There's also a patio area in which to enjoy a drink or meal on fine days.

Licensees Michael Murphy and Laura Peel have been here only since October of 2005, but bring a wealth of enthusiasm to their roles as hosts. Plans are afoot for some exterior refurbishment and also for new menus; at present a full menu, offering anything from cold sandwiches to a full mixed grill, is available all day, every day, with a good roast dinner on Sundays from midday until 4 p.m. To drink there's a good choice of beers and lagers including Stones bitter, together with Woodpecker cider, stout, select wines, spirits and soft drinks.

With plenty of parking available and access for guests with disabilities, this pub is well worth stopping at while exploring the area, which includes such draws as the Magna Science Adventure Centre, Clifton Park Museum and York and Lancaster Regimental Museum in Rotherham, Ulley Country Park, the Waterloo Kiln at Swinton, Conisborough Castle and the Earth Centre, Roche Abbey and the Mansion House, Cusworth Hall and Racecourse at Doncaster, as well, of course, as the impressive tourist attractions at Sheffield and several other picturesque villages including Norton, Stainforth, Fishlake, Branton and Thorne.

53 Elephant & Castle

Tingle Bridge Lane, Hemingfield, Barnsley,
South Yorkshire S73 0NT
Tel: 01226 755986

Bar Food, Restaurant Menu, Disabled Facilities

54 The Fiddlers Inn

55 Cemetery Road, Hemingfield, Barnsley,
South Yorkshire S73 0QD
Tel: 01226 754527

Real Ales, Bar Food, Restaurant Menu,
Disabled Facilities

55 Flare Path Public House

High Street, Dunsville, Doncaster,
South Yorkshire DN7 4BP
Tel: 01302 887350

Real Ales, Bar Food, Restaurant Menu

56 The Flying Childers

Nostell Place, Doncaster, South Yorkshire DN4 7JA
Tel: 01302 379000

Bar Food, No Smoking Area, Disabled Facilities

57 The Foresters Arms

Village Street, Adwick-le-Street, Doncaster,
South Yorkshire DN6 7AA
Tel: 01302 723550

Real Ales, Bar Food, No Smoking Area,
Disabled Facilities

58 The Fox

Church Street, Conisbrough, Doncaster,
South Yorkshire DN12 3HP
Tel: 01709 863136

Disabled Facilities

59 Fox & Hounds Inn

Main Street, Wadworth, Doncaster,
South Yorkshire DN11 9AY
Tel: 01302 853425

Real Ales, Bar Food, Restaurant Menu

60 Fox Inn

21 Robin Lane, Beighton, Sheffield, Yorkshire S20 1BB
Tel: 01142 512921

Bar Food, No Smoking Area, Disabled Facilities

61 The Gallows

Hangsman Lane, Dinnington, Sheffield,
Yorkshire S25 3PF
Tel: 01909 563141

Real Ales, Bar Food, Restaurant Menu, No Smoking Area

62 Gateway Inn

Station Road, Barnby Dun, Doncaster,
South Yorkshire DN3 1HA
Tel: 01302 880641

Real Ales, Restaurant Menu, No Smoking Area,
Disabled Facilities

63 George & Dragon

High Street, Beighton, Sheffield, Yorkshire S20 1EF
Tel: 01142 692458

64 The Glasshouse

1 Doncaster Road, Kirk Sandall, Doncaster,
South Yorkshire DN3 1HP
Tel: 01302 884268

Bar Food, Restaurant Menu, No Smoking Area,
Disabled Facilities

65 Goldthorpe Hotel

Doncaster Road, Goldthorpe, Rotherham,
South Yorkshire S63 9JA
Tel: 01709 892191

Real Ales

66 The Great Dane

Greenside, Shafton, Barnsley, South Yorkshire S72 8PL
Tel: 01226 714841

Real Ales, Restaurant Menu, No Smoking Area,
Disabled Facilities

67 Green Dragon Hotel

Silver Street, Thorne, Doncaster,
South Yorkshire DN8 5DT
Tel: 01405 812797

Real Ales

68 The Green Tree

Tudworth Road, Hatfield, Doncaster,
South Yorkshire DN7 6NL
Tel: 01302 840305

Real Ales, Bar Food, Restaurant Menu,
No Smoking Area, Disabled Facilities

69 Halfway House Hotel

142 Barnsley Road Highgate, Goldthorpe,
Rotherham, South Yorkshire S63 9AP
Tel: 01709 880066

Disabled Facilities

70 The Hare & Tortoise

329 Bawtry Road, Doncaster,
South Yorkshire DN4 7PB
Tel: 01302 861901

Real Ales, Bar Food, Restaurant Menu,
No Smoking Area, Disabled Facilities

71 The Harlequin

King Edward Road, Thorne, Doncaster,
South Yorkshire DN8 4DE
Tel: 01405 812597

No Smoking Area

72 The Harvester

Thorne Road, Stainforth, Doncaster,
South Yorkshire DN7 5BL
Tel: 01302 841660

Bar Food, Disabled Facilities

73 Harvey Arms

Old Bawtry Road, Finningley, Doncaster,
South Yorkshire DN9 3BY
Tel: 01302 770200

Bar Food, Restaurant Menu, No Smoking Area

74 Hatfield Arms

19 High Street, Laughton, Sheffield, Yorkshire S25 1YF
Tel: 01909 562681

Real Ales, Bar Food, Restaurant Menu, No Smoking Area

75 Hatfield Chace

Doncaster Road, Hatfield, Doncaster,
South Yorkshire DN7 6AD
Tel: 01302 840508

Real Ales, Bar Food, Restaurant Menu,
No Smoking Area, Disabled Facilities

76 The Hawk & Dove

Thorpe Green, Waterthorpe, Sheffield,
Yorkshire S20 7HH
Tel: 01142 470240

77 The Haynook

Yarwell Drive, Maltby, Rotherham,
South Yorkshire S66 8HZ
Tel: 01709 817660

No Smoking Area

78 Hellaby Hall Hotel

Hellaby Lane, Hellaby, Rotherham,
South Yorkshire S66 8HN
Tel: 01709 702701

Restaurant Menu, Accommodation, No Smoking Area,
Disabled Facilities

79 High House Hotel

27 Wentworth Road, Swinton, Mexborough,
South Yorkshire S64 8JZ
Tel: 01709 583572

80 The Highwayman

Great North Road, Woodlands, Doncaster,
South Yorkshire DN6 7HS
Tel: 01302 723559

Bar Food, Restaurant Menu, No Smoking Area,
Disabled Facilities

81 Holiday Inn Express

Moorhead Way, Bramley, Rotherham,
South Yorkshire S66 1YY
Tel: 01709 730333

Real Ales, Bar Food, Restaurant Menu,
Accommodation, No Smoking Area, Disabled Facilities

82 The Holly Bush

Church Balk, Edenthorpe, Doncaster,
South Yorkshire DN3 2PR
Tel: 01302 882473

Real Ales, Bar Food, Restaurant Menu,
No Smoking Area, Disabled Facilities

83 Horse & Groom

38 Barnsley Road, Goldthorpe, Rotherham,
South Yorkshire S63 9NE
Tel: 01709 893247

Real Ales

84 Horse & Groom
Nutwell Lane, Armthorpe, Doncaster,
South Yorkshire DN3 3JU
Tel: 01302 831658

Real Ales, Bar Food, Restaurant Menu,
No Smoking Area, Disabled Facilities

85 Ingram Arms
High Street, Hatfield, Doncaster,
South Yorkshire DN7 6RS
Tel: 01302 840333

Real Ales, No Smoking Area, Disabled Facilities

86 Ivanhoe Hotel
Melton Road, Sprotbrough, Doncaster,
South Yorkshire DN5 7NS
Tel: 01302 853130

Real Ales, Bar Food, Restaurant Menu,
No Smoking Area, Disabled Facilities

87 John Bull Inn
Waterside, Thorne, Doncaster,
South Yorkshire DN8 4JQ
Tel: 01405 814677

Real Ales, Bar Food, Restaurant Menu,
No Smoking Area, Disabled Facilities

88 Joker
Blackthorn Avenue, Bramley, Rotherham,
South Yorkshire S66 2LU
Tel: 01709 702516

Bar Food

89 Joseph Glover
Station Road, Westfield, Sheffield, Yorkshire S20 8EA
Tel: 01142 476649

Bar Food

90 The Leeds Arms
Sheffield Road, Anston, Sheffield, Yorkshire S25 5DT
Tel: 01909 567906

Real Ales, Bar Food, Restaurant Menu,
No Smoking Area

91 Lord Conyers Hotel
Old Road, Conisbrough, Doncaster,
South Yorkshire DN12 3LZ
Tel: 01709 863254

Real Ales, Bar Food, Restaurant Menu,
Accommodation, No Smoking Area

92 Lordens Hotel
Doe Quarry Lane, Dinnington, Sheffield,
Yorkshire S25 2NH
Tel: 01909 562404

Real Ales, Bar Food, Restaurant Menu

93 The Loyal Trooper
34 Sheffield Road, Anston, Sheffield, Yorkshire S25 5DT
Tel: 01909 562203

Bar Food, Restaurant Menu

94 The Mallard
Cusworth Lane, Doncaster, South Yorkshire DN5 8JN
Tel: 01302 813132

Bar Food, Restaurant Menu, No Smoking Area,
Disabled Facilities

95 The Manor Farm
Denaby Lane, Old Denaby, Doncaster,
South Yorkshire DN12 4LD
Tel: 01709 581392

Real Ales, Bar Food, Restaurant Menu,
No Smoking Area, Disabled Facilities

96 Marr Lodge
Barnsley Road, Marr, Doncaster,
South Yorkshire DN5 7AX
Tel: 01302 390355

Real Ales, Bar Food, Restaurant Menu,
No Smoking Area

97 The Mayflower
High Street, Austerfield, Doncaster,
South Yorkshire DN10 6QU
Tel: 01302 710263

Bar Food, Restaurant Menu

98 The Milestone

Doncaster Road, Denaby Main, Doncaster,
South Yorkshire DN12 4JH
☎ 01709 862153

Real Ales, No Smoking Area, Disabled Facilities

☞ On the A6023 2 miles northwest of Conisborough

🍺 Stones, John Smiths

🍴 Tues-Fri 12-3 & 5-9; Sat 12-3 & 5-9.30; Sun 12-4

🎵 Sat night disco; Mon children's disco (6-10)

🏛 Car park, disabled access, large function suite

💳 All major cards

🚫 No smoking areas

🕐 12-12

🏛 Conisborough Castle, the Earth Centre, Roche Abbey, Rother Valley Country Park

Under new owner Angela Daley, who arrived here in December of 2005, The Milestone has taken on a new lease of life, offering great hospitality to all guests. Hearty snacks are served at lunch and dinner, and the Sunday carvery is worth making a special trip for.

98 The Milestone

Doncaster Road, Denaby Main, Doncaster,
South Yorkshire DN12 4JH
Tel: 01709 862153

Real Ales, No Smoking Area, Disabled Facilities

See panel above

99 The Milestone

12 Peak Square, Crystal Peaks, Sheffield,
Yorkshire S20 7PH
Tel: 01142 471614

Real Ales, Bar Food, Restaurant Menu,
No Smoking Area, Disabled Facilities

100 The Millhouse

Barnsley Road, Doncaster, South Yorkshire DN5 8QE
Tel: 01302 391617

Real Ales, Bar Food, Restaurant Menu, No Smoking Area, Disabled Facilities

101 Millstone

Westgate, Tickhill, Doncaster,
South Yorkshire DN11 9NF
Tel: 01302 745532

Real Ales, Bar Food, Restaurant Menu,
No Smoking Area, Disabled Facilities

102 Moorthorpe Hotel

Burton Street, South Elmsall, Pontefract,
West Yorkshire WF9 2AH
Tel: 01977 642930

Accommodation, No Smoking Area, Disabled Facilities

103 Mosborough Hall Hotel

High Street, Mosborough, Sheffield,
Yorkshire S20 5EA
Tel: 01142 484353

Restaurant Menu, Accommodation, No Smoking Area, Disabled Facilities

104 The New Inn

South Bank, Stainforth, Doncaster,
South Yorkshire DN7 5AW
Tel: 01302 841614

Bar Food, Restaurant Menu, No Smoking Area, Disabled Facilities

105 The Northfield Hotel

Holmsley Lane, South Kirkby, Pontefract,
West Yorkshire WF9 3HX
Tel: 01977 648629

Real Ales, Bar Food, Restaurant Menu,
No Smoking Area, Disabled Facilities

See panel opposite

106 The Oak

Northgate, Tickhill, Doncaster,
South Yorkshire DN11 9HZ
Tel: 01302 742351

Real Ales, Disabled Facilities

107 Old Anchor Inn

Main Street, Fishlake, Doncaster,
South Yorkshire DN7 5JH
Tel: 01302 841423

Real Ales, Bar Food, Restaurant Menu,
No Smoking Area

105 The Northfield Hotel

Holmsley Lane, South Kirby, Pontefract,
West Yorkshire WF9 3HX
☎ 01977 648629

Real Ales, Bar Food, Restaurant Menu, No Smoking Area, Disabled Facilities

☛ Off the A628/A638 10 miles southeast of Wakefield

🍴 Mon-Sat 12-7; Sun 12-3

🎵 Thurs night quiz; music Fri-Sun

�parking Parking, disabled access, beer garden, children's play area, function suite

🕐 Mon-Thurs 12-12; Fri-Sun 12-1am

🏛 Nostell Priory, Wakefield, Harewood House, Leeds, Castleford

Set back from the main road, The Northfield Hotel was built in 1928 and is a large and impressive inn with Yorkshire beers and lagers, good food at lunch and dinner six days a week, tempting roasts on Sundays – all home-cooked – and a warm and friendly atmosphere.

108 The Old Bells

High Street, Campsall, Doncaster,
South Yorkshire DN6 9AG
Tel: 01302 700423

Real Ales, Bar Food, Restaurant Menu,
No Smoking Area

109 Old Crown Inn

Barnsley Road, South Kirkby, Pontefract,
West Yorkshire WF9 3BH
Tel: 01977 642421

Real Ales, No Smoking Area

110 The Old Hall Inn

1 High Street, Great Houghton, Barnsley,
South Yorkshire S72 0EN
Tel: 01226 758706

Real Ales

111 The Old Mill Hotel

Mill Lane, South Kirkby, Pontefract,
West Yorkshire WF9 3DT
Tel: 01977 640001

Real Ales, Disabled Facilities

112 The Old Moor Tavern

Everill Gate Lane, Wombwell, Barnsley,
South Yorkshire S73 0YQ
Tel: 01226 755455

Bar Food, Restaurant Menu, No Smoking Area,
Disabled Facilities

113 Owston Park Lodge

Doncaster Road, Owston, Doncaster,
South Yorkshire DN6 9JG
Tel: 01302 700571

Bar Food, Restaurant Menu, No Smoking Area,
Disabled Facilities

114 The Paddock

Goodison Boulevard, Doncaster,
South Yorkshire DN4 6NL
Tel: 01302 536433

Bar Food, Restaurant Menu, No Smoking Area,
Disabled Facilities

115 Palfreys Lodge

Acacia Road, Doncaster, South Yorkshire DN4 6NR
Tel: 01302 534511

Bar Food, Restaurant Menu, No Smoking Area,
Disabled Facilities

116 The Plough

2 High Street, Arksey, Doncaster,
South Yorkshire DN5 0SF
Tel: 01302 872472

Real Ales, Bar Food, No Smoking Area

117 The Plough

Greaves Sike Lane, Micklebring, Rotherham,
South Yorkshire S66 7RR
Tel: 01709 812710

Real Ales, Bar Food, Restaurant Menu,
No Smoking Area

See panel on page 222

118 The Poacher

Radburn Road, New Rossington, Doncaster,
South Yorkshire DN11 0SH
Tel: 01302 864161

Disabled Facilities

117 The Plough

Micklebring, Rotherham, South Yorkshire S66 7RR
☎ 01709 812710

Real Ales, Bar Food, Restaurant Menu, No Smoking Area

- ☛ Parallel to the M18 8 miles northeast of Rotherham
- 🍺 Black Sheep, John Smiths, guest ales
- 🍴 12-2 & 6.30-9.30
- 🎵 Quiz night Monday
- ⚓ Parking, disabled access, beer garden
- 💳 All major cards
- 🚫 No smoking in dining area
- 🕐 Mon-Sat 12-2.30 & 6.30-12; Sun 12-9
- 🏛 Magna Science Adventure Centre, Rotherham; the Earth Centre and Conisborough Castle, Conisborough

On an elevated site hidden away on a minor road, The Plough is an attractive and welcoming pub with a handsome interior and a huge beer garden commanding superb views over the surrounding countryside. Real ales and a good range of lagers, wines, spirits, cider, stout and soft drinks ensure there's something to quench every thirst.

The accent is firmly on great food here, with a menu and daily specials board boasting dishes such as home-made steak pie, wholetail scampi, Sicilian chicken, steaks, mixed grill and surf & turf, together with delicious salads including Cajun chicken and roast beef. All dishes use the freshest local ingredients and are expertly prepared.

119 Prince Of Wales

High Street, Wombwell, Barnsley,
South Yorkshire S73 0DA
Tel: 01226 752312

Real Ales

120 The Punch Bowl

Fieldside, Thorne, Doncaster,
South Yorkshire DN8 4AE
Tel: 01405 813580

Real Ales, Bar Food, Restaurant Menu,
Accommodation, No Smoking Area

121 Queen Hotel

135 High Street, Mosborough, Sheffield,
Yorkshire S20 5AF
Tel: 01142 485848

Bar Food

122 The Queens Hotel

Tickhill Road, Maltby, Rotherham,
South Yorkshire S66 7NQ
Tel: 01709 812494

Real Ales

123 The Railway Hotel

Moss Road, Askern, Doncaster,
South Yorkshire DN6 0JS
Tel: 01302 700289

124 Railway Tavern

Church Street, Bentley, Doncaster,
South Yorkshire DN5 0BE
Tel: 01302 874312

Real Ales

125 The Red Bear

The Green, Thorne, Doncaster,
South Yorkshire DN8 5AT
Tel: 01405 813425

Disabled Facilities

126 Red Lion

Market Place, Tickhill, Doncaster,
South Yorkshire DN11 9LX
Tel: 01302 759563

Real Ales, Bar Food, Restaurant Menu,
Accommodation, No Smoking Area, Disabled Facilities

127 The Red Lion

Sheffield Road, Conisbrough, Doncaster,
South Yorkshire DN12 2BY
Tel: 01709 864005

Real Ales, Bar Food, Restaurant Menu,
No Smoking Area, Disabled Facilities

128 Red Lion

Holywell Lane, Braithwell, Rotherham,
South Yorkshire S66 7AF
Tel: 01709 812886

Real Ales, Restaurant Menu, No Smoking Area,
Disabled Facilities

129 The Red Lion Hotel

High Street, Askern, Doncaster,
South Yorkshire DN6 0AB
Tel: 01302 700514

130 The Red Rum

Cemetery Road, Grimethorpe, Barnsley,
South Yorkshire S72 7NR
Tel: 01226 716334

Real Ales, Bar Food, Restaurant Menu

131 The Ridgeway Arms

Quarry Hill, Mosborough, Sheffield, Yorkshire S20 5AZ
Tel: 01142 477111

Bar Food, Restaurant Menu, No Smoking Area,
Disabled Facilities

132 Ridgewood

Thorne Road, Edenthorpe, Doncaster,
South Yorkshire DN3 2JD
Tel: 01302 882841

Bar Food, No Smoking Area

133 The Rising Sun

Hatfield Road, Thorne, Doncaster,
South Yorkshire DN8 5QZ
Tel: 01405 812688

Bar Food, Restaurant Menu, No Smoking Area,
Disabled Facilities

134 Robin Hood Inn

Main Street, Aughton, Sheffield, Yorkshire S26 3XJ
Tel: 01142 871010

Real Ales, Bar Food, Accommodation, No Smoking Area

135 Rock Tavern

Highthorn Road, Kilnhurst, Mexborough,
South Yorkshire S64 5UP
Tel: 01709 583587

Real Ales, Disabled Facilities

136 The Roland Arms

117 Mansfield Road, Aston, Sheffield,
Yorkshire S26 2BR
Tel: 01142 876199

Real Ales, Bar Food, Restaurant Menu,
No Smoking Area

137 The Royal Oak

44 High Street, Beighton, Sheffield, Yorkshire S20 1EA
Tel: 01142 697410

Real Ales, Bar Food, No Smoking Area,
Disabled Facilities

138 The Royal Oak

53 High Street, Mosborough, Sheffield,
Yorkshire S20 5AF
Tel: 01142 510131

Real Ales, Disabled Facilities

139 The Rusty Dudley

43-45 Doncaster Road, Goldthorpe, Rotherham,
South Yorkshire S63 9HJ
Tel: 01709 888069

Bar Food, Disabled Facilities

140 Rutlands Inns

Hollings Lane, Thrybergh, Rotherham,
South Yorkshire S65 4LQ
Tel: 01709 850820

Bar Food, Restaurant Menu

141 The Sandhill

2-6 Turner Street, Great Houghton, Barnsley,
South Yorkshire S72 0DL
Tel: 01226 757375

Real Ales

142 Sandhill Club House

Middlecliff Lane, Little Houghton, Barnsley,
South Yorkshire S72 0HW
Tel: 01226 755079

Real Ales, Bar Food, Disabled Facilities

143 The Saxon Hotel
Station Road, Kiveton Park, Sheffield,
Yorkshire S26 6QP
Tel: 01909 770517

Bar Food, No Smoking Area

144 Scarborough Arms
Sunderland Street, Tickhill, Doncaster,
South Yorkshire DN11 9QJ
Tel: 01302 742977

Real Ales, No Smoking Area

145 The Scotsman
Cow Lane, Havercroft, Wakefield,
West Yorkshire WF4 2BE
Tel: 01226 701675

146 Sharon Law
Doncaster Road, Barnsley, South Yorkshire S71 5EF
Tel: 01226 282050

Real Ales, Bar Food, Restaurant Menu,
No Smoking Area, Disabled Facilities

147 The Sheppey
Littlewood Way, Maltby, Rotherham,
South Yorkshire S66 7BG
Tel: 01709 815240

Real Ales

148 Ship Inn
Newington, Doncaster, South Yorkshire DN10 6DJ
Tel: 01302 710334

Real Ales, Bar Food, Restaurant Menu,
No Smoking Area

149 Sir Jack
Bawtry Road, Bramley, Rotherham,
South Yorkshire S66 1YZ
Tel: 01709 530306

Bar Food, Restaurant Menu, No Smoking Area,
Disabled Facilities

150 Southmoor Hotel
55 Southmoor Road, Hemsworth, Pontefract,
West Yorkshire WF9 4LX
Tel: 01977 625526

Real Ales, Accommodation

156 The Star
Doncaster Road, Conisborough,
South Yorkshire DN12 3NG
☎ 01709 512197

Bar Food

🖝 On the A630 5 miles southwest of Doncaster
🎵 Sun karaoke and quiz, disco Fri & Sat night
🅿 Parking, beer garden
🕐 12-12
🏛 Conisborough Castle, the Earth Centre, Tropical Butterfly House, Wildlife and Falconry Centre (North Anston), Rother Valley Country Park (Wales)

Just a short distance from Conisborough Castle, The Star is a friendly family-run pub with a full range of lagers, beers, cider, stout, wines, spirits and soft drinks. Located at a busy junction in the heart of Conisborough, the inn is large and impressive. The interior is spacious and welcoming, while outside, from the beer garden, there's a lovely view of Conisborough

Castle.

The kitchen has recently been refurbished, and meals and light bites will be served beginning in 2006 – please ring for details. Jenny, Sean and Simon and their efficient, welcoming staff offer all their guests a warm welcome and a high standard of service and hospitality. Handy for visits to the Castle, Conisborough's Earth Centre and many other sights in the region, it makes a perfect place to stop for a relaxed drink while touring the area.

151 The Spinney Hotel

Forest Rise, Doncaster, South Yorkshire DN4 9HH
Tel: 01302 852033

Real Ales, Bar Food, No Smoking Area,
Disabled Facilities

152 The Sportsman

Bawtry Road, Bramley, Rotherham,
South Yorkshire S66 2TW
Tel: 01709 543328

Real Ales, Bar Food

153 The Squirrel Inn

Laughton Road, Dinnington, Sheffield,
Yorkshire S25 2PT
Tel: 01909 562554

Bar Food, Restaurant Menu, No Smoking Area,
Disabled Facilities

See panel on page 226

154 St Leger Arms

4 High Street, Laughton, Sheffield,
Yorkshire S25 1YF
Tel: 01909 562940

Real Ales, Bar Food, Restaurant Menu,
Accommodation

155 The Staithes

Old Doncaster Road, Wath-upon-Dearne,
Rotherham, South Yorkshire S63 7EJ
Tel: 01709 873546

Real Ales, Bar Food, No Smoking Area

156 The Star

Doncaster Road, Conisbrough, Doncaster,
South Yorkshire DN12 3AG
Tel: 01709 512197

Bar Food

See panel opposite

157 The Star Inn

High Street, Barnby Dun, Doncaster,
South Yorkshire DN3 1DY
Tel: 01302 882571

Real Ales, Bar Food, Restaurant Menu,
Accommodation, No Smoking Area, Disabled Facilities

See panel above

157 The Star Inn

High Street, Barnby Dun, Doncaster,
South Yorkshire DN3 1DY
☎ 01302 882571

Real Ales, Bar Food, Restaurant Menu, Accommodation, No Smoking Area, Disabled Facilities

☞	Off the A18 5 miles northeast of Doncaster
🍴	12-2 & 5-8
🛏	rooms for 2006
🎵	Disco second Sat night of the month
🍺	Parking, beer garden, function room
🕐	Mon 4.30-11; Tues-Sun 12-11
🏛	Norton, Stainforth, Fishlake, Thorne

In the quiet village of Barnby Dun, The Star Inn is a convivial pub dating back to the early 1900s, freshly painted and perfectly maintained. The meals, served at lunch and dinner every day, are all home cooked, the three qualified chefs creating dishes such as steak and ale pie, all-day breakfast, steaks, seafood and more.

158 The Station Hotel

West End Lane, New Rossington, Doncaster,
South Yorkshire DN11 0DX
Tel: 01302 865023

Real Ales

159 The Station Inn

Station Road, Conisbrough, Doncaster,
South Yorkshire DN12 3DD
Tel: 01709 863250

Real Ales, Bar Food, Restaurant Menu

See panel on page 227

160 Station Hotel

Kiveton Park Station, Sheffield, Yorkshire S26 6NP
Tel: 01909 773201

Bar Food, Restaurant Menu

153 The Squirrel Inn

Laughton Road, Dinnington, Sheffield S25 2PT
☎ 01909 562554

Bar Food, Restaurant Menu, No Smoking Area,
Disabled Facilities

☛ On the B6060 east of J31 of the M1, 12 miles
east of Sheffield

🍴 12-2

♫ Occassional live music, quiz night Sun

⛱ Parking, disabled access, patio, children's play
area

🚫 No smoking area

🕐 Mon-Fri 12-11; Sat & Sun 12-12

🏛 Maltby, Rotherham, Tickhill, Bawtry, North
Anston, Doncaster

With a full range of lagers, beers, wines,
spirits, cider, stout and soft drinks,
there's something to quench every thirst at

The Squirrel Inn. Meals are served at lunchtime
– simple and hearty dishes cooked using the
freshest local ingredients. Plans are also afoot
to provide evening meals – please phone for
details. This convivial inn lies just off the main
street in Dinnington, on a huge site within a
busy housing area. Spacious and attractive, the
inn is a happy marriage of traditional comfort
and modern service. Tastefully decorated and
furnished, the inn boasts a warm and
welcoming ambience. Owner Wayne Brunt is
ably assisted by his friendly and helpful staff,
providing all their guests with first-class
hospitality. The inn makes a very attractive

place to stop for a relaxing drink or lunch
while exploring the many sights and attractions
of the region: a region of great age and
antiquity and, in many places, real beauty, both
natural and man-made. Sheffield has the
Kelham Island Museum, the City Museum and
Mappin Art Gallery in Weston Park, and The
Millennium Galleries, which have helped to
establish the city as a cultural force in the
north of England. Sheffield's Bishop's House
Museum dates from around 1500 and is the
earliest timber-framed house in the city.
Southeast of Sheffield, Renishaw Hall has
beautiful formal Italian gardens and 300 acres
of wooded park. Rother Valley Country Park
provides excellent water sports facilities, and
the charming riverside town of Doncaster is
perhaps best known as the home of the St
Leger, Britain's oldest classic horse race.
Elsewhere in the county visitors can discover
the delights of Roche Abbey, Conisborough
Castle and Brodsworth Hall.

159 The Station Inn

Station Road, Conisborough, Doncaster,
South Yorkshire DN12 3DD
☎ 01709 863250

Real Ales, Bar Food, Restaurant Menu

- ☛ Via the Mexborough Road exiting Conisborough, 5 miles south of Doncaster on the A630
- 🍺 Tetleys Cask
- 🍴 Sundays 12-4
- 🎵 Karaoke Fri & Sat night
- ⚒ Car park, disabled access, function suite
- 🕐 Sun-Thurs 10am-midnight; Fri & Sat 10am-2am
- 🏛 Conisborough Castle, the Earth Centre, Doncaster, Roche Abbey, Renishaw Hall

The Station Inn is a large and spacious hostelry with a good selection of Tetleys cask-conditioned ales and a friendly, relaxed atmosphere. Dorothy Kaye took over at the helm of this fine inn in December of 2005, and brings a wealth of enthusiasm to providing first-class hospitality to all her guests.

161 Station Hotel

Station Road, Blaxton, Doncaster,
South Yorkshire DN9 3AA
Tel: 01302 770218

Real Ales, Bar Food, Restaurant Menu,
Accommodation, No Smoking Area

162 Station Inn

Doncaster Road, Darfield, Barnsley,
South Yorkshire S73 9JA
Tel: 01226 752096

Real Ales, Bar Food, Restaurant Menu,
No Smoking Area

163 The Styrrup

Stripe Road, Rossington, Doncaster,
South Yorkshire DN11 0XY
Tel: 01302 868639

Bar Food, Restaurant Menu, Disabled Facilities

164 Sun Inn

Main Street, South Hiendley, Barnsley,
South Yorkshire S72 9BP
Tel: 01226 711469

Real Ales

165 The Sun Inn

York Road, Doncaster, South Yorkshire DN5 8RN
Tel: 01302 784109

Real Ales, Bar Food, No Smoking Area

166 The Talisman

Chestnut Grove, Conisbrough, Doncaster,
South Yorkshire DN12 2JA
Tel: 01709 862482

Real Ales, Bar Food, Restaurant Menu

See panel on page 229

167 The Tavern

Doncaster Road, Denaby Main, Doncaster,
South Yorkshire DN12 4ET
Tel: 01709 864029

Real Ales

168 Three Horseshoes

Barnsley Road, Brierley, Barnsley,
South Yorkshire S72 9JT
Tel: 01226 711246

Real Ales, Bar Food, Restaurant Menu,
No Smoking Area, Disabled Facilities

169 Three Horseshoes Inn

Doncaster Road, Branton, Doncaster,
South Yorkshire DN3 3NL
Tel: 01302 379011

Bar Food, Restaurant Menu, No Smoking Area,
Disabled Facilities

170 Thurnscoe Hotel

Houghton Road, Thurnscoe, Rotherham,
South Yorkshire S63 0JX
Tel: 01709 893168

Restaurant Menu, Accommodation, No Smoking Area

175 The Travellers Rest

Westgate, Tickhill, Doncaster,
South Yorkshire DN11 9NQ
☎ 01302 744497

Real Ales, Bar Food, Restaurant Menu, No Smoking
Area, Disabled Facilities

- ☛ At the junction of the A631/A60, 8 miles south of Doncaster
- 🍺 John Smiths, Hardy & Hanson Dark Mild, guest ale
- 🍴 12-2 & 6-9
- ♫ Live music monthly (Sat), quiz night Thurs, occasional music quiz night Tues
- ♿ Parking, disabled access, patio, function room
- 💳 All major cards
- 🚫 No smoking in restaurant
- 🕐 Mon-Thurs 12-11.30; Fri & Sat 12-12; Sun 12-11
- 🏛 Doncaster, Maltby, Swinton, Rotherham

The Travellers Rest is an impressive redbrick inn dating back to 1881. This superb village pub has a modern exterior built onto the traditional interior. Spacious inside, it is also extremely cosy and welcoming, with several lovely little nooks inviting comfort and conversation dotted with sofas and other comfortable seating. The décor is traditional, adding to the inn's warm and friendly ambience .

Owners Ian Bell arrived here late in 2005 and brings a wealth of enthusiasm to providing first-class service and hospitality; together with his partner and capable, conscientious staff, they offer a pleasant experience to all guests. To drink, there is a choice of real ales together with a good range of lagers, cider, stout, wines, spirits and soft drinks. The food here is all freshly prepared, with a changing menu including hearty favourites such as steaks and roasts. The separate, no-smoking restaurant is tastefully furnished and decorated.

Tickhill, just a few miles south of Doncaster, is a quiet and charming place that is also convenient as a

stopping-off point while visiting the sights and attractions of the region, which include other handsome villages such as Finningley, Cadeby and Bawtry, the Tropical Butterfly House, Wildlife and Falconry Centre at North Anston, Rother Valley Country Park in Wales, Thorpe Salvin Hall, Roche Abbey and Renishaw Hall, as well as Conisborough Castle and the Earth Centre in Conisborough.

166 The Talisman

Chestnut Square, Conisborough, Doncaster,
South Yorkshire DN12 2JA
☎ 01709 862482

Real Ales, Bar Food, Restaurant Menu

- ☛ Just off the A630 (Sheffield Road) in Conisborough
- ⑂ Sunday 12-6; free light bites
- ♫ Fri & Sat night karaoke, quiz and bingo Sun & Weds night
- ⚓ Parking, disabled access
- 🕐 Mon-Thurs & Sun midday-12.30am; Fri-Sat 11am-1am
- 🏛 Conisborough Castle, the Earth Centre, Roche Abbey, Renishaw Hall, Thorpe Salvin Hall

The Talisman is a handsome redbrick modern-built pub close to the centre of Conisborough. New owners Clare and Shaun Lawrence have been here since September of 2005, and bring enthusiasm to their role offering great service and hospitality to all their guests. With a range of lagers, cider, stout, wines, spirits and soft drinks, there's something for every taste. Free light bites are served every evening, and the Sunday carvery provides a choice of delicious roasts with all the trimmings. Handy for a relaxed drink while visiting Conisborough sights such as the Castle and Earth Centre, and interesting and historic attractions in nearby Maltby, Renishaw and Thorpe Salvin, the ambience is always warm and welcoming at this friendly local.

171 Toby Carvery

Lyndale Avenue, Edenthorpe, Doncaster,
South Yorkshire DN3 2LB
Tel: 01302 880275

Bar Food, Restaurant Menu, No Smoking Area,
Disabled Facilities

172 Travellers Inn

The Green, South Kirkby, Pontefract,
West Yorkshire WF9 3AB
Tel: 01977 642284

Disabled Facilities

173 The Travellers Inn

Bawtry Road, Bramley, Rotherham,
South Yorkshire S66 2TS
Tel: 01709 540550

Real Ales, Bar Food, Restaurant Menu,
No Smoking Area, Disabled Facilities

174 Travellers Rest

Brookhouse, Laughton, Sheffield S25 1YA
Tel: 01909 562661

Real Ales, Bar Food, Restaurant Menu

175 The Travellers Rest

Westgate, Tickhill, Doncaster,
South Yorkshire DN11 9NQ
Tel: 01302 744497

Real Ales, Bar Food, Restaurant Menu,
No Smoking Area, Disabled Facilities

See panel opposite

176 Upton Arms

2 High Street, Upton, Pontefract,
West Yorkshire WF9 1HG
Tel: 01977 650495

Bar Food, Restaurant Menu

185 The White Hart Hotel

High Street, Askern, Doncaster,
South Yorkshire DN6 0NY
☎ 01302 702645

Bar Food, Restaurant Menu, No Smoking Area,
Disabled Facilities

- 🚩 Just off the A19 7 miles north of Doncaster
- 🍴 Mon-Sat 11-2 & 5-7; Sun 12-4
- 🎵 Poker night Tues, pool night Thurs, karaoke Fri & Sat
- ⚓ Parking, disabled access
- 💳 All major cards
- 🚫 No smoking areas
- 🕐 Mon-Thurs 11-11; Fri-Sat 11am-1am; Sun 12-11
- 🏛 Doncaster, Norton, Stainforth, Fishlake, Thorne, Branton

A roadside inn with new owners, The White Hart Hotel is an excellent example of a typical Yorkshire inn, with a very pleasing interior and a warm and friendly staff. Michaela and Wes Fox offer all their guests a

stone ceilings and traditional features. Light bites and snacks are served all day, while meals are served at lunch and dinner every day, with a menu that makes the most of fresh and healthy ingredients to create hearty favourites such as roast of the day, pork or lamb chops, liver and sausage and Cajun chicken. The snacks include burgers, quiche and warm baguettes, salads, sandwiches and more. All dishes are home cooked. The White Hart is also available for private parties and celebrations, and can look after all your catering needs. Future plans include the refurbishment of the guest bedrooms. Meanwhile, the inn makes a good place to stop for a quiet drink or meal while exploring the region, which boasts attractions including those at nearby Doncaster – the Mansion House, Doncaster Racecourse, Cusworth Hall and Brodsworth Hall – as well as Brockhole Riding and Visitor Centre, and the Stainforth and Keadby Canal (great for walks and abundant in natural wildlife).

high standard of service and quality. They've been here only a short time but bring experience and zeal to providing great food and drink and a relaxed ambience throughout the inn. From the outside, where there is a large area for parking, the inn presents a friendly face to the world, with casement windows and a pristine appearance. Inside the inn is both spacious while managing to be cosy, with an interior brimming with warm woods,

177 Victoria Hotel

77 Kirkby Road, Hemsworth, Pontefract,
West Yorkshire WF9 4BX
Tel: 01977 610574

No Smoking Area

178 Victoria Inn

South End, Thorne, Doncaster,
South Yorkshire DN8 5QN
Tel: 01405 813163

Real Ales, Bar Food, Restaurant Menu,
Accommodation, No Smoking Area

179 The Waverley

Station Road, Stainforth, Doncaster,
South Yorkshire DN7 5QA
Tel: 01302 844577

180 The Weatherby

Park Hill, Swallownest, Sheffield, Yorkshire S26 4UN
Tel: 01142 548821

Real Ales

181 The Wheel

Plumbley Hall Road, Mosborough, Sheffield,
Yorkshire S20 5BL
Tel: 01142 484991

No Smoking Area

182 The White Hart

Top Road, Barnby Dun, Doncaster,
South Yorkshire DN3 1DB
Tel: 01302 882959

Bar Food, No Smoking Area, Disabled Facilities

183 The White Hart

Main Street, Wadworth, Doncaster,
South Yorkshire DN11 9AZ
Tel: 01302 857622

Bar Food, Restaurant Menu, No Smoking Area,
Disabled Facilities

184 The White Hart

Market Place, Thorne, Doncaster,
South Yorkshire DN8 5DG
Tel: 01405 813104

Real Ales, Bar Food, Restaurant Menu

185 **The White Hart Hotel**

High Street, Askern, Doncaster,
South Yorkshire DN6 0AB
Tel: 01302 702645

Bar Food, Restaurant Menu, No Smoking Area,
Disabled Facilities

See panel opposite

186 The White Rose

Grange Lane, New Rossington, Doncaster,
South Yorkshire DN11 0QZ
Tel: 01302 868476

187 The White Swan

9 Blyth Road, Maltby, Rotherham,
South Yorkshire S66 8HX
Tel: 01709 819777

Real Ales

188 The Windmill

19 Queen Street, Thorne, Doncaster,
South Yorkshire DN8 5AA
Tel: 01405 812866

Real Ales, Disabled Facilities

189 The Winning Post

Warmsworth Road, Doncaster,
South Yorkshire DN4 0TR
Tel: 01302 853493

Real Ales, Restaurant Menu

190 The Woodlands

Great North Road, Woodlands, Doncaster,
South Yorkshire DN6 7HS
Tel: 01302 728439

Disabled Facilities

HIDDEN PLACES GUIDES

Explore Britain and Ireland with *Hidden Places* guides - a fascinating series of national and local travel guides.

Packed with easy to read information on hundreds of places of interest as well as places to stay, eat and drink.

Available from both high street and internet booksellers

For more information on the full range of *Hidden Places* guides and other titles published by Travel Publishing visit our website on

www.travelpublishing.co.uk
or ask for our leaflet by phoning **0118-981-7777** or emailing **info@travelpublishing.co.uk**

VISIT THE TRAVEL PUBLISHING WEBSITE

Looking for:

- *Places to Visit?*
- *Places to Stay?*
- *Places to Eat & Drink?*
- *Places to Shop?*

Then why not visit the Travel Publishing website...

- Informative pages on places to visit, stay, eat, drink and shop throughout the British Isles.

- Detailed information on Travel Publishing's wide range of national and regional travel guides.

www.travelpublishing.co.uk

TRAVEL PUBLISHING ORDER FORM

To order any of our publications just fill in the payment details below and complete the order form.
For orders of less than 4 copies please add £1 per book for postage and packing.
Orders over 4 copies are P & P free.

Please Complete Either:

I enclose a cheque for £ [   ] made payable to *Travel Publishing Ltd*

Or:

Card No: [   ]   Expiry Date: [   ]

Signature: [   ]

Name: [   ]

Address: [   ]

Tel no: [   ]

Please either send, telephone, fax or e-mail your order to:
Travel Publishing Ltd, 7a Apollo House, Calleva Park, Aldermaston, Berkshire RG7 8TN
Tel: **0118 981 7777**   Fax: **0118 982 0077**   e-mail: **info@travelpublishing.co.uk**

	Price	Quantity
HIDDEN PLACES REGIONAL TITLES		
Cornwall	£8.99	....
Devon	£8.99	....
Dorset, Hants & Isle of Wight	£8.99	....
East Anglia	£8.99	....
Lake District & Cumbria	£8.99	....
Northumberland & Durham	£8.99	....
Peak District	£8.99	....
Sussex	£8.99	....
Yorkshire	£8.99	....
HIDDEN PLACES NATIONAL TITLES		
England	£11.99	....
Ireland	£11.99	....
Scotland	£11.99	....
Wales	£11.99	....
HIDDEN INNS TITLES		
East Anglia	£7.99	....
Heart of England	£7.99	....
North of England	£7.99	....
South	£7.99	....
South East	£7.99	....
Wales	£7.99	....
West Country	£7.99	....
Yorkshire	£7.99	....

	Price	Quantity
COUNTRY PUBS AND INNS		
Cornwall	£5.99	....
Devon	£7.99	....
Sussex	£5.99	....
Wales	£8.99	....
Yorkshire	£7.99	....
COUNTRY LIVING RURAL GUIDES		
East Anglia	£10.99	....
Heart of England	£10.99	....
Ireland	£11.99	....
North East	£10.99	....
North West	£10.99	....
Scotland	£11.99	....
South of England	£10.99	....
South East of England	£10.99	....
Wales	£11.99	....
West Country	£10.99	....
OTHER TITLES		
Off the Motorway	£11.99	....

Total Quantity: [   ]

Post & Packing: [   ]

Total Value: [   ]

Reader Reaction Form

The *Travel Publishing* research team would like to receive reader's comments on any pubs and inns covered (or not covered) in this guide so please do not hesitate to write to us using these reader reaction forms. We would also welcome recommendations for suitable entries to be included in the next edition. This will help ensure that the *Country Pubs and Inns series of Guides* continues to provide a comprehensive list of pubs and inns to our readers. To provide your comments or recommendations would you please complete the forms below and overleaf as indicated and send to:

**The Research Department, Travel Publishing Ltd,
7a Apollo House, Calleva Park, Aldermaston, Reading, RG7 8TN.**

Your Name:

Your Address:

Your Telephone Number:

Please tick as appropriate:

Comments ☐   Recommendation ☐

Name of Establishment:

Address:

Telephone Number:

Name of Contact:

Reader Reaction Form

Comment or Reason for Recommendation:

....
....
....
....
....
....
....
....
....
....
....
....
....
....
....
....
....
....
....

Reader Reaction Form

The *Travel Publishing* research team would like to receive reader's comments on any pubs and inns covered (or not covered) in this guide so please do not hesitate to write to us using these reader reaction forms. We would also welcome recommendations for suitable entries to be included in the next edition. This will help ensure that the *Country Pubs and Inns series of Guides* continues to provide a comprehensive list of pubs and inns to our readers. To provide your comments or recommendations would you please complete the forms below and overleaf as indicated and send to:

**The Research Department, Travel Publishing Ltd,
7a Apollo House, Calleva Park, Aldermaston, Reading, RG7 8TN.**

Your Name:

Your Address:

Your Telephone Number:

Please tick as appropriate:

Comments ☐   Recommendation ☐

Name of Establishment:

Address:

Telephone Number:

Name of Contact:

Reader Reaction Form

Comment or Reason for Recommendation:

....

....

....

....

....

....

....

....

....

....

....

....

....

....

....

....

....

....

....

Reader Reaction Form

The *Travel Publishing* research team would like to receive reader's comments on any pubs and inns covered (or not covered) in this guide so please do not hesitate to write to us using these reader reaction forms. We would also welcome recommendations for suitable entries to be included in the next edition. This will help ensure that the *Country Pubs and Inns series of Guides* continues to provide a comprehensive list of pubs and inns to our readers. To provide your comments or recommendations would you please complete the forms below and overleaf as indicated and send to:

**The Research Department, Travel Publishing Ltd,
7a Apollo House, Calleva Park, Aldermaston, Reading, RG7 8TN.**

Your Name:

Your Address:

Your Telephone Number:

Please tick as appropriate:

Comments ☐   Recommendation ☐

Name of Establishment:

Address:

Telephone Number:

Name of Contact:

Reader Reaction Form

Comment or Reason for Recommendation:

....

....

....

....

....

....

....

....

....

....

....

....

....

....

....

....

....

....